WITHDRAWN

TEMPORAL MAN

TEMPORAL MAN

The Meaning and Uses of Social Time

Robert H. Lauer

PRAEGER

PRAEGER SPECIAL STUDIES • PRAEGER SCIENTIFIC

Library of Congress Cataloging in Publication Data
Main entry under title:

Temporal man.

   Bibliography: p.
   Includes indexes.
   1. Life. 2. Time. 3. Self (Philosophy) 4. Social
change. I. Lauer, Robert H.
BD435.T37   128   81-11917
ISBN 0-03-059719-6   AACR2

Published in 1981 by Praeger Publishers
CBS Educational and Professional Publishing
A Division of CBS, Inc.
521 Fifth Avenue, New York, NY 10175 USA

© 1981 by Praeger Publishers
All rights reserved
Library of Congress Catalog Card Number:
ISBN: 0-03-059719-6

123456789 145 987654321
Printed in the United States of America

To
Robert Boguslaw
sine qua non

PREFACE

This book investigates a central and fascinating aspect of human life—social time. We cannot say merely _time_ but must add the adjective _social_. The reason for this will become abundantly clear in the first chapters. Briefly, however, the point is time is not something that exists independently of human life, something that is objectively "out there" somewhere (as Sir Isaac Newton defined it), but is something that is always socially constructed. All of us live in social time, but most people are probably unaware that they do so.

Social time is an inevitable and pervasive aspect of human behavior and social life. The following examples are but a few of the numerous insights to be gained by those who probe into the temporal meaning of life:

> It was once possible to identify the grade of an official in the British Civil Service according to the time the official arrived at work.
> Temporal adjustments required by long-range jet travel may lead to headaches, burning eyes, digestive problems, sweating, and nightmares.
> An individual's performance in a mental task depends upon the time of day.
> Increasing the time pressure under which an individual works may lead that individual to strive for less ambitious goals.
> Working with a computer may be more or less stressful depending upon the time taken by the computer to respond to the worker.
> The dominant temporal orientation of a society will affect the rate and direction of change in that society.

These are but a few of the numerous findings that are emerging from the growing interest in and study of the temporal. Psychologists, philosophers, anthropologists, sociologists, and others are probing into the temporal dimension of human life with increasing intensity and presenting us with an intriguing variety of findings.

In spite of considerable work on the temporal, however, there is as yet no systematic effort to take the diverse materials and present them together as an exploration of the temporal aspects of all human life. This volume is an attempt to correct that deficiency: to utilize the work coming out of the various disciplines, to provide a useful conceptual framework, and to examine the wide range of materials from different disciplines through the lens of that framework. I have, of course, also used some of my own research on temporality. Hopefully, this book will stimulate even more research and further development of the conceptual framework. As our understanding of the temporal nature of human life expands, we may be able to go beyond the state of the Concord laboring man described by Thoreau: "He has no time to be anything but a machine."

I am grateful to those who encouraged me to pursue the study of time and who helped my developing perspective with their critical reactions to my early efforts. George Rawick was particularly insightful and helpful. His extensive knowledge in many disciplines corrected some of my flaws and opened up some new directions for my work. Robert Boguslaw, to whom the book is dedicated, was the first person to encourage me to pursue the problem of temporality. He supported my early efforts and provided in his own person a model of scholarship disciplined by both an academic and a moral commitment.

CONTENTS

		Page
PREFACE		vii

CHAPTER

1	CONFRONTING TIME	1
	The Centrality of the Temporal	3
	Philosophical Time	7
	Psychological Time	10
	Social Time	13
	Summary: Confronting the Devouring Monster	15
	Notes	17
2	THE MEANING OF SOCIAL TIME	21
	Social Time versus Clock Time	21
	Social Time as Conceptualization	26
	The Structure of Social Time	28
	Social Time and Social Process	41
	Conclusion	45
	Notes	46
3	THE INDIVIDUAL IN TIME	52
	The Self As Process	54
	Temporal Socialization	57
	The Temporal Dimensions of Self-Concepts	63
	The Oriented Individual	67
	The Disoriented Individual	70
	The Actualizing Individual	73
	Notes	80
4	SOCIAL TIME AND HUMAN INTERACTION	86
	Interaction as Process	86
	Interaction in Social Time	87
	Social Time and Status Relationships	95
	Social Time and Power Relationships	99

CHAPTER		Page
	Social Time and Conflict Relationships	102
	Notes	107
5	SOCIAL TIME AND SOCIAL CHANGE	112
	Social Time and Planning	113
	Social Time and Modernization	117
	A Case Study: Nineteenth-Century China and Japan	121
	Conclusion	143
	Notes	145
BIBLIOGRAPHY		152
NAME INDEX		174
SUBJECT INDEX		176
ABOUT THE AUTHOR		181

1
CONFRONTING TIME

Time is the greatest of all mysteries.[1] And its mystery becomes evident as soon as we begin to think about it, for our experience with time continually leads us into puzzles and paradoxes. Consider, for instance, the individual's experience, which is in a sense both intimate and impersonal.

> Though awareness and conceptions of time are products of the human mind, time itself seems to possess an existence apart, its passage impersonal and inexorable. As an old Italian proverb put it, "Man measures time and time measures man." This intimate and personal, yet aloof and detached character constitutes the paradox of human time.[2]

Or consider the contradiction between our commonsense experience of time and the nature of time according to relativistic physics (a contradiction, incidentally, that was the initial stimulus for my own study of the meaning of time). In our experience, time seems to be an absolute, unchanging, inexorable process. But relativistic physics teaches that time is relative to motion. In particular, time slows down in the direction of motion, and measurably so as the motion approaches the speed of light. Thus, in a spaceship that traveled at 260,000 kilometers per second, the travelers would spend one year in space for every two years that elapsed on earth.[3]

As a final example of the mystery of time, consider the fact that there seems to be an inverse relationship between our growing understanding and increasing efforts to control time, on the one hand, and our sense of being enslaved and oppressed by time, on the other hand. As Sebastian de Grazia succinctly stated: "What kind of rule is this? The more timesaving machinery there is, the more pressed a person is for time."[4] De Grazia notes that the more timesaving technologies we develop, the more "time-harried faces" we see. Our efforts to become masters seem to keep plunging us deeper into bondage.

Is time, then, a human good or a human millstone? Reactions to time have been diverse. People have both cursed the passage of time and welcomed it. They have seen in the temporal both the great destroyer and the wellspring of meaning. They have both identified time as somehow of their essence and scorned time as somehow peripheral to their ultimate being.

People, in other words, have confronted the temporal with ambivalent feelings. But the confrontation is inevitable. Indeed, if one were to write a history of concern with the temporal, one would find oneself compelled to probe into the primordial consciousness. Even at the most primitive level of human life, we have evidence of human awareness of and concern with temporality. Long before humans conceptualized numerical, temporal, and spatial differences, they had already acquired the "subtlest sensitivity to the peculiar periodicity and rhythms of human life."[5] In the mythical consciousness of the archaic human, there was an inner sense, an intuitive grasping, of the temporality of life. Although they could not conceptualize time in quantitative terms, archaic humans could and did give expression to their temporal nature through various rites that marked such events as birth, pregnancy, puberty, marriage, and death.

Human awareness of and concern with temporality is particularly evident in our unique concern for the dead—a distinctively human trait that has apparently characterized all people in all places and at all times. Archaeological evidence indicates that Paleolithic man had three basic concerns: food supply, birth, and death. The rituals surrounding death testify not only to a belief in some kind of postmortem existence, but also to the individual's anticipation of his own death. Thus, even at the dawn of human culture, "man was urgently aware of the temporal character of his life," aware of the fact that life had a beginning and that it would also have an inevitable end.[6]

But this awareness of and concern with the temporal has not always found adequate expression in human thought. The world's great thinkers have approached the subject in diverse ways, and some have either denied or ignored the fact of temporality as the essence of human life. In the remainder of this chapter, we will see some of this denial and neglect in various disciplines as well as some of the efforts to rectify the neglect as we explore the way in which thinkers from diverse disciplines have grappled with the temporal. First, we will look at how some physicists, economists, planners, and others have incorporated the temporal into their perspectives. Their efforts underscore the fact that the temporal is the essence of human existence and also illustrate the utility of adding the temporal dimension to our varied analyses. We will then examine more closely the way in which philosophers, psychologists, and sociologists have dealt with time (more closely because these disciplines were particularly important in the development of this book).

In subsequent chapters, I will fully develop a sociological approach to temporal analysis. A conceptual and theoretical framework for investigating social phenomena in temporal terms will be discussed. I will show the significance of that framework by applying it to analyses of the individual, of interaction, and of processes of social change. These analyses should demonstrate the significance of social time for human existence. By that point, hopefully, the "greatest of all human mysteries" will be a topic of greatest fascination.

THE CENTRALITY OF THE TEMPORAL

Certain ideas that were to find fuller development in the twentieth century emerged in the 1890s. One was the problem of the meaning of time and duration in psychology, philosophy, literature, and history.[7] Considerable impetus was given to interest in the problem by revolutionary changes in theoretical physics in the first years of the twentieth century, when time was declared to be dependent upon physical processes. Time, in other words, lost its absolute character. It could no longer be conceived in Newtonian terms as that which "of itself, and from its own nature, flows equably without regard to anything external." In relativistic physics, various observers cut out their space and their time in different fashions.[8] The world no longer contained a time that was independent of human processes and, in particular, of human consciousness. Furthermore, we could no longer treat space and time as separate and fixed frameworks. Rather, we must now deal with space-time if we are to fully understand physical processes.

Stimulated in part by the intriguing implications of the new physics, thinkers in various fields began to explore the meaning of temporality. It became increasingly clear that any viable theory must deal with temporality, whether the level of analysis is the physical, the infrahuman, or the human. Philosophers, historians, psychiatrists, musicians, linguists, analysts of drama and literature, and others all found that there were significant temporal dimensions to their fields of study.[9]

For example, in the field of economics Gary Becker and others have made considerable and fruitful use of time by looking at the implications of the allocation of time in both the market and nonmarket sectors. In particular, Becker has shown that the cost of time must be entered as a variable into analyses of both work and nonwork activities. The neglect of time in the past has led to some flawed understandings. Consider, for instance, the question of productivity. While productivity in the service sector (including retailing, transportation, education, health, and others) seems to have advanced more slowly over the past decades than productivity in the goods sector, we may get a different picture if we use household time as a variable in our analysis. Becker supports his argument with the example of the barbering industry.[10] Typical productivity measure indicate little advance in barber shops. But the activities performed by the shops have changed considerably. In the 1920s, shaving was an important part of the output. By the 1950s, shaving was a negligible activity of barbers. Men used the new home safety and electric razors to shave themselves, saving the time that they had to spend in the shop each day. If we constructed a measure of productivity for general barbering activities (which would include shaving), the measure might show the same kind of advance that has been evidenced by goods.

In other words, time is a scarce resource in our society and, as such, must be an integral part of economic analyses. Households are not merely passive consumers of goods and services. They are production units that employ a variety of resources, including time, to produce such nonmarketable commodities as health and prestige. Time becomes a resource by allocating it among members of the household. Those who are efficient at market activities would devote more time to them and less to consumption activities than other members. If a member becomes more efficient in a market activity, there will be a reallocation of time among the others, who will spend a greater proportion in consumption activities than they did formerly. In essence, the way the time of any particular member is allocated depends upon the skills and opportunities of all other members. Time is a resource that is allocated so as to maximize the production of valued, nonmarketable commodities.

Becker applies his theory of time allocation to a great many areas. We might note one other. Time is a measure of the satisfaction obtained from many market goods, for in numerous cases the satisfaction is directly proportional to the amount of time with which the goods are consumed:

> A boat moored to the dock all season, the daily newspaper tossed out without being unfolded, or a quick

lunch gulped down between appointments contributes less produce and hence less utility than would a leisurely (time consuming) use of each of these items. So an understanding of the use of time seems necessary for an understanding of the consumption of most market goods and services.[11]

The notion of the allocation of time has proven to be useful in a number of disciplines other than economics. They do not all use the term in the same fashion, but planners, geographers, social scientists, and others have gained many insights by studying the way people allocate their time. Time allocation studies, or time budgets as they are sometimes called, have been gathered for over half a century. They provide us with information on the way in which people allocate their time throughout each day, each week, or any time period of interest. We can chart all of the activities, showing how much time (and what time of the day or week) is devoted to the various activities. And of what use is such information? John Robinson begins his study of how Americans use their time by noting that the allocation of time is "of ultimate concern to every society. Even if it only enters indirectly or unconsciously into policy deliberations, the matter of whether time is spent wisely or unwisely bears heavily on the quality of societal life."[12]

We may illustrate the usefulness of time allocation studies by looking at a few of the ways they have been employed to investigate social phenomena. First, they have shown the diverse patterns of activities of males and females and of people in different age groups. We get a clearer picture of the similarities and differences in the activity patterns of the various groups within a society and between the various societies.[13] For instance, we have discovered how different groups or people in differing nations allocate their time among such activities as work, household chores, child care, personal needs, and various educational, recreational, and other leisure activities. Such information bears directly upon our evaluation of the quality of life. Thus, a comparison of 12 nations with regard to male-female differences in time use concluded that women in all the nations have a common problem, namely, too much work and too little time. Employed women tend to have considerably less free time than employed men because the women still accept the burden of household chores. The employed woman, however, just about doubles the amount of time spent on housework on her days off from work: clearly she must use them to catch up on these obligations rather than profit from them for rest and recuperation.[14] In none of the 12 nations surveyed, including the United States and the Soviet Union, was this problem resolved. The time allocation studies show the inequities faced by working women in nations throughout the world, inequities that depress the quality of life for those women.

Time allocation studies also help us to identify the values of people. Of course, a certain amount of time must necessarily be spent in caring for the necessities of life. But there is also a considerable amount of discretionary time, and we can tell something of people's values by examining the amount of time they allocate to such matters as religious activities, reading, watching television, working second jobs, volunteer work, and so forth.

Time allocation studies are useful to planners. They show activity patterns of people, including the amount of time people allocate to various activities. Planners can use these results to guide policymaking decisions for transportation, urban renewal, and other urban programs. For example, F. Stuart Chapin studied activity patterns in the metropolitan Washington, D.C., area and reported numerous findings that are directly relevant to the work of planners.[15] Among other things, he identified the way in which residents divided up their discretionary time differently at various times of the week; the variations by work status, sex, presence of children, race, and status; and the amount of time spent in passive versus active kinds of leisure. Such information, he notes, enables urban planners to understand how people use a city, to get a portrait of the rhythms of city life, and to identify the variations in patterns of activity among different segments of the population who follow diverse life-styles.

Many other uses have been made of time budgets, from the monitoring of social relationships to measuring the effectiveness of executives to predicting marital cohesion.[16] In all of the uses discussed, the allocation of time is treated as a social indicator, that is, as an index that is a measure of social well-being. Social indicators allow us to develop a social accounting system so that we can assess where we stand and where we are going with respect to our values and goals. The use of social indicators also enables us to evaluate specific programs and determine their impact. Time budgets are useful social indicators and are likely to find increasing utility in the future as more and more policymakers recognize the centrality of the temporal in social life.

In sum, in spite of considerable neglect there has been increasing concern with, and recognition of, the centrality of the temporal in numerous disciplines throughout the twentieth century. Temporality, as J. T. Fraser has persuasively argued, is inherent in all things, from particulate matter to human societies.[17] Increasingly, researchers from a broad range of backgrounds are investigating the temporal implications of everything from the physical world to human social life.

As suggested, however, the way in which the temporal is investigated will vary from one discipline to another. Some researchers are interested only in quantitative time. Others find that qualitative as well as quantitative time is important in their work. The present work is an attempt to take into account all of the dimensions of time that bear upon social life. These dimensions emerged out of an examination of the treatment of time in numerous disciplines, including physics, philosophy, psychology, anthropology, sociology, and, to some extent, history, economics, and a few others. Basically, I wanted to see what others were saying about time before I developed a sociological analysis. I have profited from all of the works I read, but have been particularly influenced by philosophical, psychological, and sociological efforts. We will, therefore, look at these in more detail. Our examination of the first two will highlight the distinctiveness of the sociological approach. An examination of prior sociological works will show the foundations upon which the present work is built.

PHILOSOPHICAL TIME

The first serious effort to deal with the problem of time was that of Aristotle in his Physics.[18] Aristotle asked the question, "In what sense, if any, can time be said to exist?" Although philosophers have concerned themselves with other aspects of temporality, including the problem of the source of our ideas about time, the dominant concern has been with the answer to Aristotle's question, and particularly with the problem of the reality or nonreality of time. Furthermore, if the reality of time is asserted, an additional question is raised: does that time inhere in "things in themselves" or is it real only in the consciousness of man?

Some philosophers have argued that the temporal is of ultimate significance, while others have declared it to be relatively unimportant or even illusory. A common conclusion (and, in my judgment, an unfortunate one) is that the temporal dimension of human life does not possess the ultimate importance of the nontemporal or the eternal. Thinkers who are otherwise quite diverse in their perspectives—Plato, Kant, Bradley, and so forth—agree in denying any ultimate significance to the temporal mode of perception.[19]

Perhaps the only point of agreement in the philosophical debates is that the problem of developing a logical theory about time from the fact of the experience of time is overwhelming.[20] As a result, numerous thinkers have concluded that the problem of time presents us with irresolvable contradictions, time is essentially an irrational concept, and because reality is rational, it follows that time is not part of reality. Ultimate reality must be timeless, unchanging. This kind of reasoning has prevailed in both the East and West; time has been defined as illusion and placed at the level of appearance. Once having placed it here, the philosophers have left it there with contempt.[21]

To those of us whose whole lives seem to be structured if not tyrannized by the clock, the philosophical debate about the reality of time may sound like something of an anomaly. But the philosopher is concerned with issues that are of broader significance than any individual life. Often the manner in which the issue has been expressed has been in terms of the apparent contradiction between being and becoming, or permanence and change. The contradiction can be illustrated by considering an ancient Greek example: a stream. As the water flows by, one gets the impression that the stream is quite the same over a stretch of time. There is movement, but no fundamental change. Yet it could be argued that the stream is changing, that the quality of the water or the depth and width of the stream are slowly, even if imperceptibly, changing. The notion that the stream does not fundamentally change, therefore, is an illusion of perception. On the other hand, it could be argued that the stream remains fundamentally the same, and that whatever minute changes one notes are mere appearance that do not alter the basic nature of the stream.

In other words, a typical solution to the problem of change versus permanence has been to make one real and the other only apparent, so that either change (becoming) is somehow reduced to permanence (being) or permanence (being) is somehow reduced to change (becoming).[22] The latter solution is represented by Heraclitus while the former is commonly associated with Zeno. Heraclitus stressed the "flux of things," the fact that no man can step into the same stream twice. But he did not see a threat in the temporal flux as have some other thinkers. Rather, Heraclitus was led to a "passionate affirmation of existence"; he discovered a "hidden harmony" in the temporal flux so that "there is no peace and beatitude in the negation of change, in perfection with tension. . . ."[23]

If it is possible to find harmony in change, to see the meaning of human existence rooted in the passage of time rather than stifled by that passage of time, why have so many philosophers opted for the changeless and eternal as true reality? Why has the temporal so often been treated as only of peripheral significance for human life? I suggest two possible reasons. One is that the devaluation of the temporal may reflect a prior devaluation of human life and existence. If it is argued that the universe has been emptied of "both the Glory of God and Glory of Man," so that the human is a creature whose presumed significance is only a form of self-delusion,[24] then the temporal flux in which people exist may also be of little import.

A second possible reason is the effort of humans to transcend in some way their own finitude. Paleolithic man created rituals for the dead in a search for transcendental meaning, and subsequent generations have sought that meaning in the affirmation of the ultimate significance of the eternal rather than of the temporal. This may be seen particularly in certain strands of thought such as Hinduism. In the Indian conception, time is static, reality is unchanging, and temporal existence is "ontologically nonexistence, unreality."[25] That is, the temporal world that we apprehend through our senses is illusion, lacking reality because of its bounded duration. In the vision of infinite time, on the other hand, is knowledge and liberation. To transcend the temporal is to transcend karma, the symbol of man's slavery.[26] The endless cycles of human existence through reincarnation are man's bondage. Liberation comes through breaking the chains of the temporal process.

This static notion of reality even finds expression in the language. In the classical Indian languages, there were no words that corresponded to the idea "to become." Further, there were no linguistic ways of distinguishing between the ideas of becoming and being. Ultimate reality was conceived to be atemporal, for true existence is Brahman, the Absolute, Pure Consciousness, beyond all time. Time, space, and causality are all illusory:

> . . . the reality of the tangible universe is only apparent and derivative. The empirical reality of things is derived from the Absolute Reality of Brahman, as the apparent reality of a mirage is derived from the reality of the desert.[27]

In light of such ideas about temporality, it is understandable that the Hindu, whether philosopher or not, would seek freedom by withdrawing into his or her inner being rather than by actively striving to manipulate the external world.

The philosophical approach, then, deals primarily with the reality or nonreality of time. Included in this problem are questions about the locus of the time that is real (if it is real) and the relationship between our experience of time and the actuality of time. I have followed those philosophers who accept the reality of time and, in particular, those process philosophers who assert the dynamic nature of all being. We shall meet some of their philosophical ideas in the next chapter, along with a discussion of the problem that confronts sociologists as well as philosophers: what is the relationship between our perception of time and the actuality of time?

PSYCHOLOGICAL TIME

Psychological interest in, and studies of, time increased rapidly after 1930. Looking at the number of entries in the <u>Psychological Abstracts</u>, we find that there were 32 on time in 1930, representing 0.62 percent of all entries. By 1967, there were 460 entries, and these represented 5.7 percent of the total. The greatest increase, incidentally, occurred after 1960.

It is not merely that interest has grown, however, but also that it has expanded in scope. Early psychologists were primarily concerned with the study of time perception. In more recent times, psychologists have integrated their studies of temporal experience with studies of various facets of personality. The more recent studies include the investigation of time orientations, time perspectives, and "the study of 'macro-events' revolving around the relationships between persons' past, present and future within their phenomenological frames of reference."[28]

A comprehensive study of psychological work in the area of the temporal has been provided by Paul Fraisse, who has grouped the work into three categories: the conditioning of time, the perception of time, and the mastery of time.[29] The conditioning of time refers to the biological level of adaptation and characterizes the behavior of both humans and lower animals. That is, changes occur in the organism as a result of the conditioning of the environment; that environment subjects the organism to regular changes. For example, circadian (24-hour) rhythms in animals are nearly always acquired rather than instinctual. As an illustration, Fraisse tells of an experiment in which bees were trained to come for food at a particular hour in Paris and were then flown to New York. On the next day, they came for their food at the same time of day—that is, the Paris time rather than the New York time.

Such rhythmic patterns are common not only in animals but in humans. The baby has no innate preference for day or night sleep, but simply has numerous periods of sleep throughout the 24-hour period. The preference for night rather than day and for longer and fewer periods is learned in the social environment. Likewise, babies may be taught to eat at three-hour intervals, four-hour intervals, or on demand. European parents have customarily followed the first pattern; Americans have varied, sometimes striving for four-hour intervals and sometimes allowing the child to indicate its own pattern.

The second category of psychological study, the perception of time, deals with the way in which we adapt to change by apprehending changes when they occur. Psychologists have been interested in the specific limitations of this apprehension, that is, the shortest interval of time in which change can be perceived and the longest interval of time that can be considered the "present." For example, we perceive a sentence spoken by someone else as a whole; the words obviously occur over some period of time, but they are apprehended as a unit. This unit of apprehension is the psychological present, and a number of efforts have been made to measure it in terms of both the shortest and longest interval possible for humans.

Finally, the control over time, the third category of study, refers to the investigation of those phenomena through which we form representations of changes and thus gain some control over them. Memory, for example, enables us to reconstruct the past and to anticipate the future. In this way, we create both a past and a future, a temporal horizon that forms the framework which provides significance to our behavior. Such an ability should not be taken lightly; in fact, some thinkers would argue that our ability to incorporate past and future into our behavior is what distinguishes us from the lower animals.

In sum, the psychological investigation of time focuses upon the individual's experience of the temporal. It seeks to understand both the source of the psychological sense of time and the consequences for behavior. It strives to understand the nature of the experience of temporal phenomena and to integrate that experience into various other psychological processes. While our concerns will go beyond these, they will also include them; the psychologists have demonstrated well the centrality of the temporal at the individual level.

As pointed out, however, psychological interest in the temporal has greatly increased in more recent years. Why did earlier generations of psychologists neglect the temporal if indeed it is central to our understanding of human behavior? Probably the most important reason is to be found in the dominance of behaviorism, which virtually assured psychology of a neglect of the temporal. As Robert E. Ornstein points out, it was with "Watson's purging of 'mentalism' from psychology in the early 1900s" that "time's tributary almost dried up. The flow of research on consciousness as a whole began to slacken, the work on time even more so."[30] The reason for this attenuation of research, Ornstein claims, is the incompatibility of an objectively oriented psychology with the study of experiential phenomena. The individual studied by behaviorists acts on the basis of external stimuli. The individual's consciousness is an unnecessary facet of the scientific understanding of behavior.

Behaviorists, then, have not rejected all temporal studies—only those that involve a phenomenological approach. Behaviorists are concerned with such temporal aspects of human life as schedules of reinforcement. But from the point of view of the cognitive psychologist—or of any social scientist who accepts the importance of cognitive processes—the behaviorists have ignored or rejected as irrelevant some of the most significant temporal facets of human life.

In the related field of psychoanalysis, a different situation has existed. Freud contended that time is a mode of perception but that the unconscious mental processes are timeless. In other words, time does not alter the content of the unconscious processes.[31] Furthermore, the "flow of time" that marks our conscious existence does not apply to the unconscious. This disparity between the conscious and unconscious processes may be illustrated by the phenomenon of dreaming. In the dream, we may perceive a sequence of events holistically, Godlike, simultaneously. Linear time with its rigidity and logically ordered sequence does not constrain us in our dreams. Joost A. M. Meerloo sums up the matter well:

> The time as experienced in dreams is without localization in time line and without any direction. Past and present often are painted beside each other in a distorted symbolic way. . . . The unconscious has no conception of time as duration and continuity. Only analysis and interpretation make it into a continual process.[32]

As a result of this perspective, psychoanalysts have been concerned with the developmental aspects of time perception, but have not generally viewed time as of the essence of human existence. Although we exist as temporal beings, the deepest levels of our existence—the unconscious processes—are taken to be timeless. But this, it seems, is inadequate, for it presents us as temporally fragmented creatures.

At any rate, the discipline of psychology has experienced a surge of interest in the temporal facets of human existence. Americans have lagged behind the French in this respect, but the interest is growing and the significance is being affirmed. In recent years, journals have published papers that relate the temporal to issues, ranging from the minor matter of whether human electrodermal activity has the same diurnal variations as other physiological measures to the important question of psychological well-being. American psychologists—or at least some of them—are reaffirming the critical significance of human temporality.

SOCIAL TIME

In the next chapter, I will fully explicate the meaning of social time. Here I want to note the work of three sociologists that may be regarded as pioneering efforts to develop a sociology of time: Pitirim Sorokin, Georges Gurvitch, and Wilbert E. Moore. Each, in one way or another, has influenced the present effort. We should note that apart from these three and a few minor efforts, the temporal ordering of behavior has received sparse attention in sociology until the 1970s. Sociologists have been concerned with the invariant or recurrent patterns of social behavior. Of course, all sociologists recognize the existence of processes in social life, but actual research typically fails to incorporate the temporal dimension.[33]

Of those sociologists who did attend to the temporal, Pitirim Sorokin was one of the earliest and most prolific writers on the topic. Sorokin emphasized that social time differs from astronomical time, the former being an expression of "the change or movement of social phenomena in terms of other social phenomena taken as points of reference."[34] Nevertheless, there is a significant correlation between social time and astronomical time in modern life, for in a clock-tyrannized society, activities are not accorded a span of time that would seem to be necessary by the nature of those activities but are bound instead by "mechanically imposed units of watch time."[35] Watch time is imposed upon all human activity, including working, sleeping, eating, loving, quarreling, studying, and praying. According to Sorokin, we are obsessed by the mechanistic timing of all activities. And, indeed, it is not difficult to find numerous illustrations that support his argument. Consider the mother who makes her son sit for hours on a toilet because it is "time" that he is trained or the man who devotes his life to showing businesses how to maximize the value of every minute of their employee's time. Or consider the woman who can write an article for a religious magazine describing how she kept a meticulous record of her time and concluding: "I see where I can pinch a minute or be frivolous with ten. It is almost like handling money."[36]

Sorokin also explored various facets of temporality, such as synchronicity and order, rhythm and phases, the periodicity of rhythms, and tempo. For example, we find in social life such two-phase rhythms as depression-prosperity cycles in business, movements of idealism-materialism in philosophy, and even such mundane matters as movements of transportation between two terminal points. We find such three-phase rhythms as the familiar thesis, antithesis, and synthesis of Hegel and Marx, the rhythm of social movements from the ideological phase through the organizational phase to the power phase, and so forth.

Obviously, social time includes far more than the minutes and hours of the clock, however much modern people may be obsessed with that clock. Georges Gurvitch, the second of the three sociologists, was a philosophically oriented thinker who argued that there are different kinds of time for various spheres of reality. The time that is applicable to social reality, according to Gurvitch, is "the most complex and most enigmatic to comprehend."[37] For purposes of understanding social life eight different kinds of time are important—enduring time, deceptive time, erratic time, cyclical time, retarded time, alternating time, time in advance of itself, and explosive time.[38]

Gurvitch is a provocative writer, but much of his work has probably sounded more like verbal artistry than scientific analysis, particularly to empirically oriented American sociologists. For example, time in advance of itself is time in which the future becomes present. It is the time, in theory, of the proletariat and also of competitive capitalism. It is the time of the active masses (in contrast to the passive masses, who are characterized by erratic time). Thus, like Sorokin, Gurvitch stressed the fact that social time is more than clock time; in fact, it is "not always measurable and even more not always quantifiable."[39]

A very different approach to the study of temporality has been offered by Wilbert E. Moore, who most often refers to or implies clock time in his discussion.[40] Such time presents itself to man both as a scarce resource and as a mode of ordering one's life. With respect to the latter, Moore posits three elements: synchronization, sequence, and rate. The first refers to the necessity for simultaneous actions; the second to the fact that certain actions require a specific ordering; and the third emerges as a result of the fact that the frequency of events during a particular period of time may be a crucial factor.[41]

In contrast to Sorokin and Gurvitch, Moore tends to focus upon time as a quantitative variable. As a variable in analysis, time may be either dependent or independent. As an independent variable, time is the context within which certain processes occur, for example, we can use time to compare rates of transition or of diffusion in differing systems. As a dependent variable, time becomes a strategy. Temporal strategies involve the deliberate manipulation of time (in terms of rates, for example) in an effort to gain or secure power, to secure loyalty of members to an organization, and so forth. More than one labor problem has involved the efforts of both management and workers to control the pace of the assembly line, and more than one organization has measured the loyalty and commitment of its members in terms of the amount of time they give to the organization.

Moore has also called attention to the importance of temporal orientations and perspectives: "The future is the cause of the present in substantial degree. . . ."[42] That statement could well represent the call to intellectual arms of a burgeoning group of thinkers who have become obsessed with the study of the future. Both liberal and radical sociologists may be found who say essentially the same thing with regard to the future: our capacity for both constructive and destructive acts demands that we now grapple seriously with the question of creating the future rather than merely trying to predict or adapt to the future.

Despite these noteworthy sociological efforts to deal with temporality, sociologists on the whole have neglected the temporal. Perhaps this has happened because sociology was born in the midst of convulsive changes. The nineteenth-century world in which sociology emerged was a world of turbulence, and many of the early sociologists were concerned with the factors that make for stability and integration. In general, sociologists have always been more concerned with structures than with processes (though there are some exceptions). And structures, unlike processes, do not necessarily demand a consideration of temporality.

SUMMARY: CONFRONTING THE DEVOURING MONSTER

Although thinkers from diverse disciplines have grappled with the problem of time, the study of the temporal is in its infancy.[43] And although the temporal is central to human existence, many thinkers have either ignored or minimized temporality. As I have shown, there are a number of reasons for this neglect. First, the temporal has sometimes been suppressed because of logical necessity, that is, the devaluation, denial, and/or neglect of the temporal may follow logically from the premises of a system of thought. This has been true in philosophical idealism and in Freudian thought.

A second reason for the neglect has been a mechanistic view of science. Although the physical sciences no longer proceed on the basis of a Newtonian world, the human sciences have tended to proceed upon the assumption that a mechanistic science can apprehend all of reality. The human sciences have tended to assume what Alfred North Whitehead called "simple location."[44] In this view, the world is composed of material entities that are simply here or there in space, in time, or in space-time; these entities require no reference beyond themselves for their explanation. They are "indifferent to the division of time," so that the passage of time "is an accident rather than of the essence. . . . "[45] Some sociologists have assumed simple location in social life by proceeding as if the historical, the temporal, could be ignored in analyzing social phenomena.

A third reason for temporal neglect has been a low view of human life and/or of mundane existence. Eastern philosophy has tended to view present existence as a bondage rather than as the essence of life. To the extent that the human essence or human existence is devalued, the problem of temporality will also be demoted to a place of relative insignificance.

Finally, the temporal has been neglected because of existential anxiety. It is said that when Rousseau threw away his watch in order that it could no longer remind him of the time, "he was full of joy and thanked heaven."[46] The story well illustrates an aspect of modern thought: the existential anxiety that is generated by the awareness of temporality. Mircea Eliade calls this anxiety the "terror of history," and maintains that the rejection of history by archaic man is a "reidentification with the modes of nature" in order to maintain his freedom and creativity. The latter, from the mythical point of view, are lost on the individual who "wills to be historical," since that individual is no longer free to be what he or she was, to annul personal history by the "periodic abolition of time and collective regeneration."[47]

In his 1949 Howison lecture, George Boas also commented upon the "disagreeable" implications of the "acceptance of time."[48] Change, he argued, involves loss, so that time has been viewed as the "great destroyer." People have, therefore, fled from time because the world of change is both illogical and evil. Such a viewpoint is exemplified in Shakespeare's sonnets, in which the poet rages against the "bloody tyrant, Time" who slowly but inexorably deprives his beloved of her youth and beauty. And nothing, the poet laments, is able to withstand "Time's scythe."

An interesting experiment relating to this idea of time as a destroyer was conducted by Robert H. Knapp and John T. Garbutt.[49] The two researchers correlated various time metaphors with n Achievement (need to achieve) scores; that is, they tried to determine whether people with a high need to achieve thought about time in distinctive ways. One metaphor used was that of time as "the devouring monster." This they found to yield the highest negative correlation of all metaphors with n Achievement—the higher the need to achieve, the stronger the rejection of the notion of time as a devouring monster. They suggested that the image of the devouring monster may be an "obnoxious threat" to the person who has a high need to achieve since the implication is that time is a destructive force that threatens to destroy even the self.

Thus, both archaic and modern people find that the awareness of temporality generates anxiety. This has led to efforts to ignore or deny or in some way transcend the temporal. In the case of the archaic person, the "myth of the eternal return" performed this function. In the case of moderns, a variety of religious and philosophical perspectives have been employed. Existentialism, for example, makes time a matter of central concern, but the purpose is to "'transcend' this situated mode of man's existence."[50]

In the following chapters we will confront the devouring monster. However, I will proceed upon the assumptions that time is not the great destroyer, social reality is a process, and humans are temporal creatures. Time, as G. W F. Hegel stated, is both our "destiny and necessity."[51] Social time therefore reflects both the necessities and the destiny of human existence.

NOTES

1. Robert MacIver, The Challenge of the Passing Years (New York: Simon and Schuster, 1962), p. 47.
2. Alden E. Wessman and Bernard S. Gorman, "The Emergence of Human Awareness and Concepts of Time," in The Personal Experience of Time, ed. Bernard S. Gorman and Alden E. Wessman (New York: Plenum Press, 1977), p. 3.
3. See L. D. Landau and G. B. Rumer, What Is Relativity? (New York: Basic Books, 1960), pp. 47-51.
4. Sebastian de Grazia, Of Time, Work, and Leisure (Garden City: Anchor Books, 1962), p. 313.
5. Ernst Cassirer, The Philosophy of Symbolic Forms, vol. 2 (New Haven: Yale University Press, 1955), p. 108.
6. S. G. F. Brandon, "Time and the Destiny of Man," in The Voices of Time, ed. J. T. Fraser (New York: George Braziller, 1966), p. 143.
7. W. Stuart Hughes, Consciousness and Society (New York: Random House, 1958), p. 64.
8. Louis de Broglie, The Revolution in Physics (New York: The Noonday Press, 1953), p. 100.
9. A good introduction to the way in which thinkers from diverse disciplines have used or analyzed time is J. T. Fraser, ed., The Voices of Time (New York: George Braziller, 1966).
10. Gary S. Becker, The Economic Approach To Human Behavior (Chicago: University of Chicago Press, 1976), pp. 103-4.
11. Ibid., p. 142.
12. John P. Robinson, How Americans Use Time: A Social-Psychological Analysis of Everyday Behavior (New York: Praeger, 1977), p. 3.

13. Robinson, How Americans Use Time; John Farley, "Activities and Pastimes of Children and Youth: Age, Sex, and Parental Effects," Journal of Comparative Family Studies 10 (Autumn 1979):385-410; John P. Robinson, Philip E. Converse, and Alexander Szalai, "Everyday Life in Twelve Countries," in The Use of Time: Daily Activities of Urban and Suburban Populations in Twelve Countries, ed. Alexander Szalai (The Hague: Mouton, 1972), pp. 113-44.

14. Robinson, Converse, and Szalai, "Everyday Life," p. 121.

15. F. Stuart Chapin, Jr., Human Activity Patterns in the City (New York: John Wiley, 1974).

16. See C. Neil Bull, "The Use of Time-Budgets To Monitor Social Relations" (Paper presented at the Midwest Sociological Society, March 1973); Ross A. Webber, Time and Management (New York: Van Nostrand Reinhold, 1972), pp. 91-92, 154 f.; and Karoly Varga, "Leisure and Divorce: Marital Cohesion in the Time-Budget," New Hungarian Quarterly 11 (Winter 1970):137-50.

17. J. T. Fraser, Time As Conflict (Basel and Stuttgart: Birkhauser Verlag, 1978).

18. See Richard M. Gale, ed., The Philosophy of Time (Garden City: Doubleday, 1967), pp. 1 ff.

19. G. J. Whitrow, The Natural Philosophy of Time (New York: Harper & Row, 1961), p. 289.

20. Hans Meyerhoff, Time in Literature (Berkeley and Los Angeles: University of California Press, 1955), p. 7.

21. George Boas, The Acceptance of Time, University of California Publications in Philosophy, vol. 16 (Berkeley: University of California Press, 1950), p. 250.

22. A. Cornelius Benjamin, "Ideas of Time in the History of Philosophy," in The Voices of Time, ed. J. T. Fraser (New York: George Braziller, 1966), p. 10.

23. Cassirer, The Philosophy of Symbolic Forms, p. 135.

24. See Joseph Wood Krutch, The Modern Temper (New York: Harcourt, Brace, 1929), pp. 135-41.

25. Mircea Eliade, "Time and Eternity in Indian Thought," in Man and Time, ed. Joseph Campbell (New York: Pantheon Books, 1957), p. 181.

26. Mircea Eliade, The Myth of the Eternal Return (New York: Pantheon Books, 1954), p. 117.

27. Swami Nikhilananda, The Upanishads, vol. 1 (New York: Harper & Brothers, 1949), p. 39.

28. Melvin Wallace and Albert I. Rabin, "Temporal Experience," Psychological Bulletin 57 (1960): 213.

29. Paul Fraisse, The Psychology of Time, trans. Jennifer Leith (New York: Harper & Row, 1963).

30. Robert E. Ornstein, The Psychology of Consciousness, 2d ed. (New York: Harcourt Brace Jovanovich, 1977), pp. 101-2.

31. Sigmund Freud, Collected Papers, vol. 4 (London: Hogarth Press, 1925), p. 119.

32. Joost A. M. Meerloo, "The Time Sense in Psychiatry," in The Voices of Time, ed. J. T. Fraser (New York: George Braziller, 1966), p. 247.

33. Julia S. Brown and Brian G. Gilmartin, "Sociology Today: Lacunae, Emphases, and Surfeits," American Sociologist 4 (November 1969): 287.

34. Pitirim A. Sorokin and Robert K. Merton, "Social Time: A Methodological and Functional Analysis," American Journal of Sociology 42 (March 1937): 618.

35. Pitirim A. Sorokin, Social and Cultural Dynamics, vol. 2 (New York: American Book, 1937), p. 235.

36. Marilyn L. Bailey, "How Well Spent Is Your Time?" Home Life, November 1971, pp. 50-51.

37. Georges Gurvitch, "Social Structure and the Multiplicity of Times," in Sociological Theory, Values, and Sociocultural Change, ed. Edward A. Tiryakian (New York: Harper & Row, 1963), p. 173.

38. Georges Gurvitch, The Spectrum of Social Time (Dordrecht, Holland: D. Reidel, 1964), pp. 30-33.

39. Ibid., p. 19.

40. Wilbert E. Moore, Man, Time, and Society (New York: John Wiley, 1963).

41. Ibid., p. 5.

42. Wilbert E. Moore, Order and Change: Essays in Comparative Sociology (New York: John Wiley & Sons, 1967), p. 300.

43. Anthropology is one discipline that has devoted considerable and fruitful attention to time. Anthropologists have sought to point out cultural differences, to identify cultural sources of temporal ideas, and to show the manner in which temporal ideas function in the whole of a given culture. Because anthropologists have been less remiss than others to deal with temporality, I have omitted them from this chapter, but their contributions will appear throughout the book.

44. Alfred North Whitehead, Science and the Modern World (New York: Macmillan, 1925), p. 50.

45. Ibid., p. 51.

46. John Cohen, Humanistic Psychology (New York: Collier Books, 1958), p. 118.

47. Eliade, The Myth of the Eternal Return, pp. 155-57.

48. Boas, The Acceptance of Time, p. 250.

49. Robert H. Knapp and John T. Garbutt, "Time Imagery and the Achievement Motive," Journal of Personality 26 (1958): 426-34.
50. Meyerhoff, Time in Literature, p. 18.
51. G. W. F. Hegel, The Phenomenology of Mind, trans. J. B. Baillie (New York: Harper, 1967), p. 800.

2

THE MEANING OF SOCIAL TIME

Our quest for understanding must continually surmount the obstacles of everyday language. "Time," for example, immediately presents us with the image of the clock. But social time is not equivalent to clock time, for by social time, I refer to the patterns and orientations that relate to social processes and to the conceptualization of the ordering of social life. In this chapter, I will offer materials that stress the distinction between social and clock time, and then explicate more carefully the meaning of social time and its significance for social life.

SOCIAL TIME VERSUS CLOCK TIME

Actually, a diverse group of thinkers have recognized and argued that social time must be distinguished from clock time. The philosopher Henri Bergson, for example, insisted that the homogeneous time of Newtonian physics is not the time that reveals to us the essence of man.[1] Philip Bock, an anthropologist, has shown how an Indian wake can be meaningfully analyzed in terms of "gathering time," "prayer time," "singing time," "intermission," and "meal time."[2] None of these "times" has any particular relationship to clock time; the mourners move from one time to another by consensual feeling rather than by the clock. And, finally, certain kinds of psychological disorders may be viewed in terms of the individual living wholly in the present, as though both past and future were severed from consciousness.[3]

The point of each of the above examples is that we can clearly distinguish between social and clock time; the former is a more inclusive concept and may or may not be related to the latter. The same lack of necessary correlation between social time and clock time may be seen in the mythical consciousness. In mythical thought, magic can be employed to negate the temporal order that inheres in causality. A warrior who is wounded by an arrow may attend to his pain by hanging the arrow up where it is cool or by applying ointment to the arrow. This implies a reversibility of clock time, a wrenching of the present back into the past in order to alter the course of events. For mythical people, temporal intervals are not simple, homogeneous series; rather, they contain an inherent quality, an essence and efficacy of their own.[4] Thus, the objectivity represented by clock time is unknown to the mythical person.

This is not to say that people who lack or minimize clock time also lack either regularity or temporal measurement. Both regularity and measurement may be achieved by natural and/or social phenomena. P. E. Ariotti gives a number of examples of natural events that have been used for timing human activities:

> The arrival of the cranes in ancient Greece, Hesiod noted, marks the time for planting, the return of the swallows the end of pruning. Even more reliable are celestial events. . . . The South African Bushmen, who lack all systematic knowledge of astronomy, note the rising of Sirius and Canopus and reckon the progress of winter by their movement across the night sky.[5]

An example of social activities used to mark time is provided by the Nuer, whose temporal concepts reflect both the ecological setting of the culture and the relationships within the social structure. Thus, the Nuer calendar is based upon cyclic ecological changes. Fishing dams are constructed and cattle camps formed in the month of _kur_, and when "one is doing these things it must be _kur_ or thereabouts." Likewise, the camps are broken and the people return to the villages in the month of _dwat_, and "since people are on the move it must be _dwat_ or thereabouts."[6]

E. R. Leach points out that among the Kachin people of North Burma there is no word that is the equivalent of the English "time." Where we would speak of the "time" of the clock, the Kachin use _ahkying_; but a long "time" is _na_, and a short "time" is _tawng_. Spring "time" is _ta_ and a "time" of one's life is _asak_, and so forth. In other words, there is no external objectivity to which the Kachin people refer in their various conceptualizations of time.[7]

Similarly, Sorokin has noted that such divisions of time as the week reflect social conditions rather than mechanical Newtonian divisions. Most societies have some kind of week, but the week may consist of three, four, five, six, seven, eight, nine, or sixteen or more days. In many instances, these are reflections of the cycle of market activities. The Khasi week is eight days because the Khasi hold market every eighth day, and the names of the days of the week are names of places where principal markets occur.[8]

Some peoples exhibit a social time that is not only different from clock time but actually hostile to or scornful of the latter. Certain peasants in Algeria live with indifference to the passage of clock time and despise haste in human affairs. They have no notion of exact times of appointment, lack exact times for eating, and label the clock as "the devil's mill."[9]

This is not to say, however, that clock time is unimportant or irrelevant. I have only argued that there is no _necessary_ correlation with social time. But clock time takes on paramount importance in a social context like the modern West where the watch becomes something of a tyrant. In such a context, activities that previously could only be analyzed in terms of a social time, where social phenomena were expressed in terms of other social phenomena, now become explicable in terms of their ordering according to the clock. Great portions of human life become subservient to the dictates of the clock. As Johnathan Swift expressed it, Gulliver never did anything without looking at his watch. "He called it his oracle, and said it pointed out the time for every action of his life." The Lilliputians concluded that the watch was Gulliver's god.[10]

When we turn from literature to actual behavior, we find many examples of an obsession with clock time. For instance, in The Use of Time, published in 1947, the author states at the outset that he is 43 years old, which means that he probably has "only 227,760 hours to go." He then proceeds to detail how he will maximize the use of those remaining hours of his life. For example, he has been sleeping eight hours a night, though he can do with six. Thus:

> Here, then, is the first big saving I can effect—two hours a day for 26 years amounts to 18,980 hours. Converted into 20-hour days, that is equivalent to about two years and two months, but since these salvaged hours would all be waking-hours and no deduction need be made from them for sleep, this change in my daily schedule will virtually lengthen my life about two years and eleven months![11]

Rather than being analyzed in terms of significant events or stages, human life is turned into a lengthy succession of minutes and hours, and the individual's existence becomes a compulsive and frantic effort to avoid waste.

We have only begun to explore the implications of this tendency to order all of modern life by the clock. The deeper we probe, the more facets of our existence will we discover to be affected in one way or another by clock time. In some cases, we will see that clock time is an independent variable that requires us to revise our understanding about some social process. Richard J. Gelles and Robert R. Faulkner illustrate this in their study of the role of time in television news work.[12] The two researchers found that time is a major factor in the production of unscheduled "hard" news (hard news refers to events such as fires, homicides, and accidents that have a certain urgency to them). They summarize their research in three propositions. First, the news value of an event is directly proportional to the time invested in covering it. An event may turn out to be relatively minor, in the sense of not involving the trauma or the shock value that had been anticipated. But when a film crew invests time in the event and a story is needed for the news program, the event will likely be run in the evening news. Second, what is news depends upon when it happens and how long it lasts:

> Although viewers tend to believe what they see on the evening news is a compilation of the universe of "news" events for that day, the practical reality is that what is telecast each evening is a compilation of events which news workers were able to learn about, get to, capture on film, process and edit.[13]

Third, bias in the news reflects occupational assumptions and temporal constraints more than political or social views of the news workers. The news media have often been criticized for selecting events and commenting on them in terms of the biases of the reporters. But Gelles and Faulkner found that more important than political or social biases were the assumptions about what will make good news on television and the severe time constraints on those attempting to locate, film, and write about events in time for the program each evening. "Because of deadline pressures, it is inevitable that events are reduced to surface actions; visuals of the most 'dramatic' event; and brief concise narratives making a few points in a simple manner."[14]

While clock time is of paramount importance in a modern industrial society, we need to keep two mitigating facts in mind. First, even in a modern society the clock may be a relatively peripheral part of social life. Not all people in such a society function under the ineluctable tyranny of the clock. A survey that comprised a representative sample of the French population showed that approximately 21 percent of the respondents felt that there was no urgency about being punctual and could not say that they had experienced the feeling of wasting time.[15]

A second fact that needs to be recognized is that while I have posed the question as one of social time versus clock time in order to underscore the more inclusive and fundamental nature of the former, clock time actually becomes a part of the social time of any group. That is, social meanings are imposed upon clock time such that, for example, different units of clock time will have differing meanings. Eviatar Zerubavel illustrates this in his analysis of the temporal order of the hospital.[16] As a purely quantitative phenomenon, any unit of clock time is equal to any other unit, whether we are talking about minutes, hours, days, weeks, and so forth. But different days mean quite different things to people. Thus, hospital administrators must be quite careful about "fairness" in scheduling. All personnel must share in duty on weekends. Why working two weekends in succession is "unfair" may not be wholly clear to an administrator, but fairness is nevertheless considered to be the most important moral standard in scheduling coverage.[17] Similarly, evening or night duty is considered more undesirable than day duty and all personnel are expected to take their share of the less desirable times. Obviously, different units of clock time have differing meanings to people.

The way in which clock time is a part of social time is also illustrated in Murray Melbin's analysis of night as a kind of frontier.[18] Again, from a quantitative point of view the night hours are no different from the day hours. But the night is invested with much different meaning. Melbin argues persuasively that the trend toward increasing activity at night continues the geographic expansion that led people to cover the earth, that is, night is a temporal frontier with many of the characteristics of spatial frontiers. Advance into the frontier occurs in stages. The people who make the advance are fewer in number and more homogeneous. There is more solitude, fewer social constraints, and less likelihood of persecution (for instance, street people and homosexuals may encounter less chance of harassment because surveillance diminishes at night). Pockets of activity are smaller and more isolated from each other. The point is that the frontier nature of the night reflects the fact that we invest differing portions of clock time with diverse meanings.

In sum, the extent to which the social time of any society or any group is dominated by clock time is a matter of empirical investigation. Social time is not to be equated with clock time, but clock time may be an important component of the social time of a people. Although clock time is mechanical, it is invested with social meanings. Even though it may be dominant, the varying units of clock time will have differing meanings to people. Finally, while clock time may be defined independently of social life (if we look at it as a purely physical phenomenon), social time has no reality that is independent of or external to social processes.

SOCIAL TIME AS CONCEPTUALIZATION

Social time, as noted above, is a conceptualization of the ordering of social life; it conceptualizes social processes at both the micro and macro levels. Whether the subject of analysis is the social self, an organization, a society, or a span of history, the process may be conceptualized in terms of social time. The self may be analyzed in terms of its "time structure," as a social process, or in accord with the inherent temporality of consciousness, and so forth. An organization may be analyzed in accordance with its existence in a time stream, so that a viable firm must strive to anticipate the future, in an effort to control both that future and its own state of readiness for it.[19]

In fact, an entire society may be differentiated from other societies according to its temporal ideas, including its basic orientation toward the past, present, or future. And, finally, a span of history may be understood and differentiated from other spans in terms of the tempo of change, the legitimated sequences of activities, or its images of past, present and future.

Furthermore, these conceptualizations are both inevitable and necessary for social life. They are inevitable in that temporality is a facticity that demands response. They are necessary in that they legitimate social processes, that is, they explain and validate those processes. Thus, they become a part of the shared meanings that are essential to any viable social life.

Emile Durkheim argued the point that temporal concepts are inevitable and necessary from a somewhat different perspective. He identified time as one of the collective representations, the latter being the "most general relations which exist between things" and which impose themselves upon all the members of a society.

> If men did not agree upon these essential ideas at every moment, if they did not have the same conception of time, space, cause, number, etc., all contact between their minds would be impossible, and with that, all life together.[20]

In point of fact, people do not have the same conceptions of such things as time, space, cause, number. But Durkheim was correct in stressing the importance of similar conceptions for a viable social life. In the case of social time, differing conceptions may lead to serious problems in interaction at both the interpersonal and intergroup levels. Misunderstandings, maladjustment between actors, and conflict may result from divergent conceptions, as will be demonstrated in Chapter 4 with the discussion of conflict relationships.

It is important to note at this point that I am speaking of social time in two senses—what Abraham Kaplan called act meanings and action meanings.[21] That is, social time refers both to these processual meanings that the actors hold, and to those imposed upon their behavior by the researcher. This involves a long-standing debate in sociology, namely, whether social phenomena are to be understood in terms of subjective meanings or in terms of ecological factors (the "social facts" of Durkheim). It seems the effort to insist that the social is to be explained in terms of one or the other of these perspectives is ill-advised, for both are necessary.

On the one hand, subjective meanings are a factor in behavior. We have already seen examples of how meanings are important for understanding the temporal life and behavior of people. "Process is the becoming of experience," as Whitehead stated.[22] In subsequent chapters, we will encounter many more examples of the significance of meaning. Here we might take note of a study by S. Albert that shows rather dramatically how subjective processes affect behavior.[23] Subjects were given a variety of tasks that, by varying the speed of a clock, some believed took 45 minutes while others thought 3 hours had elapsed. The actual time in all cases was 1 hour and 30 minutes. Individuals tended to forget word lists and, in some cases, the order in which they were presented more when they thought 3 hours rather than 45 minutes had elapsed. They were more likely to regard a description of someone as positive, on the other hand, if they thought they had read the description 3 hours ago rather than 45 minutes ago. And, finally, estimates of time intervals varied depending upon whether an individual had been in the presumed 45-minute or 3-hour session. All subjects worked the same length of time, but memory, impressions of people, and time estimates differed depending upon how long the individuals <u>thought</u> they had been working.

On the other hand, we can demonstrate that social phenomena can be explained by ecological or supraindividual factors. As Durkheim showed in his study of suicide, the pattern of "observable physical activity itself" may be shown to lead to certain kinds of results. Again, we will see many examples in subsequent chapters. For instance, there is a relationship between psychic disorganization and temporal disorientation; the researcher can identify the temporal disorientation even though it is not part of the conscious experience of the subjects.

At this stage of development of the social sciences, it is not possible to state the exact relationship between act meanings, action meanings, and human behavior. But clearly the conceptualization of social time must include both act meanings and action meanings.[24] Thus, the conceptual scheme outlined below may be used by the social scientist in analyzing social phenomena; it is also the conceptual scheme that actors use to define situations. I will discuss this point further after examining the conceptual elements of the structure of social time.

THE STRUCTURE OF SOCIAL TIME

To speak of the structure of social time is to recognize that we are dealing with a complex phenomenon and to attempt an analytical breakdown of that phenomenon into facets that are amenable to empirical research. A considerable number of dimensions have already been identified, particularly in the psychological literature, but the terminology is not standardized. The following classification is therefore an effort to bring order into a somewhat chaotic situation by identifying the three broad aspects of social time that are necessary for analysis. Each of these aspects will then be further broken down into significant subareas.

Temporal Pattern

Amos Hawley identified the temporal as one important aspect of ecological organization. He asserted that there is an implicit temporal pattern in every spatial pattern, and identified rhythm, tempo, and timing as elements of the temporal pattern.[25] Moore offers a slightly different set of elements: synchronization, sequence, and rate.[26] I suggest five basic elements in the temporal pattern of any social phenomenon: periodicity, tempo, timing, duration, and sequence. The following discussion will serve to clarify the meaning of these elements and illustrate their applicability at various levels of social reality.[27]

Periodicity

Periodicity refers to various rhythms of social life. It characterizes activities related to both the needs and the activities of people. For example, Hawley pointed out that in terms of material needs every community has a "functional routine" that is peculiar to itself, but that in all communities "the search for food, shelter, and mates recurs with a more or less regular periodicity."[28] People also have transcendental needs, and these too are pursued with some regular periodicity. In a modern society, people may attend church weekly in pursuit of transcendental needs or they may engage in regular activities related to some cause. Humans have always had transcendental needs. Thus, Eliade points out that mythical people everywhere possess temporal periods that are based upon observed "biocosmic rhythms" and that form a part of the larger system of "periodic purifications . . . and of the periodic regeneration of life."[29] The actual length of these periods varied considerably in terms of clock time.

When we look at activities, we find an enormous range that follows some kind of periodic pattern. There are cyclic variations in physiological functions, such as body temperature and blood pressure. There are cyclic variations in creativity, crime, violence, marriage and birth rates, religious and scientific activity, labor problems, and even wars. The cycles may occur in terms of hours, days, weeks, months, seasons, or years.[30]

Periodicity is an inexorable aspect of human life. We may not always be able to assign precise units of clock time to activities, but we will still find periodicities that are regular in occurrence even though they are somewhat irregular by the clock. For example, Dorothy Nelkin studied the behavioral patterns of migrant workers and found a number of daily, weekly, and seasonal rhythms to the existence of the workers.[31] Precise units of clock time could not be assigned to the periodicities of migrant life, but the periodicities were identifiable and they were consequential for the life-style of the workers.

Nelkin found that the migrant workers seemed to alternate between periods of compact and diffuse time. Thus, there is a striking contrast between migrant time, which is "present oriented, irrational, and highly personal," and the typical American time, which is "future oriented, rational, and impersonal."[32] Furthermore, the social time of the migrants, being a "series of disconnected periods" rather than a "continuous and predictable process," accounts in part for such adjustive behavior as excessive drinking and gambling, volatile social relationships, and such personal characteristics as apathy. Living in a context of alternating periods of compact and diffuse time that are unpredictable as to length and also as to whether they will be gratifying or debilitating, the migrant workers employ coping mechanisms that are common to oppressed and deprived peoples.

Periodicity is also important at the organizational level. One important aspect of organizational life regards the periodicity of meeting (in the case of voluntary organizations) or of functioning (in the case of industry, hospitals, and so forth). A voluntary association can be engaged in a process of systematic self-destruction or of assured high turnover of membership if it seeks to gather its members too often; such organizations must legitimate their demands on members' time and must create the novelty necessary to maintain interest.

Finally, we may note periodicity at the individual level. Leroy G. Augenstine investigated periodicity in task performance and concluded that during the course of performing tasks in the laboratory setting, periodic characteristics are manifested by subjects that are "not built into the task itself."[33] Another interesting illustration involves periodicity in man-machine interaction; SAGE operators have been found to experience less stress with five-second responses than ten-second responses from computers. The faster response is more in accord with conversational timing, and, therefore, "more natural and comfortable for humans" than the slower response time.[34] It is uncertain whether such periodicities are rooted in physiological processes of the individual or whether they reflect a particular social context. There are the physiological rhythms—diurnal variations in blood pressure and temperature among others.[35] Nevertheless, I suspect that periodicity of the type in the above two studies is a social phenomenon, so the results would vary from one social context to another.

There is one periodicity at the individual level that probably results from a combination of physiological, psychological, and social factors, namely, people's preferred periodicity for working. When individuals control their work patterns, they seem to choose "alternate bouts of intense labor and of idleness."[36] In fact, there is evidence that when workers are able to control their work periodicity both their satisfaction and their productivity will be maximized.[37] Such evidence is particularly interesting in light of the fact that numerous studies of work organizations, examining diverse variables, have shown little or no relationship between satisfaction and productivity, that is, there is little if any correlation between worker satisfaction and productivity or between either of those variables and indexes that are correlated with the other.[38] It may be that self-control of work periodicity is the one variable that can maximize both satisfaction and productivity.

At any rate, the importance of control over the periodicity of one's work is sufficiently established to help explain the agony and conflict that resulted when workers had to adapt to the mechanical regularity of the factory. Factory work violates an individual's preferred periodicity, so that much of the agony of industrialization involved temporal conflict. We will examine this conflict in more detail in the next chapter when we discuss temporal socialization.

The modern worker continues the struggle against the mechanical ordering of work (consider, for instance, the sabotage of the assembly line in the auto assembly plant). And the modern worker continues to demonstrate a preference for nonmechanical rhythms of work, rhythms that are congruent with either the perceived demands of the individual's body or the processes of the individual's life. What the optimal rhythm is, we do not know. It may differ for every individual, or there may be a modal type for various groups or societies. But in any case, it is not the rigid, mechanical rhythm of the typical factory.

It is interesting, in this regard, that the utopian community of the Bruderhof allows some flexibility in work patterns. Men may come into the factory from 10 to 20 minutes late with impunity as long as no individual does so habitually. And even though mass production techniques are utilized, the needs and abilities of the unique individual are generally given primacy over the requirements of the system.[39] Work rates are adjusted in order to enhance the general well-being rather than to maximize productivity.

Periodicity, in sum, is an important facet of human life, and is the first aspect of the temporal pattern. It refers to the recurrence of phenomena with some kind of regularity. This regularity may be measured by clock time or by comparing social phenomena with other social phenomena. And as with the other aspects of the temporal pattern, periodicity characterizes human life at all levels.

Tempo

Tempo is the second facet of the temporal pattern; it simply refers to rate. As such, it comprises a number of different phenomena. For example, tempo may be the frequency of activities in some unit of social time, or it may refer to the rate of change of some phenomenon. With regard to the latter, it is well known that certain changes have assumed exponential forms and some have been characterized by a loglog form when plotted over a period of time.[40] We may raise the question of whether an experience is the same when it occurs at two different rates; for example, is the industrialization experience of the United States basically different from that of the Soviet Union and China because of the different rates?[41] There is some evidence to support the notion of the importance of tempo in experience. A study of Vietnam veterans found that one problem resulted from the rapidity with which they were brought home. That is, the sudden transition from combat to the United States via jet flights required a psychic adjustment that was often traumatic.[42]

Tempo also includes the perceived rapidity of time and experience, and the rapidity of various modes of social life (urban versus rural, work versus leisure, and others). In an organizational setting, the tempo can be a focal point of conflict, as demonstrated by numerous industrial studies that have investigated labor-management struggles over productivity and worker output.

Tempo also has a number of important consequences at the individual level. Control over the tempo of one's work seems to be important for a healthy self-concept.[43] And the tempo of change in the social order seems related to emotional health; the more rapid the change, the greater the stress on the individual. This is the theme of Alvin Toffler, who coined the phrase "future shock" to describe the psychic disruption that results from experiencing too much change in too short a time.[44] The next chapter will provide some experimental support for this thesis. Here I will simply note that there is historical evidence as well.[45] For example, although the Japanese have traditionally changed their culture and their society, the very rapid tempo of the deliberate transformation of the Meiji era produced considerable stress. The 1868 revolution saved Japan from Western domination, but the generation that experienced the brunt of the hectic rate of change suffered "extraordinary mental agonies."[46]

A final example of the utility of tempo is provided by Max Heirich, who points out that rate is one measure of the intensity of an event. While rate cannot be equated with intensity (since the content of an event may generate that intensity independently of the rate), a sufficiently large change within a small unit of time is bound to generate intensity independently of content.[47]

Timing

Timing, the third element in the temporal pattern, is what Moore calls synchronization. It involves the adjustment of various social units and processes with each other. It is, in fact, the necessity of synchronizing activities that has led to the stress on clock time in the modern world. In a primitive society, the synchronization of activities is a comparatively simple matter, and is accomplished through the mechanism of localized methods and customs, such as the time it takes to cook rice, the time that the cock crows, and so forth. But with an increasing scope of interaction and the necessity of somehow interacting with diverse social times, the need grows for a time that will enable differing groups to coordinate their activities. Hence the emergence of the purely quantitative, bleached of any local color, even flowing, infinitely divisible, time of the classical mechanics.[48]

Timing can be a crucial factor in the initiation of planned social change, as a number of studies of primitive societies have demonstrated, as any astute politician well knows, and as numbers of frustrated change agents have discovered for themselves. And timing is of obvious importance in numerous social contexts such as industrial processes, military campaigns, and political campaigns. The psychiatrist, the political leader, the comedian, and the lover, among others, will all fail or succeed in accordance with their sensitivity to the appropriate timing of their activities.

Some observers claim that one of the serious problems of the modern family is the difficulty of synchronizing family life because of the diverse activities in which each member of the family is engaged. Difficulties have also been pointed out in the efforts of rural emigrants to adjust to the stringent temporal demands of industrial life; the individual's habitual functioning must be synchronized with the industrial process, and, as noted, such synchronization may disallow the individual's self-actualization.

A final example of the importance of timing is provided by institutionalized disturbed children. Such children can be permitted to engage in activities such as competitive sports for limited amounts of time; the process of the game and their own psychic processes can only mesh for a certain period and then the two processes conflict and lead to destructive behavior.[49]

In sum, timing refers to the adjustment of two or more processes to each other so that their activities do not conflict, that is, so that they do not preclude joint implementation. This is an important problem not only when a new behavioral pattern is imposed upon an old one, but also when the multiplicity of activities that comprise a complex social milieu must be so adjusted as to provide adequate scope of operation for all.

Duration

The fourth element of the temporal pattern, duration, has been the concern of psychologists more than of sociologists. Psychological concern is related to that duration of which the individual is conscious—the so-called "specious present" which varies, wrote William James, from a few seconds to around a minute. Longer or shorter periods, James argued, are conceived symbolically by adding to or dividing the "vaguely bounded unit" that is the specious present.[50]

But duration has significance beyond the psychological level. In a half-satiric, half-serious way, C. Northcote Parkinson has set forth a number of laws that relate to duration and behavior in organizations.[51] Perhaps the best known of these (and one, we should note, which has found empirical support) is that work expands to fill the time available for its completion. The duration assigned for any task, in other words, is likely to be the duration required for the completion of that task even though it might be completed in a much shorter period of time if the worker were free to function at his or her own pace. Parkinson also developed a Law of Triviality and a Law of Delay. The former states that the amount of time spent on any item in the agenda for a meeting is inversely proportional to the money involved with that item; people may quibble far more about a $50 expenditure than one involving $10,000. The Law of Delay asserts that delay is the deadliest form of denial. Parkinson suggests a formula that puts the law into mathematical form, so that given such information as the expected life of a person who suggests some reform, the duration between the time the reform is proposed and the final solution, the number of irrelevant issues raised during the discussion, and the age of the "prohibitive procrastinator" (the person who never says "no" but only says "in due course"), we may compute the amount of delay that is equivalent to a denial.

Parkinson's laws bear upon the effectiveness and efficiency of an organization. While stated tongue-in-cheek, they reflect some realities of organizational life, including the fact that the duration of various organizational processes is crucial to the effectiveness and efficiency of that organization.

Expected duration may also be an important variable. In his listing of the properties of groups, Robert K. Merton said that the expected duration of the group would be one differentiating factor of importance since it would presumably affect such matters as the self-selection of members, group structure, and power distribution.[52] Merton also maintained that the expected duration of membership on the part of participants is significant. An evident example is the employee who has already accepted a job elsewhere.

Finally, perceived duration is a useful variable. Psychologists have been investigating for some years the effects of various phenomena such as the perceived importance of time, anxiety, boredom, and others on the perception of time. Perceived differences in duration might be one measure of the meaning of various activities to participants. And the knowledge that perceived duration is important can be used and misused in planning various processes. For example, morale may be improved among workers if the time is subjectively made to pass more quickly, and there are a number of methods whereby the apparent length of a period of time can be manipulated.[53]

Sequence

The final element of the temporal pattern, sequence, derives from the fact that there are activities requiring the ordering of actions.[54] One evident utility of sequence is as a measure of values. "Work before play" is an ordering of activity that reflects a value hierarchy. An interesting experiment by Bertha Friedman involved time and money as measures of values. She measured values relating to physical activity, theoretic-scientific interests, and aesthetic interests, and found that subjects made similar choices on both the time and money scales. That is, when cost in time or money was equalized, similar preferential orderings were made for various activities. In American culture, time is indeed money.[55]

Of course, the sequential ordering of activities may reflect necessity rather than values, as in industrial processes. Furthermore, conflict may arise at the point of disagreement over whether the sequence actually does represent necessity or whether it represents values. This kind of conflict is perhaps most common in organizational settings where disputes arise over the necessity of sequential ordering that is demanded by bureaucratic rules.

Sequential ordering may reflect habit also. The rituals of primitive societies may be ordered in accord with custom. Modern rituals also fall into this category, although some are more appropriately conceived as reflections of values. The ritual of the male removing his hat before entering an elevator is a habitual sequence; the ritual of the male removing his hat before the playing of the national anthem is a sequence demanded by values.

To sum up, the temporal pattern has five elements: periodicity, tempo, timing, duration, and sequence. This pattern is social in nature, which is to say that the form assumed by the five elements in any particular case is not demanded by any inexorable physiological processes or environmental conditions. As Hawley has well stated, people do not possess clearly defined physiological rhythms with which to adapt to physical rhythms or to the behavior of others. Rather, people must "rely upon a constructed time system for the ordering of interrelated behavior."[56] The temporal system is one important aspect of the social time of any group or activity. But there are two additional aspects of great significance: the temporal orientation and the temporal perspective.

Temporal Orientation

Temporal orientation refers to the ordering of past, present, and future. Both individuals and groups may be differentiated according to whether their behavior is primarily related in some fashion to past, present, or future. There may be two points of objection to this statement. On the one hand, it may be objected that past, present, and future comprise an organic whole that cannot be separated.[57] But while this objection may be true in the sense that the three are inseparable in social life, it is not true for purposes of analysis, where we are always making artificial separations.

A second objection might be raised with respect to ordering past, present, and future among various groups. One might argue, for example, that an actor's orientation to a situation always contains an "expectancy aspect," which implies that all orientations are to a future state of the situation as well as to the present.[58] But this is only true in the limited sense that actors generally do not anticipate their demise in the situation. It is not true that orientation to the future is a universal and inherent aspect of all social action, for a future orientation means that the future is a dominant factor in present behavior, and this kind of orientation is by no means universal.

An example of an orientation that hardly seems to include the "expectancy aspect" is the Navajo view of time. Early efforts to get the Navajos to engage in range control and soil conservation programs were enormously frustrating because the Navajos simply had no view of temporality that would lead them to act on the basis of an expected future. To the Navajo, the only real time, like the only real space, is that which is the here and now. There is so little reality to the future that a promise of future benefits is not even worth thinking about.[59]

It is, therefore, necessary to speak about a basic orientation toward past, present, or future. The way in which a society or a group or an individual orders these three modes of time will be consequential for behavior. Florence R. Kluckhohn and Fred L. Strodtbeck have argued that a knowledge of the rank ordering of the three modes can tell us much both about a social unit and about the direction of change of that unit.[60] Americans have typically placed the dominant emphasis on the future. This does not mean ignoring either the past or the present. But there are undesirable connotations in the label "old-fashioned," while at the same time few Americans express total contentment with the present state of affairs. The result, Kluckhohn and Strodtbeck point out, is that Americans value change highly as long as that change does not contradict what is perceived to be the "American way of life." In other words, there is a direct relationship between the extent of future orientation and the amount of change, although the change is expected to be the kind that does not threaten the existing order.

On the other hand, we would expect resistance to change where there is a past orientation. For example, we would expect serious problems in efforts to industrialize where a future orientation is lacking. One such effort—among the Chippewa Indians, who traditionally lacked any concern for the future—encountered such problems as workers who would quit as soon as they had sufficient money for immediate needs.[61]

Temporal orientations are not immutable, however. They may change, and along with that change will come various behavioral changes. Thus, a shift of orientation to the present may have significant consequences in a number of contexts.[62] In a crowd, the orientation is drawn into the present; some of the unusual behavior of crowds, from lynching to struggling at the counter of a department store sale, is a function of the fact that the crowd has neither a past nor a future. Similarly, in a marriage the partners may begin to act in accordance with proximate feelings rather than stable values if the relationship is perceived to be of uncertain duration. In other words, whenever a situation is structured so that people function primarily in a present that lacks a meaningful past and future, various kinds of deviant and debilitating behavior tend to result.

On the other hand, where a changed orientation is resisted, serious consequences can follow. The intersection of a traditional orientation with pressures toward modernization can cause much societal agony. A society may initiate the process of industrialization and carry on industry without engaging in the planning that we ordinarily associate with a future-oriented industrial society. Problems arose in a factory in Cantel, Guatemala, because the management was not sensitive to market variations nor to the problem of equipment obsolescence.[63] Even worse was the situation in Iran, where the past is of prime importance and the future of minimal significance, where businessmen invested considerable sums of money in factories without any plans of how to use them.[64]

Temporal orientation, then, is an important variable in societal behavior; it is also significant at the individual level. A number of psychological studies have shown that temporal disorientation is a concomitant of various kinds of emotional disorders, alcoholism, and certain kinds of deviance such as delinquency. In general, these studies set forth a picture of individuals whose lives are "nothing but instants," to use Kierkegaard's pungent phrase. The individual seemingly responds to the proximate situation, without references to past or to future. In such cases, the individual does not merely rank order present over past and future, but is, rather, wholly immersed in the present. We shall look at this phenomenon more closely in the next chapter when we explore the social psychological implications of temporal man.

Temporal Perspective

Temporal orientation and temporal perspective have often been used in the literature as synonymous terms. The more common term is temporal perspective. I will not use temporal perspective to refer to rank ordering; instead, temporal perspective will refer to the image of the past, present, and future that prevails in a society, a social group, or for an individual. While the rank ordering of past, present, and future is of significance, it is insufficient for gaining an adequate understanding of social time.

Assume, for example, that a group is future oriented, in the sense that it ranks the future highest in its hierarchy of values. What does this mean for present behavior? It will mean something very different depending upon the particular image of the future. A group striving to experience a situation like Thoreau's Walden will exhibit very different behavior from a group that is impelled by Engels' scientific socialism, though both may be future oriented. As Fred L. Polak has impressively argued, the image of the future significantly affects present behavior, but that behavior will vary considerably in accord with the content of the future image. In fact, the future may be said to be the cause of the present in both a positive and negative sense. In a positive sense, an image of the future functions to direct present behavior in accordance with specific values. We may view a society as being magnetically _pulled_ towards a future fulfillment of their own preceding and prevailing, idealistic images of the future, as well as being _pushed_ from behind by their own realistic past.[65]

In a negative sense, the lack of an image of the future implies, in Spengler's terms, happened history rather than willed history. Polak argues that there is a contemporary aversion to images of the future, with the result that we are left "standing at the edge of a bottomless abyss, facing death, destruction, chaos."[66] Those who speak about the decline of our culture have failed to identify the "torn and still" images of the future that characterize our age. These broken and rejected images are the "gaping wound from which the lifeblood of the culture is draining away."

Polak devotes considerable attention to delineating the images of the future of various societies—ancient Greece, ancient Israel, ancient Christianity, modern socialism and Marxism, numerous utopian writers, and so forth—and relating these images of the future to directions of change.

To speak of the image of the past, present, and future is to take a position that has been held in some disrepute, particularly with regard to a future image. Philosophically, it can be argued that any kind of conclusion concerning the future is unwarranted, since there is no way to establish the truth of such conclusions.[67] C. D. Broad maintained that the future is literally nothing, that any statements about the future are neither true nor false, there being no fact with which such statements can correspond.[68]

Nevertheless, people act on the basis of the future. Whatever the philosphical status of the reality or nonreality of the future (and of time in general), it is sociologically significant in that it is consequential for present behavior. As Whitehead argued, "The future is there in the present, as a general fact belonging to the nature of things. . . ."[69] A number of psychologists have agreed with this position, affirming the future as a phenomenal reality. Fraisse claims that the temporal perspective is not fully developed until "through symbolic experiences we become capable of conceiving a future which is a creation in relation to our own history."[70]

Some sociologists have also recognized the importance of the future as a factor in human behavior. But past and present images must not be neglected, for all three images convey meanings and are therefore consequential for behavior. Succeeding chapters will demonstrate this again and again. Here I offer one illustration of the importance, indeed the necessity, of a utopian image of the future for planned change. In the Third World, where efforts at conscious self-direction are flowering, we also find the creation of images of the future. In particular, socialist convictions are being shaped through created images of the future. Celso Furtado has written that one of the reasons Brazilian youth have responded to Marxism is that it provides them with a view of the social process that "opens the way to a conscious policy of social reconstruction."[71] And Nehru related the way in which Marxist thought gave him a new perspective on the temporal process, including an image of the future. A linear concept of time was combined with a utopian image of the future to become a source of both inspiration and directives for self-determined change. Modernization may begin with the conviction that society can and should be transformed, that change is desirable.[72] But if so, this conviction must be incorporated into an image of the future that legitimates and gives directives to change.

To sum up, then, the three primary constituents of social time are the temporal pattern, the temporal orientation, and the temporal perspective. These three apply to any social entity, including the individual, and are necessary for an adequate understanding of the behavior of temporal man. I have called these three the structure of social time, have differentiated them into their component parts, and have illustrated their utility.

A number of points concerning the above framework should be kept in mind. First, the variables have been developed on the basis of hundreds of studies in both professional and popular literature. Thus, these variables appear to be significant in analyses of temporality. Second, as noted, the framework may be used to identify both act and action meanings. Both actors and observers make use, sometimes implicitly and sometimes explicitly, of this framework to understand social phenomena or to define situations. At times, then, act meanings and action meanings may be equivalent. Observers may analyze and actors may define the tempo of life as excessively rapid for human well-being. The two sets of meanings may also be equivalent because actors accept the observers' analyses and define their situations accordingly. For instance, a good deal of recent research has focused on various physiological rhythms in human beings and the impact of those rhythms on behavior. The research has been translated into popular articles to some extent. One writer advises people to "exploit" their biological rhythms by such actions as completing demanding jobs just before dinner, taking tests in the late afternoon, and cutting out carbohydrates on the day of any flight east.[73] As people accept the analyses of their individual periodicities and act accordingly, act and action meanings converge.

Act and action meanings may also be incongruous. The observer may identify facets of temporality of which the actor is unaware. Some actors might define themselves as uncreative, whereas observers might note it is the temporal structure of their existence that is stifling their creativity. Incongruity can also arise when actors make temporal definitions of which the observer is unaware; in such cases, the behavior of the actors may be enigmatic. For example, people seem to behave in strange ways because they have defined the duration of the world's existence or of their own lives as short, or because they are attempting to live in harmony with what they believe to be the natural rhythm of the universe or of their bodies, and so forth.

This leads to a third point about the framework. If observers may use it to analyze social phenomena, and if actors use its various concepts in defining situations, certain questions arise. First, how does the framework fit into an analysis of the social process? What the observer analyzes, after all, is a dynamic phenomenon. Can a static framework be useful for such an analysis? It can be if we keep in mind that the framework is static with respect to form but dynamic with respect to content. Any analytical framework is static in form. The dialectic, for instance, retains the same form even while the contents of the process being analyzed change. Similarly, a concept such as perceived duration may be used to analyze interaction as long as we keep in mind that the perceptions may change during the course of the interaction.

Another question that needs to be addressed relates to the

cause of particular temporal definitions, that is, why do people define situations in accordance with one temporal definition rather than another? What is the source of the temporality that people use to define their situations? These questions will be briefly addressed below in an outline of the way in which social time relates to the process of social life in general.

SOCIAL TIME AND SOCIAL PROCESS

The above structure of social time is incorporated into a basic perspective on social reality that forms the basis for the remaining chapters in this book. The general perspective may be summarized in the following series of propositions.

<u>Every social phenomenon is processual in the sense of exhibiting movement over time.</u> Movement is used here rather than change because the former is a more inclusive term; movement includes such things as cyclic patterns, while change always involves some kind of development (though not necessarily in a positive sense).

The affirmation of social reality as process is not, of course, novel. In fact, it is deeply rooted in sociological tradition. Albion Small wrote that "all sociologists since Comte have more or less consciously assumed this concept [i.e., the concept of social process] as their major premise."[74] In their introductory textbook, published in 1937, R. M. MacIver and Charles H. Page declared that society "is a becoming, not a being; a process, not a product."[75] Furthermore, the processual nature of society applies to primitive as well as modern societies. In the latter, change occurs at a slower pace, but we cannot "assume that they are really unchanging, and that the crust of custom, on which writers like Maine and Bagehot laid such stress, holds them inexorably."[76]

Many other writers could be quoted, but the concern here is to express my own affirmation of the processual nature of social reality and to point out that such an affirmation is fully in accord with past sociological theorists as well as with present perspectives such as the Marxist and symbolic interactionist.

<u>The movement of a social phenomenon may assume diverse patterns; the change of any social phenomenon involves a dialectical process.</u> Movement may be linear, cyclic, or follow a variety of other patterns. Moore, for example, has described ten geometric patterns that may be found in various theories of change.[77] There is a twofold point to be made here: one is that all social phenomena exhibit movement of some kind, and the other is that certain kinds of movement—such as the cyclic—do not necessarily involve change.

A common type of movement that has received minimal

attention by sociologists is the cyclical. According to one of the foremost students of cyclical phenomena, "more than 500 different phenomena in 36 different areas of knowledge have been found to fluctuate in rhythmic cycles—that is, in oscillations that recur at reasonable regular time intervals."[78] We have already noted some of the cyclic phenomena of interest in sociology: wars, creativity, crime, marriage and birth rates, religious and scientific activity, and labor problems. There appears to be a recent renaissance of interest in cyclic phenomena; that interest ranges from the physiological, emotional, and intellectual cycles of individuals through the correlation between lunar cycles and murder rates to the periodic fluctuations in national values.[79] The point is that movement is pervasive in social life, and that what may appear to be significant change in the short run may be in reality cyclic variations.

Change is also pervasive, but it follows a dialectical pattern rather than diverse pattern. In other words, change is a particular kind of movement. "Dialectical" is an abused concept, and a few words must be said about its meaning here. To say that change follows a dialectical pattern is to say that change is a process whose driving mechanism is contradiction. Contradiction, in turn, has two basic components to its meaning [80] One component is the unity and conflict of opposing forces. The opposing forces involved may be ideas, material factors, or a combination of the two. Thus, I do not limit the dialectical process to a materialist one; it may also be a process involving conflict between ideologies or conflict between ideology and material conditions. The second component of meaning in contradiction, then, is incompatibility; that is, the opposing forces that are in conflict cannot function together indefinitely. Ultimately the opposing forces generate change.

<u>All movement may be conceptualized in terms of social time</u>. As noted, social time includes temporal patterns, orientations, and perspectives; these three dimensions should suffice to describe any kind of movement. For example, when we talk about cyclic phenomena, we are dealing with an element of the temporal pattern—periodicity.

We may characterize movement not only in terms of social time, but also use that characterization to distinguish between the consequences of diverse kinds of movement. For example, the period of transition among African nations from colonial status to nationhood varied from roughly one to nine years. The transition involved an interim during which the colonial power and the nationalist movement shared power At least two consequences resulted from the relative duration of the process.[81] First, the longer it took the colonial power to begin relinquishing its control, the shorter the interim of shared power. And, second, the longer the time of shared power, the more moderate were the promises made to the people by the leaders of the nationalist movement. Thus, differential duration of the phases of the sequence had diverse consequences for the societies involved.

Another example of the differentiating ability of social time involves tempo. A good portion of the world is in the process of development, but the tempo of development varies considerably. Tempo is an important variable here because the level of political turmoil in a developing society is a function of the tempo of socioeconomic change: the greater the tempo, the higher the level of turmoil.[82]

Finally, we should note that the direction of movement may also be conceptualized in terms of social time. Temporal orientations and perspectives are particularly important in characterizing direction. Wendell Bell and James A. Mau have even argued that social change may be explained with a "cybernetic-decisional model," which views action as the consequence of decisions regarding alternative futures; the image of the future then becomes "of critical importance in influencing which of the alternative futures becomes present reality."[83] It seems this gives too much scope to human intentions. We must allow for the unanticipated consequences of behavior and for structural constraints upon human intentions and desires. Nevertheless, the temporal perspective is a significant variable in a theory of change and in understanding the direction of movement. Humans may not be wholly free to implement their intentions, but neither are they wholly thwarted in their efforts to do so.

Because humans are cognitive creatures, they strive to understand and control the process of existence; to that end, they construct symbols of social time that legitimate their social existence. Man has always striven to "catch and condense his subjective experience of time and duration" in symbols.[84] But the creation of those symbols involves more than the provision of understanding. It introduces a mechanism of social control, for legitimation is the process of explaining and justifying; legitimation explains by "ascribing cognitive validity" and justifies by providing "normative dignity."[85] That which makes sense and is defined as right is likely to persist.

It is for this reason that the rate of change in primitive societies is very slow. Such societies tend to be past oriented, conceptualizing the social process in terms of the past and legitimating social processes by the extent to which they conform to the past. In the mythical concept of time, for example, social life is made sacred by its association with the mythical past and existence is only comprehensible to the mythical mind in terms of the primordial past.[86]

The use of temporal symbols for social control may also be seen in the calendar. In the Mayan civilization, the public calendars were made of stone. The material reflects the rigidity that was imposed upon social life by the calendar, which became "universal, unchanging, detailed and obligatory. Instead of serving as a means of providing order in social life, it easily became the means of establishing a tyrannous control over social life."[87] The Mayan calendar was not unique in serving as a tool of social control; in many ancient civilizations, the priestly caste was entrusted with the care of the calendar and thereby gained enormous power. In fact, the control of the calendar (which is, in essence, the control of the symbols of social time) retains significance in the modern world, as evidenced by the first part of the <u>Book of Common Prayer</u> (where the care of the calendar is still entrusted to the church) and by an Anglican discussion of the problem of the erosion of the Christian year and the Christian Sunday.[88]

Thus, whether we are talking about the mythic consciousness, about Richard Baxter's contribution to the legitimation of capitalism when he wrote about wasting time in terms of sacrilege,[89] or about contemporary concern over religious and secular holidays, work tempo in industry, and so forth, we are dealing with various examples of symbols of social time that legitimate social processes. Conflict over the symbols reflects a struggle for power. The lack of conflict reflects a high degree of social control.

<u>Because humans are social creatures, their temporal symbols are socially constructed; that is, they emerge out of human interaction, and particular symbols tend therefore to characterize particular groups</u>. Anthropologists have detailed the way in which temporal systems reflect both the ecology and social structure of primitive societies. It is not only divergent and separated groups that exhibit varying temporal systems. Five groups of people living within American society have been found to have significant differences in temporal orientation: the Zuni, the Rimrock Navajo, the Spanish-Americans of Atrisco, the Mormons of Rimrock, and the Texans of Homestead.[90]

There are also class differentials in temporality. The so-called colored people's time (CPT) was a way of conceptualizing social time that characterized lower-class blacks. CPT reflects what a middle-class observer might label as unrealistic behavior since a scheduled event could occur at any point over a span of hours or could even fail to occur.[91] But CPT indicates the experience of oppression rather than gratification of a group existing in the capitalistic process, a group that created symbols of social time that rejected the process by rejecting the temporality characteristic of the process.

One commonly identified class difference in temporality is future orientation and perspective. Angela O'Rand and Robert A. Ellis, for example, found class differences in the way individuals

THE MEANING OF SOCIAL TIME / 45

anticipate the future and orient their behavior toward it.[92] The researchers compared a sample of trainees for the Job Corps with a sample of male university freshmen. The former group largely consisted of persons from socioeconomic backgrounds that were lower than the latter group. The lower-class youth had a much more constricted view of the future, so that few of them thought beyond getting married and having children. The middle-class youth, on the other hand, "are thinking ahead to the time when their own children are growing up and going out into the world."[93] Temporal differences also had consequences for the role performance. Dropouts from the trainee program, for instance, had more constricted views of their future than those who remained.

Thus, our temporal definitions, which have such significance for our behavior, arise out of the groups in which we participate. At least in terms of an individual's initial definition of any situation, it is his or her reference groups that will provide the particular mode. We learn our symbols of social time from our interaction within particular groups, and we use those symbols to define subsequent situations.

<u>Because social life is complex, every society will have diverse systems of social time; conflict arises at the point of intersection of these diverse systems.</u> Such conflict has already been illustrated above in the case of the Micmac Indians. As the next chapter will show, conflict may also arise between an individual and his social context; such individuals may be defined as either deviant or mentally ill.

As suggested by this brief discussion, and as will be demonstrated in the following chapters, the structure of social time, combined with these five basic propositions, will help to explain numerous social phenomena. Social reality is a process, and process may be apprehended in terms of social time.

The remainder of the book will utilize social time to examine human life at varying levels from the individual to societal. I will explore pertinent topics at each level, and show the meaning of social time for diverse facets of human life as well as the ways in which man uses social time.

CONCLUSION

In this chapter I have attempted to show in detail the meaning of social time, and have provided a conceptual framework that will be used in the remainder of the book. As I examine the individual, human interaction, and social change, I shall make full use of the temporal pattern, orientation, and perspective. These conceptual tools should be applicable to the analysis of any social phenomenon. I have also specified the assumptions about the nature of social reality and social time that underlie the analyses in the remaining chapters. We shall see these assumptions emerge again and again. For instance, we began with the proposition that all social phenomena are processual. We shall discuss the way in which the self is a process and the significance of interaction as a process. Sometimes the assumptions are implicit and sometimes explicit. But in all cases they form the foundation for the various analyses. With our assumptions stated and our conceptual framework spelled out, we are ready to plunge into specific areas of sociological concern.

NOTES

1. Henri Bergson, Time and Free Will, trans. F. L. Pogson (New York: Harper & Row, 1910).
2. Philip Bock, "Social Structure and Language Structure," Southwestern Journal of Anthropology 20 (Winter 1964): 393-403.
3. Paul Fraisse, The Psychology of Time, pp. 184 ff.
4. Ernst Cassirer, The Philosophy of Symbolic Forms, pp. 51-53, 108.
5. P. E. Ariotti, "The Concept of Time in Western Antiquity," in The Study of Time II, ed. J. T. Fraser and N. Lawrence (New York: Springer-Verlag, 1975), p. 69.
6. E. E. Evans-Pritchard, The Nuer (London: Oxford University Press, 1940), p. 100.
7. E. R. Leach, Rethinking Anthropology (London: The Athlone Press, 1961), p. 124.
8. Pitirim A. Sorokin, Sociocultural Causality, Space, Time (New York: Russell & Russell, 1964), pp. 191 ff.
9. E. P. Thompson, "Time, Work-Discipline, and Industrial Capitalism," Past and Present 38 (December 1967): 58-59.
10. Jonathan Swift, Gulliver's Travels (New York: Holt, Rinehart and Winston, 1961), p. 20.
11. Godfrey Lebhar, The Use of Time, 3d ed. (New York: Chain Store, 1958), p. 7.
12. Richard J. Gelles and Robert R. Faulkner, "Time and Television News Work: Task Temporalization in the Assembly of Unscheduled Events," Sociological Quarterly 19 (Winter 1978):89-102.
13. Ibid., p. 99.
14. Ibid., p. 100.
15. Jean Stoetzel, "The Contribution of Public Opinion Research Techniques to Social Anthropology," International Social Science Bulletin 5 (1953):499.

16. Eviatar Zerubavel, Patterns of Time in Hospital Life (Chicago: University of Chicago Press, 1979).

17. Ibid., p. 117.

18. Murray Melbin, "Night As Frontier," American Sociological Review 43 (February 1978): 3-22.

19. Neil W. Chamberlain, Enterprise and Environment: The Firm in Time and Place (New York: McGraw-Hill, 1968), p. 202.

20. Emile Durkheim, The Elementary Forms of the Religious Life, trans. Joseph Ward Swain (New York: The Free Press, 1915), p. 30.

21. Abraham Kaplan, The Conduct of Inquiry (San Francisco: Chandler, 1964).

22. Alfred North Whitehead, Process and Reality (New York: The Free Press, 1979), p. 193.

23. S. Albert, "Time, Memory, and Affect: Experimental Studies of the Subjective Past," in The Study of Time III, ed. J. T. Fraser, N. Lawrence, and D. Park (New York: Springer-Verlag, 1978), pp. 269-90.

24. Some of the points made here have been put forth by W. D. Hitt, who contrasts the behaviorist and phenomenological approaches in psychology to the study of man. He gives evidence to support each approach on each of ten important aspects of significance to the nature of man. See "Two Models of Man," American Psychologist 24 (1969): 651-58.

25. Amos H. Hawley, Human Ecology (New York: The Ronald Press, 1950), pp. 288 ff.

26. Wilbert E. Moore, Man, Time, and Society, p. 8.

27. The elements are applicable, as already suggested, across societies as well as across various levels within a society. For an application of the scheme to the Navajo see Douglas R. Givens, An Analysis of Navajo Temporality (Washington, D.C.: University Press of America, 1977).

28. Hawley, Human Ecology, p. 290.

29. Eliade, The Myth of the Eternal Return, p. 52.

30. See, for example, H. B. Green, "Temporal Stages in the Development of the Self," in The Study of Time II, ed. J. T. Fraser and N. Lawrence (New York: Springer-Verlag, 1975), pp. 1-19; M. Melbin, "City Rhythms," in The Study of Time III, ed. J. T. Fraser, N. Larence, and D. Park (New York: Springer-Verlag, 1978), pp. 444-65; and Zick Rubin, "Seasonal Rhythms in Behavior," Psychology Today, December 1979, pp. 12-16.

31. Dorothy Nelkin, "Unpredictability and Life Style in a Migrant Labor Camp," Social Problems 17 (Spring 1970): 478.

32. Ibid., p. 480.

33. Leroy G. Augenstine, "Evidence of Periodicities in Human

Task Performance," in *Information Theory in Psychology*, ed. Henry Quastler (Glencoe: The Free Press, 1955), p. 216.

34. Harold Sackman, *Computers, System Science, and Evolving Society* (New York: John Wiley & Sons, 1967), pp. 434-35.

35. Paul Fraisse provides many examples of this inherent periodicity, extending his analysis to the infrahuman and plant worlds. It is so common that he calls it a "general law for all organisms." See Fraisse, *The Psychology of Time*, pp. 17-48.

36. Thompson, "Time, Work-Discipline," p. 73.

37. George Strauss, "Group Dynamics and Intergroup Relations," in *Of Men and Machines*, ed. Arthur O. Lewis, Jr. (New York: E. P. Dutton, 1963), pp. 321-27; Bertil Gardell, "Technology, Alienation and Mental Health: Summary of a Social Psychological Study of Technology and the Worker," *Acta Sociologica* 19 (1976): 83-93.

38. See Curt Tausky, *Work Organizations* (Itasca, Ill.: F. E. Peacock, 1970), pp. 183-87.

39. Benjamin Zablocki, *The Joyful Community* (Baltimore: Penguin Books, 1971), p. 134.

40. Hornell Hart, "Social Theory and Social Change," in *Symposium on Sociological Theory*, ed. Llewellyn Gross (Evanston: Row, Peterson, 1959), pp. 196-238. Inventions, social movements, and others tend toward a logistic trend, while long-term developments of basic capacities tend toward a loglog trend.

41. This point has been suggested by Victor Gioscia, "On Social Time," in *The Future of Time*, ed. Henri Yaker, Humphry Osmond, and Frances Cheek (Garden City: Doubleday, 1971), p. 102.

42. Veterans World Project, *Wasted Men: The Reality of the Vietnam Veteran* (Edwardsville, Ill.: Southern Illinois University Foundation, 1972), p. III-9. This report was developed in cooperation with the U.S. Office of Education, Division of Manpower Development and Training.

43. Melvin L. Kohn, *Class and Conformity* (Homewood, Ill.: Dorsey, 1969), p. 174.

44. Alvin Toffler, *Future Shock* (New York: Random House, 1970).

45. Robert H. Lauer and Jeanette C. Lauer, "The Experience of Change: Tempo and Stress," in *Social Change: Explorations, Diagnoses and Conjectures*, ed. George K. Zollschan and Walter Hirsch (Cambridge: Schenkman, 1976), pp. 520-45.

46. Kenneth B. Pyle, *The New Generation in Meiji Japan* (Stanford: Stanford University Press, 1969), p. 3.

47. Max Heirich, "The Use of Time in the Study of Social Change," *American Sociological Review* 29 (June 1964): 390.

48. Sorokin, Sociocultural Causality, Space, Time, p. 169.
49. Leonard W. Doob, Patterning of Time (New Haven: Yale University Press, 1971), p. 83.
50. William James, The Principles of Psychology, vol. 1 (New York: Dover Publications, 1890), p. 642.
51. C. Northcote Parkinson, Parkinson's Law (New York: Ballantine Books, 1957); The Law of Delay (London: John Murray, 1970).
52. Robert K. Merton, Social Theory and Social Structure (Glencoe: The Free Press, 1957), p. 312.
53. Robert D. Meade, "Time On Their Hands," Personnel Journal 39 (1960): 130-32.
54. Moore, Man, Time, and Society, p. 8.
55. Bertha B. Friedman, Foundations of the Measurement of Values (New York: Columbia University Press, 1946), pp. 196-216.
56. Hawley, Human Ecology, p. 295.
57. Ernst Cassirer, An Essay On Man (New York: Bantam Books, 1944), p. 54; James, The Principles of Psychology, p. 609.
58. Talcott Parsons and Edward A. Shils, eds., Toward A General Theory of Action (New York: Harper & Row, 1951), p. 68.
59. Edward T. Hall, The Silent Language (Garden City: Doubleday, 1959), p. 23.
60. Florence R. Kluckhohn and Fred L. Strodtbeck, Variations in Value Orientations (Evanston, Ill.: Row, Peterson, 1961), p. 14.
61. Robert E. Ritzenthaler, "The Impact of Small Industry on an Indian Community," American Anthropologist 55 (January-March 1953): 147.
62. J. D. Ketchum, "Time, Values, and Social Organization," Canadian Journal of Psychology 5 (September 1951): 104-5.
63. Manning Nash, Machine Age Maya (Chicago: The University of Chicago Press, 1967), p. 21.
64. Hall, The Silent Language, p. 29.
65. Fred L. Polak, The Image of the Future, 2 vols. (New York: Oceana Publications, 1961), 1:15.
66. Ibid., 2:14.
67. This was David Hume's argument. See Frederick L. Will, "Will the Future Be Like the Past?" in Logic and Language, ed. Anthony Flew (Garden City: Anchor Books, 1965), p. 250.
68. See Richard M. Gale, ed., The Philosophy of Time (Garden City: Doubleday, 1967), pp. 174-75.
69. Alfred North Whitehead, Adventures of Ideas (New York: Mentor Books, 1933), p. 196.
70. Fraisse, The Psychology of Time, p. 172.
71. In Paul E. Sigmund, ed., The Ideologies of the Developing Nations (New York: Frederick A. Praeger, 1967), p. 410.

72. C. E. Black, The Dynamics of Modernization (New York: Harper & Row, 1966), p. 7.

73. Flora Davis, "Exploit Your Biological Rhythms," Woman's Day, April 24, 1978, pp. 103 ff.

74. Quoted in Max Lerner, Ideas Are Weapons (New York: Viking Press, 1939), p. 493.

75. R. M. MacIver and Charles H. Page, Society: An Introductory Analysis (New York: Rinehart, 1937), p. 511.

76. Ibid., p. 512.

77. Wilbert E. Moore, Social Change (Englewood Cliffs: Prentice-Hall, 1963), pp. 34-39.

78. Edward R. Dewey, Cycles—Selected Writings (Pittsburgh, Pa.: Foundation for the Study of Cycles, 1970), p. 38.

79. See Michael R. Wallerstein and Nancy Lee Roberts, "All Together on the Bio-Curve," Human Behavior, April 1973, pp. 8-15; Arnold L. Lieber and Carolyn R. Sherin, "Homicides and the Lunar Cycle: Toward a Theory of Lunar Influence on Human Emotional Disturbances," American Journal of Psychiatry 129 (July 1972): 69-74; and J. Zvi Namenwirth, "Wheels of Time and the Interdependence of Value Change in America," Journal of Interdisciplinary History 3 (Spring 1973):649-83.

80. These two components of meaning were suggested by Adam Schaff, "Marxist Dialectics and the Principle of Contradiction," Journal of Philosophy 57 (March 31, 1960):241-50.

81. Immanuel Wallerstein, Africa: The Politics of Independence (New York: Vintage Books, 1961), pp. 60-61.

82. Ivo K. Feierabend and Rosalind L. Feierabend, "Coerciveness and Change: Cross-National Trends," American Behavioral Scientist 15 (July/August 1972):914-15.

83. Wendell Bell and James A. Mau, "Images of the Future: Theory and Research Strategies," in The Sociology of the Future, ed. Wendell Bell and James A. Mau (New York: Russell Sage Foundation, 1971), p. 18.

84. Meerloo, "The Time Sense in Psychiatry," p. 246.

85. Peter L. Berger and Thomas Luckmann, The Social Construction of Reality (Garden City: Doubleday, 1966), p. 93.

86. Cassirer, The Philosophy of Symbolic Forms, p. 105.

87. F. W. Dillistone, Traditional Symbols and the Contemporary World (London: Epworth Press, 1973), p. 104.

88. Ibid., pp. 108-19.

89. Max Weber, The Protestant Ethic and the Spirit of Capitalism, trans. Talcott Parsons (New York: Charles Scribner's Sons, 1958), pp. 157-58.

90. Kluckhohn and Strodtbeck, Variations in Value Orientations.

91. Jules Henry, "White People's Time, Colored People's Time," Trans-Action 2 (March/April 1965):31.
92. Angela O'Rand and Robert A. Ellis, "Social Class and Social Time Perspective," Social Forces 53 (September 1974), 53-62.
93. Ibid., p. 57.

3

THE INDIVIDUAL IN TIME

What is man? The question has been asked repeatedly since it was posed by the ancient Psalmist. And the answers have been diverse. Humans have been said by some to be basically good and by others to be basically evil. They have been identified as both rational and irrational, as both self-directed and as impelled by forces external to them. The debate about human nature has been endless, but we do not yet have a generally acceptable viewpoint. However, one thing is certain: whatever else we may be, humans are immensely complex creatures. As Pascal said in one of his striking passages:

> What a chimera then is man! What a novelty! What a monster, what a chaos, what a contradiction, what a prodigy! Judge of all things, imbecile worm of the earth; depository of truth, a sink of uncertainty and error; the pride and refuse of the universe! [1]

But thinkers have not been deterred by this complexity and have continued to discuss human essence and to build theories on the basis of or assumption about a particular idea regarding that essence. In social psychology, for example, the Gestaltists proceed on the assumption that humans basically seek to establish an organized, meaningful perspective about their world. Reinforcement theorists assume that we are basically creatures who act according to the pleasurable or painful consequences of our behavior. Role theorists assume humans are socially determined. And psychoanalytic theorists see individuals as creatures locked in a struggle between their own biological impulses and the constraints of the social environment. [2]

When we look at an individual as a temporal creature, however, the essence is process. That is, the human is a creature engaged in a pilgrimage. He or she is not a set of reflexes, buffeted about and directed by external forces. He or she is, rather, a self-conscious creature, a self-directed being whose evolution is a function of an ongoing dialectic with the social environment.

In this chapter, I will examine the individual in time, that is, the social psychological dimensions of temporal man. At this level, the propositions set forth in the last chapter translate in the following way. First, the essence of the individual, like that of every other social entity, is process; each person is a developing being, a creature who always lives to some extent in the past, present, and future. An individual is more like the unfolding of a broadening stream than the inertness of a still pool. Therefore, if the question Who are you? is posed to an individual, the answer must necessarily be somewhat different today than it was in the past and it will continue to change in the future. We are changing creatures, not merely in the sense that we age, but in the sense that change is the core of our being.

Suppose, for example, that a student is asked the question of who he is shortly after he enters the university. He will probably say, "I am a student" rather than "I am a freshman," and he will probably still identify his selfhood in terms of being a student when he is a senior. But the meaning of being a student will have changed; and it will have changed not simply because the meaning of senior differs from that of freshman, but also because the student himself will have changed (among other changes, a number of studies show a tendency toward increasing liberalization as a result of college education).

I will begin by examining the processual self, movement at the individual level. We will then look at the way in which the individual has been and continues to be temporally socialized. As noted in the last chapter, the symbols of social time legitimate social life, and legitimate means both to justify and to explain. That which is justified will, of course, be defended and perpetuated; thus, we are all subject at all times to continuing socialization into those temporal patterns that have been defined as legitimate. Since legitimation also means explanation, we are led to a third topic—the temporal dimensions of the self-concept. The same symbols of social time that explain reality will be employed to explain the self, to define the nature of the self.

The final three sections of this chapter relate to the fact that humans are creatures who act and develop on the basis of meanings. We act on the basis of our definition of situations, and situations are always defined, in part, in temporal terms. In other words, we always orient ourselves to a situation in temporal terms. We will explore this notion of the oriented individual and its counterpart—the disoriented individual (who represents the conflict of diverse systems of social time). Finally, we will look at a particular kind of process at the individual level—self-actualization—and the way in which social time relates to that process.

THE SELF AS PROCESS

Older ideas of the self were of some kind of inner substance, an invisible but living entity that governed behavior. Modern theory of the self has discarded religious and metaphysical ideas, and defines it as a group of psychological processes. That is, the self is an evolving plexus of attitudes—a changing configuration of beliefs, feelings, and behavioral tendencies.

The idea of the self as process is not novel, of course. Hegel argued that all "true reality" is the "process of reinstating self-identity, of reflecting into its own self in and from its other, and is not an original and primal unity as such. It is the process of its own becoming. . . ."[3] The self, in other words, is a dialectical process rather than a substance.

A number of other thinkers have followed Hegel in emphasizing the processual nature of reality and of the self. Phenomenologists like Husserl, Heidegger, and Merleau-Ponty have identified time and the self; time is a function of the intentional structure of consciousness—in fact, consciousness may be said to constitute time.[4] Every real experience is characterized by duration; temporality is intrinsic to experience, not only in the sense that it inheres in each experience, but also in the sense that diverse experiences are united by the temporal bond.

Philosophers of process also view the self as process rather than substance. Contrary to the commonsense view that the individual is the most concrete reality, there is something more concrete, argues Charles Hartshorne, "and that is the actual history of the individual, the succession of 'states,' for instance, experiences, which constitute the reality of the individual through time."[5] This is not to say that the self is amorphous, that identity is an illusion. Rather, identity is an abstract conception: "Concretely there is a new man each moment. . . . But of course, in many important personality traits it may be the same man all the time."[6]

A fundamental assumption of this point of view is that the self is an emergent phenomenon; it arises out of the social process. As Whitehead has pointed out, this reverses the position of Kant that the world emerges from the subject.[7] Rather than presupposing a subject that encounters and reacts to a datum, we presuppose a datum that is met with feelings, and progressively attains the unity of a subject.[8] Thus, the self emerges from an encounter of the individual with reality; both in its genesis and in its evolution, the self derives from participation in social life.

Since the self emerges from participation in social life, we would expect part of the processual nature of the self to be rooted in societal changes. Consider the selfhood of the Roman Catholic priest during the decade of the 1960s. Certain attitudes and, therefore, a certain conception of the self were appropriate to anyone who called himself a priest in 1960. By 1970, dramatic changes in the Catholic Church had led to alterations in the notion of priesthood, so that the priest of 1970 was likely to possess a considerably different set of attitudes than the priest of 1960 or 1950. Moreover, those who had been priests over that period of time found their self-conceptions changing or being subjected to considerable pressures toward drastic change.

Changes in the self may also be rooted in dramatic personal experiences, conversion, or simply in new social situations. The various crises of life—birth of a child, vocational decisions, marriage, death of a loved one, physical or emotional illness, and so forth— leave their imprint upon the pilgrimage of the self. Physical illness may drastically alter a man's image of himself as a strong being. Feedback from teachers may cause a young woman to view herself as a creative being for the first time in her life. Or the direction of development may shift as a result of a new life situation—a job, a move to a new community, marriage or divorce, and others.

All of these reemphasize the fact that the self is an emergent phenomenon, arising out of the social process. Furthermore, one of the unique aspects of human life is that the social life in which the self is developing includes past, present, and future. All three are part of the phenomenal reality in which the self is functioning. Unlike animals, humans are not confined to the immediate past and the present. Memory is more fully developed in humans than in any other animal species, so that humans may incorporate the distant past into their behavior. Psychologists have demonstrated the significance of memory in delayed-reaction experiments, which investigate the ability of various species to recall information. In essence, their findings show that the "period of delay after which recall can occur tends to increase from lower mammals to human beings," that among humans the period increases during the growth period, and that this improved recall ability is due both to neural maturation and to language development.[9]

The particular way in which the past is a factor in the development of the self is crucially related to memory. Studies of memory, for example, distinguish between immediate memory (IM), short-term memory (STM), and long-term memory (LTM). IM is a kind of "buffer" process that allows us to retain information for about 500 msec. This is sufficient time for us to select certain parts of the incoming information and engage in other preprocessing activity. STM is a "working memory" that allows us to retain a certain amount of information for about 30 sec. while we process that information. And LTM is "a storage process for coded information of practically unlimited capacity and permanence."[10]

This suggests there are some inherent physiological limitations to the rate at which information can be assimilated and retained. Thus, our memory of the past depends upon the nature and volume of the information experienced, and reconstruction and incorporation of the past into present behavior depends upon memory.[11] The same memory, of course, is used to retain our constructed images of the future, which also are incorporated into present behavior. When we answer the question of who we are, we include what we have been and what we hope to be.

Temporal man, then, is a developing creature whose reality comprises past, present, and future, and whose self arises out of, and changes as a function of, social interaction. Among social psychologists, the most seminal exponent of the processual nature of the individual was George Herbert Mead, who spoke of the self as "essentially a social process going on" with the two distinguishable phases of the "I" and the "me."[12] The "me" is the organization of community attitudes within the individual; the "I" is the source of novelty, the unpredictable aspect of the self, the part that always eludes community control. The self, then, emerges out of the social process and develops in the ongoing encounter between "I" and "me."

Thus, both in philosophy and in early social psychological thought we find the intellectual foundations for the concept of temporal man. The self is process; the temporal dimension is fundamental. To neglect the temporal dimension is to neglect the essence. We shall never understand the human by simply analyzing the individual as a stable configuration of traits, qualities, or attitudes. The individual is an evolving being who lives at once in a social past, present, and future, and whose self arises out of, and develops as a result of, social interaction.

There is another aspect to movement at the individual level that has received scant attention from social scientists, namely, the various cyclical processes. These cyclical processes include emotional states, mental ability, and physical prowess, and appear to operate both on a daily basis and over periods of roughly three weeks or more. Studies have found, for example, that people are at their peak mental performance between 1:00 and 7:00 P.M., that industrial accidents are more frequent at certain times of the day, and that body temperature rhythms may not adjust to certain schedules of rotation of shift work in factories. Efforts have also been made to graph individual cycles of emotional, mental, and physical states and to correlate these with performance.[13]

While such studies may be declared to be the province of the psychologist and physiologist, they are too important to ignore. Sociologists must either utilize such insights or work with those of other disciplines in a joint effort to understand human behavior. Movement is a fundamental fact of human existence, and every kind of movement is significant for understanding that existence. It may well be that our perception of the various movements, from physiological to broad social, and their intersection with each other will provide us with a breakthrough in our efforts for insightful knowledge about human life.

TEMPORAL SOCIALIZATION

Temporality pervades the individual's social life as well as selfhood. Temporal socialization will occur, therefore, for at least two basic reasons. First, in order for a person to adequately function in society, he or she must learn the temporality that underlies the social context. All experience is temporally organized, but time is not prior to experience. That is, the individual does not organize experience temporally in accordance with some universal a priori principle, as Kant would have it; rather, he or she learns to organize experience temporally in accordance with specific social and cultural processes. Second, as noted, it is important that those processes of social life that have been defined as legitimate be learned and accepted as legitimate by newcomers; people defend and strive to perpetuate the processes of their existence that explain and justify it. This means that socialization involves the individual's entire life span. Newcomers to organizations, for example, will be temporally socialized in order to be able to function within the organization and in order that those already functioning within it do not face threats to the legitimacy of their existence. A human, in sum, is a temporally socialized creature. And this temporal socialization may be seen both in the development of temporal concepts and in the development of the temporal organization of individual life and society.

First of all, as Piaget and others have shown, there *is* a development of temporal concepts that gradually follows the differentiation of spatial order (see the third explanation below). In other words, contrary to Kant, temporality is not an a priori mode of organizing sensory data; we may clearly trace the increasingly sophisticated notions of time in children as they develop, and, as importantly, the different notions that develop in differing social contexts.

However, even if we concede that temporal concepts have a developmental nature, how can that development be explained? There are a number of different theories, all of which share the conviction that our temporal ideas derive from experience. First, the Freudian explanation stresses the activities surrounding early problems of feeding and toilet training. Freud accounted for the development of a future perspective of time in terms of the shift from the "pleasure principle" and the "primary process" to the "reality principle" and the "secondary process," a shift accomplished by learning to delay gratification.[14] Freudian thinkers posit several steps in this process of learning to delay gratification: frustration, anticipation of future gratification (which requires projection into the future and the ability to distinguish reality from fantasy), development of language, development of the sense of time afforded by the language, and internalization of temporal concepts.[15] While this is a reasonable account of the genesis of rudimentary notions of the future, it is inadequate to explain the rich complexity of temporality.

A second explanation is the linguistic, developed by Benjamin Whorf and others. Proponents of this view argue that a language molds the thought of those who use it.[16] Whorf maintained that even the grammar of language has significance for thought. On this basis, he tried to show how differences in the Hopi and standard average European grammar lead to diverse conceptions of time. The point is not simply that the language expresses our ideas about temporality, but that it shapes those ideas. Our language forces us to think about and to experience time in a particular way. Some languages, for example, can only express the present and thereby compel us to "experience time as a series of immediately felt actions."[17] Other languages, it is argued, have a variety and richness of structure that allow fine temporal distinctions.

Unquestionably, language is a significant factor in forming our temporal ideas. But caution must be exercised in leaning too heavily on such aspects of the language as grammar. As Arnoldo Momigliano points out, the absence of verbal or syntactical distinctions between past, present, and future does not preclude people from distinguishing the three temporal modes. Otherwise, "it was really for the Jews to have a Herodotus, and for the Greeks to hope in the Messiah."[18] The Greek language has a complex tense structure, while the Hebrew lacks tense forms for the verb.

A third explanation of the development of temporal concepts involves the perception of change. This follows Aristotle's idea that time is derived from the perception of motion. The kind of change involved may be in nature, or in both nature and in ourselves. Leach argues that two basic experiences provide the foundation from which all other aspects of time are derived: the experiences of recurrence in nature and of the irreversibility of life change in the individual.[19] Here he is trying to explain the historical development of temporal notions. At the individual level, Piaget follows Aristotle closely in arguing for the perception of motion as the critical factor in development of temporal concepts.[20] From a psychological point of view, asserts Piaget, "time depends on velocity . . . time is a coordination of velocities, or, better yet, of movements with their speeds. . . ."[21] Thus, we may see the development of temporal concepts as a process concomitant with the increasing ability to perceive velocity.

All of the above explanations are at least partially correct in that they all point to the importance of the social context in which temporal concepts develop. Our ideas of time do have their origin in social processes. Conceptions of time and history are neither natural nor self-evident, but are largely conditioned by the prevailing social and intellectual climate.[22] Temporal concepts develop gradually in children, and they are first grasped in relation to aspects of the child's existence. Variations in that existence lead to variations in perception of temporality by the child.

Various social contexts, then, with diverse social processes, will lead to differing conceptions of time and differing patterns of socialization. The close relationship between social time and socialization is rather dramatically illustrated in research reported by David Zern.[23] Looking at non-Western societies, Zern found that methods of time-reckoning could be arranged in a Guttman scale:

- a developed calendar that is approximately one year long;
- division of months into segments (such as weeks);
- names given to particular days;
- a series of dates that have "special ritual significance" and recur at the same time each year;
- monthly type splits that are recognized and named (whether or not a yearly calendar exists); and
- a "crude and general ability" to distinguish between various parts of the day.

The Guttman scale indicates that if any of the above elements are found in a given society, all of the following elements will also likely be found. For example, if a society has a yearlong calendar, it will also have all of the other elements. Another society might have names given to particular days and all of the elements below but would have neither a calendar nor the division of months into segments.

Zern's major hypothesis was that "child-rearing in the first year of life which is relatively frustrating (within 'viable' limits) will help produce an adult with a relatively structured and salient sense of time."[24] For his sample of 47 societies, the correlation between the structuring of time and overall indulgence was -0.441 ($p < 0.001$), strongly supporting the hypothesis. Zern also made a longitudinal study of American subjects. Both studies supported the major hypothesis, and his data indicate that childrearing is a better predictor of time structuring than such factors as cultural complexity, socioeconomic class, and general intelligence.

Thus, socialization practices in a variety of societies are strongly correlated with the social time of those societies; children are socialized in order to function effectively in terms of the prevailing social time. This may be seen in Crestwood Heights, where the occupational role was a prime determinant of the temporal structure. That is, the career created the primary attitudes toward time. And in order to prepare the child for a career, temporal socialization began at an early age. The child encountered time as a scarce adult commodity in the nursery school, where he or she also learned to take cues from others "rather than from his own immediate predilections and inclinations."[25] The stringent demands of career in Crestwood Heights created an image of time as scarce, relentless in passage, and, therefore, priceless. Children were taught to accept this strident image at an early age. Had they not learned and adopted it, they would have been hampered, if not incapacitated, in their functioning as adults in the community and, as important, would have threatened the meaning of the existence of their parents.

It follows from the close relation between social context and temporal conceptions that a shift in the existential situation should lead to a change in temporality. Such a shift occurred in those individuals who were deported and persecuted during the Second World War. They developed the habit of not thinking about the future and of suppressing memories of the past: "They now live only in the present and they have destroyed the continuity of the past into the future."[26]

Temporal socialization, then, involves both the development of our concepts of time and the temporal organization of our behavior. There are various ways in which we learn to organize our lives temporally. Temporal socialization is a lifelong process, beginning with the infant and continuing until death. One of the first encounters of the infant with temporal socialization involves the fitting of the infant's biological pattern into a pattern of sleeping and eating that is socially approved. Among the earliest experiences of an individual, then, is the experience of an imposed temporal structure, a temporal structure that in some measure conflicts with the natural temporality of the infant.

One might, in fact, conceive of the self in time in terms of the successive imposition of new temporal structures.[27] The imposition of a new temporal structure on a massive level is well illustrated in the work discipline demanded by capitalism. Labor patterns prior to the introduction of large-scale machinery were characteristically irregular. Primitive peoples typically worked in patterns that had nothing to do with clock time. But clock time did not enslave even Westerners until relatively recent times. As noted, when people are able to control the temporal patterns of their work, they tend to opt for a sequence of intense work, idleness, intense work, and so on.

But industrial capitalism—and as the Soviets demonstrated, industrialization in general, whether capitalist or socialist—seemed to demand a different kind of temporal work pattern. The temporal pattern of industrialization required mechanical periodicities, machine-determined tempos, precision timing, and ineluctable sequences. The agony of transition to such a pattern is clear in the industrialization of England, which was marked by an intense struggle between owners and workers as the former sought to impose the new pattern on the latter. The workers resisted in various ways. Many found escape either in gin or in religion. And numbers of English peasants preferred poverty to the well-paying factory during the eighteenth and nineteenth centuries.

But the owners vigorously pursued their socialization efforts. Some indeed tried to use devious methods such as preventing workers from knowing the time or adjusting clocks forward and backward to expropriate the worker's time.[28] And very quickly they tried an assortment of coercive measures. As early as 1700, we encounter "the time-sheet, the time-keeper, the informers and the fines."[29] But in the long run, it was temporal socialization that yielded the desired results. And in their socialization efforts, the owners found significant help in both religious and educational institutions. Weber has provided numerous illustrations from religious writings in which the value of time is heralded. Richard Baxter spoke about wasting time in terms of sacrilege, and as worthy of "absolute moral condemnation."[30] Religion made sacred the diligent use of time that was necessary for the development and expansion of capitalism.

The pervasiveness of this process of legitimation in the religious and educational context may be seen in the literature of the English charity and Sunday schools in the latter part of the eighteenth and first part of the nineteenth centuries. For example, a children's hymn went as follows:

> How doth the busy little bee
>   Improve each shining hour
> And gather honey all the day
>   From every opening flower.
>
> In works of labour or of skill
>   I would be busy too;
> For Satan finds some mischief still
>   for idle hands to do.[31]

Industrialization required both the willingness and the capacity to work hard for long hours, and the charity and Sunday schools were structured to develop both qualities.

Ultimately, the socialization was successful. The religious and educational institutions worked hand-in-hand with the owners and produced a new breed of human. By the 1830s, the English worker had become noted for "his regularity, his methodical paying-out of energy," and for his suppression "of the capacity to relax in the old, uninhibited ways."[32]

Americans had also internalized the new view about time. They exhorted each other to keep in mind the fact that the proper use of time is a religious obligation. In her 1841 self-improvement book for women, Catherine Beecher told her readers that Christianity teaches that we must give account to God for all of the time given to us "and that we have no right to waste a single hour."[33] Or as a writer in 1844 contended, none of God's gifts is more important than time, that we must keep busy in order to be happy and prosperous, for "want and misery follow in the train of idleness" while "industry and faithfulness mete out a sure reward."[34]

Both religious and secular writers in the popular media continue to impress upon us the importance of wisely using each minute. And the extent to which the industrial process continues to impose a "chronarchy" upon workers is illustrated in the following account of regulations in a British factory in more recent times.[35] Each worker has a daily goal and a weekly evaluation. "Work is measured by the number of hand and finger movements involved." Each week a computer printout is given to the production manager stating, for example, that a particular operator "has been loading trays for painting, that she ought to take 0.6 hours per 1,000, but that she took 4.8 hours to do 6,000, was only 75 percent efficient, and will lose points towards her six-monthly Merit Review, which in turn determines her share of the average pay-rise awarded to her grade."

This kind of temporal context is not natural to humans, as illustrated by the continuing problems of socialization in the industrial context. Ghetto residents have a notably different system of social time from middle-class and upper-class groups. An article in the Harvard Business Review noted that workers recruited from the ghetto are particularly difficult to train to live by the clock and suggests that counselors should make sure every new ghetto worker has an alarm clock: "At Westinghouse/East Pittsburgh, after the first paychecks have been distributed, the counselor accompanies the new employee to the nearest store to make sure he gets an alarm clock."[36]

In sum, we are temporally socialized so that we may be able to participate in and adapt to the temporal structure of our society, and in order that we may accede to the legitimacy of existing social processes. It is not surprising, then, that various societies are composed of people with quite different temporal configurations, nor that various groups within a complex society exhibit quite different temporal configurations. In fact, we may expect somewhat diverse systems of social time to characterize each different role in any social context. Thus, men and women in American society have tended to engage in diverse social processes. Congruent with that diversity, men have been more future oriented than women—possibly a function of the sense of male responsibility for occupation and material security.[37] The fact that such a socialized orientation is incongruous with nontraditional roles (and, thereby, congruent with traditional roles) is supported by a study of women executives. The researchers found that women may be hampered by their temporal orientation. Men tend to focus on long-range goals and recognize possible contradictions between those goals and present processes. However, women focus on short-term planning, with little concern for long-term implications.[38] As a result, women may fail to respond to those cues that will enable them to move up the corporate hierarchy.

Of course, women executives will be socialized by the corporation into a more appropriate temporality. And the dominant temporality of women may shift as a result of the women's movement. But in the meantime some women will experience difficulties that men will not have to face because of the differential temporal socialization of children.

THE TEMPORAL DIMENSIONS OF SELF-CONCEPTS

We learn to think about ourselves in temporal terms as well as how to organize our behavior temporally. Again, the way in which we think of ourselves depends upon the social time in which we live. For example, the old saying, "Idle hands are the devil's workshop," teaches us to disparage ourselves when we misuse our time. We live in a society that values highly the full use of time in productive activities. We are taught to think of ourselves as deficient in some sense when we fail to maximize the productive use of our time. Indeed, who has not experienced a sense of guilt for "stealing" a few moments for some kind of self-indulgence? The fact that "stealing" is an appropriate verbal link with time illustrates the close relationship between the temporal context and the way we think about ourselves. A member of a primitive tribe might consider us odd for thinking of ourselves as minor thieves with respect to our use of time.

The ways in which temporality enters into our self-concepts are many and diverse. We think of ourselves in terms of a career line that includes past, present, and future. We think of ourselves as living too rapidly, or not rapidly enough—the tempo of our lives may be discordant with our ideal. We think of ourselves as extending into eternity, or as robbed and tormented by ineluctable finitude— the duration of our lives comforts or haunts us. We think of ourselves in terms of a real or mythical past and an imagined future. The past becomes a snare to hope or a prod to fulfillment, and the future beckons us to an unfolding or stifles us with anxiety.

In each case, the temporality that bears upon our self-concepts is a social temporality. That is, we are not dealing with an individualized phenomenon but with social tendencies; individuals think of themselves in the temporal terms that are made available through the social context. For example, consider how the social meaning of time affects our sense of self-esteem. If time is valued in accordance with what is produced and consumed, if "time is money" in the sense that time is a commodity of market value, and if the life of the individual is conceived in terms of a duration that is comprised of such time, then self-esteem is a precarious and elusive possession. The individual will not possess any inherent value, but will be valued in accordance with instrumental, technological criteria that are applied to other commodities.[39] Under such circumstances, individuals will view themselves and evaluate themselves in terms of the productive use of their time, where "productive use" is measured in market value. In such a social context the poor will be disparaged, and will tend to view themselves as in some sense inferior or inadequate. When time is money, and life is an accumulation of temporal units that are defined in terms of market value, poverty is an indication of distorted, inadequate, or atrophied selfhood.

This, of course, has happened in the United States, where the poor are typically blamed for their condition. Specifically, the charge is made that the poor suffer mainly from an unwillingness to work.[40] But where time is money, no one is safe. No one's self-esteem is invulnerable. The affluent inhabitants of Crestwood Heights were haunted by the "feeling that time is running out," with the result that childhood was characterized by a "rushing at experience," and adulthood was lived out in the shadow of the ticking clock.[41] Time was a scarce and invaluable commodity in Crestwood Heights, and the people became commodities whose self-esteem rested precariously upon a proper use of time. Consequently, the enjoyment of leisure (nonproductive use of time) seemed beyond the capacity of the residents.

One way in which temporality affects self concepts, then, is through the social meaning of time. A second way involves the use of temporal perspectives as a source of defining and apprehending one's selfhood. People cannot answer the question of who they are apart from the fact that they share a social past and a social future with others. If an individual thinks of himself or herself as basically an autonomous creature, it is because he or she shares the individualistic ideology that has historically pervaded American life. If someone has a high self-esteem, it is in part because that person identifies with those people who glorify their past achievements and anticipate their future triumphs. If a man asks who he is and answers by saying that he is an American, he is defining himself in terms that incorporate a nation's past and its future. To use a group to define oneself is to include the past and future of that group in the way one thinks about oneself.

An example of the way in which temporal perspectives of groups affect self-concepts is provided by Robert Jay Lifton's study of Japanese youth.[42] Lifton identified three patterns of imagery used by Japanese youth to give temporal definition to their selfhood. The "mode of transformation" focuses on the future as the "only hope for overcoming the sordid and demeaning elements of existence" associated with the present and recent past. The present is judged as corrupt, a judgment that the transformationist tends to apply to his own life as well as to his society. The future is envisioned in terms that root out the feudal elements still remaining in Japanese society, and lead to a social order that facilitates individual self-realization. Thus, temporal perspectives of transformationist groups are used by individuals to define their own selfhood.

A second pattern identified by Lifton was the "mode of restoration," which also views the present in terms of its impurity, but sees the answer as a return to the ideal Japanese past. The restorationist sees himself as organically united with the past; he defines his selfhood in symbols derived from a sacred past. The third pattern, the "mode of accommodation," is an effort to combine the past, present, and future in a way that emphasizes the present, and the near past and future. This is a mode of compromise that recognizes the deficiencies of the present, but that refuses to find refuge in either an idealized past or a radically transformed future. The accommodationist, therefore, faces serious psychological tasks as he tries to define himself in terms that may be ambivalent or even antithetical. The contradictions of Japanese society generated by the clash of past, present, and future are incarnated in the accommodationist.

Thus, Lifton identified three different groups of Japanese youth, each of which had different temporal perspectives. He found that these temporal perspectives were utilized by members of the group to define their own selfhood. Images of the past, present, and future of Japanese society were utilized by individuals to answer the question of their own identity.

A third way in which temporality enters into self-concepts is through social roles. These roles give a temporal dimension to self-concepts because the roles themselves incorporate particular temporal demands and perspectives. As pointed out above, such basic roles as those of male and female may have differing temporal implications. Particularly important are the sex role and occupational roles. With respect to the latter, in Crestwood Heights the demand of the career for mobility resulted in a stress on the present and near future and a consequent blurring of both the past and the long-range future. The career-oriented man conceptualized himself in similar terms. He was unlikely, for example, to be concerned with his name or ancestry. On the other hand, he tended to possess self-esteem to the extent that he coped with the present, enjoyed well-being in the present, and so forth, rather than to the extent that he might make any long-range contributions to his society.

Particular roles, then, incorporate particular temporal demands. Those who occupy the roles, or who anticipate occupying the roles, will reflect the temporality of the role in the way they view themselves. For example, Sattler's study of young people interested in becoming high school counselors shows how an anticipated occupational role has an inherent temporality that is reflected in the temporal definition of selfhood.[43] The role of counselor demands some convictions regarding the manipulatory possibilities of the future. Those interested in being high school counselors were found to be more likely to view their own future as predictable, structured, and controllable. It is not possible to say, of course, whether the young people developed their future perspective as a result of interest in high school counseling, or whether young people with a particular perspective were attracted to an occupational role congruent with that perspective. But in either case, the perspective of the role and the individual's conception of his or her own selfhood were in harmony. If they are not in harmony, the individual faces serious internal and/or external conflict.

THE ORIENTED INDIVIDUAL

Human life is oriented life. For one thing, we orient ourselves spatially. The distance between two people who are engaged in dialogue can vary considerably, and the meaning of the interaction will likewise vary. In the United States, a very close distance may indicate either intense anger or erotic desire. Close distance in other societies is considered normal for conversation, while the typical American distance may be viewed as insulting.[44] The distance considered proper varies, but in all societies there are such spatial orientations that give meaning to behavior.

We also orient ourselves temporally. This orientation appears to develop after the spatial one in the history of the individual. According to Piaget, human perception is initially spatial in nature; gradually, the child develops concepts such as seriation and extension that orient him or her in time as well as space. Ultimately, the child apprehends more sophisticated temporal notions such as sequence, order, and causality.[45]

William James discussed temporal orientation of the adult in terms of the "specious present," the present experience of time. The present which we experience, he said, is not like a "knife-edge" but like a "saddle-back" that has a breadth "on which we sit perched, and from which we look in two directions into time."[46] Our experience of time, in other words, is never sheer immediacy, but includes to some extent both past and future.

Moreover, the temporal dimension of our experience may violate clock time. That is, our temporal perception of experience may be quite inaccurate in terms of measurement by clock time. Generally, experiences that are interesting seem short in passing but long in retrospect, while "time empty of experience seems long in passing, but in retrospect short."[47] The poet, the artist, the lover—those caught up in the ecstacy of creativity or passion—may become so absorbed in the experience that it becomes impossible to judge the amount of time that has passed. This is not to say that such experiences lack a temporal dimension—only that temporal perception becomes very inaccurate with respect to clock time.

An intriguing aspect of the spatial and temporal orientation of the individual is the manner in which the two interact. Our judgments of space and of time each depend upon both spatial and temporal conditions.[48] For example, if two lights are blinked in sequence, the time interval will seem longer if the space between the lights is increased. On the other hand, if the time interval is varied, the space will appear longer when the time interval is increased.

Thus, a part of all human behavior is the temporal orientation that is involved. It is fruitful to think of the temporal orientation of the individual in terms of the definition of the situation. We can understand human behavior by knowing what particular situations mean to the individuals involved. And that meaning always has a temporal dimension. As a time-bound animal, the human always defines situations in terms of their bearing upon the past, present, and future.

For example, a businessman may disparage certain workers who are unwilling to expend themselves for low wages by saying, "When I was in college, I swept floors for less than they are getting, and didn't think I was too good to do it." That, of course, fails to take into account that his definition of sweeping floors included a future that transcended floor sweeping. The disparaged workers also define their situation in terms of their future, but their future may be only an extrapolation of their present. A man may rebel against the idea of sweeping floors at low wages when he must conceive of his entire life in such terms; he is less likely to do so when he sees a future that will be more exciting and rewarding than his present task. Furthermore, we may understand the disparagement of the workers in terms of the businessman defining their situation as similar to his own past; he fails to recognize that their future differs radically from his own.

The way in which one gives a temporal definition to a situation is not individualistic, of course, but depends upon the individual's group memberships. In the above example, the man was a member of a middle-class group with expectations of upward mobility; the disparaged workers were of working-class groups with a sense of a restricted, bounded future. Such group differences in social time may lead to strikingly different definitions of situations.

Consider the definition of pain. Essentially, we tend to view pain as a physiological phenomenon. But different people define pain quite differently; and these differences become understandable in view of group differences in temporality. In a study of Jewish, Italian, and "Old American" (English, Scandinavian, and others) responses to pain, Mark Zborowski found some intriguing differences.[49] The Jewish and Italian responses were overtly quite similar; both involved the free expression of feelings and emotions, including complaints, groans, and crying. There was little shame involved in the public display of suffering; on the contrary, Jewish and Italian patients admitted to their overt expressions of distress and to their expectations of receiving sympathy from others.

The overt responses, however, were only a part of the total

situation. Attitudes toward the pain were quite different in the two groups. The Italian patients were primarily concerned with the immediate experience of pain, were quick to ask for relief through drugs, and tended to respond to the relief afforded by the drugs by forgetting their distress. The Jewish patients, on the other hand, were concerned about the symptomatic meaning of the pain, were reluctant to ask for or accept drugs, and tended to continue to worry even when drugs did bring relief. In other words, the Jewish patients exhibited a future concern with their illness, while the Italians were oriented toward the present experience of the illness. The Jewish patients defined the pain in terms of possible future consequences, and therefore experienced more anxiety and reacted differently toward the use of drugs. The Italian patients defined the pain in terms of present experience, and were physically and emotionally relieved when the present experience was changed from the painful state.

The third group, the Old American patients, were relatively stoic in their overt reactions to the pain, insisting that nothing was to be gained by complaints or groaning. In addition, they tried to be detached and diagnostic in their description of the pain. Like the Jewish patients, they were future oriented and expressed concern about the symptomatic meaning and long-range implications of the pain. But in contrast to the Jewish patients, the Old Americans were optimistic about their future; their image of the future included hope and a measure of health.

In sum, the Italians were oriented to the present, the Jewish and Old American patients were oriented to the future, and the Jewish patients held a pessimistic image of that future while the Old Americans held an optimistic image. The different temporal configurations led to three different experiences of and responses to the pain.

The temporal orientation and perspective has important implications for many facets of behavior, including even the fulfillment of basic physical needs. This may be seen in problems of medical care with the Spanish-speaking people of the Southwest, who are oriented to the present rather than the future. These Spanish-speaking people are neither visionaries nor dreamers, but realists who are concerned with the problems and rewards of the immediate present.[50] Some of the problems involved in the medical care of such people are minor, such as their bewildered reaction to the question of which day during the following week they would like to return to the clinic. They may not feel as if they need to return by that time and, in addition, may question the purpose of choosing one day over another. Some of the problems are more serious, however. A woman can be known to have tuberculosis and yet refuse to undergo treatment because her present experience is one of well-being; she therefore sees no point in inconveniencing herself now in order to avoid possible consequence in the nebulous future.[51]

As the above shows, situations are defined in temporal dimensions, and the varied temporal definitions have differing consequences for behavior and for experiences of the individual. The individual is always oriented temporally and employs this temporal orientation and a temporal perspective in order to define situations. The definition of the situation, in turn, leads to varied modes of behavior and differential experiences in the same (from an objective point of view) external situation.

THE DISORIENTED INDIVIDUAL

Although people orient themselves both spatially and temporally in all behavior, it is possible for an individual to be temporally disoriented. Temporal disorientation is an inability to function in the context of the social time that prevails in the individual's social milieu; it indicates a conflict between the individual's system of social time and that of the social milieu. This conflict reflects some kind of problematic selfhood. The extent to which the selfhood is problematic can vary from relatively mild emotional upset to character problems to serious mental illness. An example of the former are the college freshmen who suffered from homesickness and who had impaired future time perspectives and perceived disparities between their present and future selves that were greater than those reported by freshmen who were not homesick.[52]

More serious are the various neuroses and character disorders. In a study of dogmatism, it was found that highly dogmatic people have an unbalanced time perspective as compared to those who are less dogmatic; the highly dogmatic were found to be disturbed with respect to both the future and the present.[53] Whereas the actualizing individual (as will be shown in the next section) synthesizes past, present, and future in the context of a basic future orientation and perspective, the more rigid, dogmatic individual focuses too strongly on the future.[54] Such a time perspective is overly constricted and lacks the sense of continuity and interdependence between past, present, and future.

Neurotics seem to distort temporality in the course of using time as a defense mechanism. That is, time is distorted in order to create a temporal barricade between the individual and the source of trauma. If the threat to the individual is a present one, refuge may be sought by an obsession with the present. This obsession with the present creates a barricade that separates the individual from the past and the threat contained in that past. The forms of behavior in which obsession with the present may manifest itself include excessive punctuality, a compulsion to avoid wasting time, and so forth.[55] Whatever the form of behavior, however, it always involves a temporal disorientation; the neurotic is temporally disjointed and distended.

Delinquents have also been found to differ in temporality from nondelinquents. Both males and females who are delinquent are more present oriented than their nondelinquent peers, and are less likely to project their selves and their experiences into the future.[56] Similar results have been found in a cross-cultural study involving a comparison of delinquent and nondelinquent children in Costa Rica and the United States. In both cultures, delinquents exhibited shorter future time orientations than nondelinquents.[57]

Alcoholics are yet another group revealing constricted future orientation.[58] Compared with nonalcoholic peers, the alcoholic typically is more concerned with short-range gratification and has difficulty trying to cope with any long-range goals. The alcoholic has both a shorter future orientation, and a more nebulous future perspective than the nonalcoholic. The evidence indicates that these distortions in temporality are a response to problem drinking rather than a cause of that drinking.[59] And I would expect that the same would be true with respect to neuroses of various kinds, that is, problematic selfhood is always associated with temporal disorientation, but the latter is normally a symptom of and response to the former rather than vice versa.

In any case, whatever the direction of causality, it appears that temporal disorientation is always associated with emotional disturbances. The temporal disorientation may be one of various kinds. For example, the experience of time may be lost; the perception of time may be greatly distorted; the temporality of the self may be hopelessly at variance with that of the social context; the individual may be incapable of conceptualizing the future; or experiences of time may involve a sense of time coming to a halt or standing still.[60]

Temporality may be used both as a symptom of mental illness and as a signal of mental health. In a study of adolescents in a psychiatric hospital, tests of the time perspectives of the adolescents were analyzed, revaling that the adolescents were ready to leave the hospital after reorganizing a deficient time perspective. Adolescents who were able to utilize the "psychiatric moratorium" offered by the hospital in order to think more in terms of the future were prepared to return to their homes.[61]

The above, however, presents but one side of the coin. The

other side approaches the question of temporal disorientation not from the point of view of the individual with a problematic selfhood, but from the point of view of the social structure. That is, the individual may suffer temporal disorientation and consequent stress or disturbance because the social milieu imposes on that individual a temporality that is traumatic or even inhuman. Long ago, Radhakamal Mukerjee argued that the rhythm of urban, industrial society runs contrary to the "rhythms of life," leading to considerable individual maladjustment and disorganization.[62] For the whole of human life, he asserted, "rest and work, leisure and social contacts are governed, not by the rhythm of man's organic impulses and needs, but by that of mechanical time."[63]

We have already seen the way in which the imposition of a mechanical time traumatized people. There is perhaps only one temporal pattern of work that is more debilitating than the mechanical pattern exemplified by the assembly line—shift work. If mechanical periodicities and machine-determined tempos strain the human spirit, shift work pushes that spirit to its limit of endurance. Studies of the effects of shift work show a variety of deleterious consequences. Those who work rotating shifts experience the greater number of problems, but even those who regularly work a night or afternoon shift may have difficulties not encountered by the workers who attend to their jobs in the day. Among other things, the following are some of the problems that have been identified with afternoon, night, or rotating shift work.[64] There can be undesirable consequences for family life, including a perceived neglect of the parental role, inadequate companionship with one's mate, problems with fitting in sexual relations, and difficulty in attending family functions like weddings. Participation in voluntary associations is likely to be less. The more the worker perceives that the job interferes with various nonwork roles, the more the worker feels anxious and tense and the lower the worker's self-esteem is likely to be. Finally, there are a number of bodily functions, such as sleep, eating, and bodily movements, that can be adversely affected. Some shift workers report chronic fatigue, dulled appetites, and serious constipation. Shift work clashes with the worker's temporality at numerous points.

For some observers, it is not merely the industrial sector but the entire modern way of life that is traumatic. As suggested by Toffler's notion of future shock, the tempo of life is the critical factor in generating stress in people.

I have suggested elsewhere that, contrary to many sociological writings, there is no inherent trauma in change; rather, stress is a result of the rate and kind of change.[65] In other words, I agree with Toffler on the importance of tempo, but would modify his notion by

arguing that the kind of change involved is an intervening variable
between tempo and stress. These hypotheses were tested in a study
involving a random sample of classes at a midwestern university
during the summer of 1972. Stress was measured by the short form
of the Taylor Manifest Anxiety scale, a standard measure of a generalized state of anxiety. Perceived tempo of change was measured
by three questions derived from a factor analysis and "kind of
change" was measured by a question relating to the perceived desirability of changes that were occurring.[66]

The results supported the hypotheses. There was a statistically significant relationship between perceived tempo of change and
anxiety score. That relationship was stronger when the change was
defined as undesirable. For those who defined the change as desirable, there was a much smaller probability of having a high anxiety
score. Among those perceiving a high tempo of change, about 52
percent of those defining the change as desirable and 73 percent of
those defining it as undesirable had high-anxiety scores. Thus both
tempo and kind of change are important. And even when the change
is defined as desirable, tempo is related to anxiety, lending support
to those who contend that a high rate of change generates psychic
disruption in humans. In accordance with the present perspective,
we would say that when the tempo of change is too great, the individual is unable to orient himself or herself in order to act.[67]

Thus to speak of the disoriented individual is not to imply that
the individual possesses some flaw that has prevented him or her
from functioning in a healthy manner. The disorientation may be an
individual one, one that reflects individual psychic disturbance, but
it may also be a social problem; the temporality imposed upon the
individual by the social environment may be dehumanizing or debilitating. In either case, temporal disorientation indicates a significant
problem.

THE ACTUALIZING INDIVIDUAL

The concept of temporal man has significant implications for
self-actualization, which is the process of the individual realizing
his or her full potential. Indeed, to accept the notion of "temporal
man" is to stand with those students of individual growth who stress
struggle rather than tension reduction; individual change is a dialectical process. "We have to assume only one drive, the drive of self-actualization, and . . . the goal of the drive is not a discharge of
tension."[68] Furthermore, the growth that is demanded by the
processual nature of the self, and therefore by self-actualization,
encompasses the totality of the life span. I use the phrase "actualiz-

ing individual" to stress the point that self-actualization is a process and not a state of being. The actualizing individual is an evolving, unfolding, growing person.

Although the exact meaning of self-actualizing is not yet precise, there is a sufficient amount of data available to enable us to specify some of the temporal requisites for the actualizing individual. First, the actualizing individual affirms the processual nature of his or her existence. Life is oriented in accordance with "intentional time"; the individual actively chooses to "be."[69] Or better, the actualizing individual chooses to become. Becoming is affirmed, and the properties of becoming are incorporated into the selfhood of the actualizing individual. These properties include "open-mindedness, re-evaluation, projection, decision, action, choice, individualization, and many others."[70]

Second, the actualizing individual functions within an optimally structured temporal system. "Structure hunger" is one of the three basic needs of humans identified by Eric Berne; but while an individual can exist as long as time is structured, he or she cannot engage in self-actualization without some autonomy in the structuring of his or her time. In other words, although we cannot at this point fully specify what is optimal in the structuring of a temporal system, one facet of an optimal system is a degree of self-structuring. Too much "free" time can be as stressful as too little, but it is probably true that more people have experienced too little than too much. At various points in history people have struggled to gain a greater amount of discretionary time for themselves.[71] For example, we noted the assembly-line workers and their continuing efforts to acquire some control over the tempo of their work. Similarly, those in prison and concentration camps struggle with severe psychological problems because of their lack of control over time. In long-term incarceration, prisoners face daily the problem of making time pass, and "they talk about one thing only: the sheer psychological impossibility of facing up to so many years in prison."[72]

Similar experiences faced those in concentration camps during the Second World War. Two prisoners report that the "ghost of time" was the most severe threat to their sanity. They tried desperately to fill their time with some kind of activity, but their efforts enabled them to gain little except the precarious retention of sanity. Like other concentration camp prisoners, they lived in the immediacy of the present and lost the sense of process.[73]

The optimal structuring of the temporal system also includes the amount of time pressure faced by the individual. There is insufficient research to be able to identify the optimal amount of time pressure, but life satisfaction is related to that pressure in a curvilinear fashion. "The harried on one end and the unoccupied on the other give less satisfied responses than are made by individuals lying between."[74] The individual is more likely to be aware of the former than the latter, but contrary to some popular notions of what a halcyon existence would be like, people do not thrive in a context of total temporal freedom any more than they do in a context of temporal oppression.

A third way in which temporal structuring affects the actualization process involves its relationship with decision making. Experimental evidence indicates that our evaluation of alternatives is a function of how much time we have to make a decision. With only a few minutes to make a decision, the preferred alternative will be evaluated lower and the nonpreferred will be evaluated higher than when a longer time span is available.[75] In other words, alternatives that would otherwise be evaluated in a decisive rank ordering tend to converge in their appeal as the time span for deciding becomes shorter. This has important implications for self-actualization since we may make decisions that do not maximize our process of actualization if we are constrained to decide in too short a duration of time.

The structuring of the temporal milieu of the actualizing individual must also minimize sudden and drastic shifts in the social time in which the individual functions. The importance of this may be seen in the ability of the Japanese to adjust to old age. Such adjustment is apparently easier for the Japanese than for those of some other societies partly because of the Japanese mode of structuring time; the Japanese are not tyrannized by the clock, nor is there an emphasis on scheduling of activities, and even industrialization has failed to completely alter that pattern.[76] As typified by the residents of Crestwood Heights, on the other hand, some Westerners live in a temporal context that is despotic and coercive. The loosening of that context upon retirement can be a traumatic experience. The Japanese adjustment to old age is facilitated because the structuring of time throughout life is not so radically dissimilar to that of the later years. In short, humans find it traumatic and debilitating to suddenly be thrust from one temporal pattern to another and significantly different pattern. The actualizing individual will alter, to some extent, the temporal pattern of his or her existence throughout life, but a sudden, drastic shift of that pattern will tend to create frustration.

Thus, an affirmation of process and optimal structuring are two of the temporal requisites for an actualizing individual. A third is an optimal congruence between the temporality of the social milieu and the various movements identified above that occur in the individual's mental, physical, and emotional processes. Once again, we cannot identify the precise point at which the congruence is optimal, but it is clear that the disparity can be too great. Even the lower animals evidence congruence between their intrinsic temporality and that of their environment. In an experiment with cockroaches, the 24-hour rhythm of the insects' neurosecretory cells was established. One group of the roaches was kept in light during the night, and in the dark during the day, until their internal rhythms were 12 hours out of phase with those of normal cockroaches. Next, neurosecretory cells from the out-of-phase roaches were implanted into the normal cockroaches, resulting in two contradictory clocks within the roaches. All the cockroaches developed malignant tumors, mostly in the intestine.[77]

To the extent that certain physiological processes are similar at all levels of life, the experiment with roaches could have significant implications for human health. Indeed, various periodicities have already been discovered that include a greater susceptibility to disease at certain points in physiological cycles, periodic variations in the intensity of an illness, and others.[78] Experiments with animals underscore the potential significance of the various human physiological cycles. As illustrated, "an animal—whether human or guinea pig—is virtually a different creature, physically and chemically, at different times of day."[79] Yet we now prescribe drugs three or four times a day at regular intervals, ignoring the very different effects of those drugs at various times of the day. When rats were given a near lethal dose of amphetamine, their mortality rate varied from 6 to 78 percent, depending upon the time of day the drug was administered. In another experiment, some rats were given a sufficient quantity of phenobarbital to kill half of them. In one group, none of the rats died; in another group, they all died. The only difference was the time that the drug was given!

It would be surprising if humans did not have similar diverse reactions to drugs depending upon the time at which they ingested the drugs (that is, the point in their own physiological rhythms when they took a drug). Furthermore, it may well be that some of the other problems that we have discussed are related to some kind of violation of the individual's periodicity. For instance, why is there a direct relationship between experienced anxiety and the perceived rate of change? Perhaps part of the explanation of such a relationship may be found in a disparity between the individual's temporality and the social time in which he or she must function. We have barely begun to explore such relationships, but the evidence we have—including the problems of shift workers, the physical and emotional effects of jet travel, and so forth—demands that we probe deeper into the relationships between movements at the individual level and the social time in which the individual exists.

A final temporal requisite for the actualizing individual is the incorporation of a future image into his or her phenomenal reality. "If we do not know what we may become, we cannot know what we are."[80] We must have some notion of our potential future if we are to understand ourselves and engage in the process of actualizing our potential. An early exponent of the importance of the phenomenal future was Lawrence Frank, who also recognized that future orientation is a variable rather than an attribute. Thus, Frank argued that if our future orientation is too short, "life becomes insignificant, meaningless and dreary, since the present leads to nothing of enduring value."[81] But if that orientation is too great, focusing on the remote future, "the present is rendered equally valueless and dreary because nothing humanly desirable or satisfying is permissible."[82]

John Cohen has also insisted that human life would be meaningless without the psychological future.[83] He points out that all present behavior has implicit relationships with the future, and that even among the animals there is the "germ of futurity." For example, bees can be trained to come for sugar at regular intervals. After a while, they will come in advance of that interval as though they had learned to anticipate their food.

Both Frank and Cohen argue that human life gains its meaning from its relationship to the future. Abraham Maslow took this a step further by relating the future to self-actualization. He argued that the future is a reality to the actualizing self in the form of "ideals, hopes, duties, tasks, plans, goals, unrealized potentials, mission, fate, destiny, etc."[84] Without a future that contains gratification, the individual falls into hopelessness and emptiness.

Are we being ethnocentric at this point? Is the insistence that the actualizing individual possess an orientation to the future due to our Western bias? Are we so tyrannized by the clock and so consumed by our cultural emphasis on the future that we are unable to conceive of an alternative temporal orientation for the actualizing self? Consider the present-oriented Chippewa. Even after the introduction of light industry, the Chippewa did not develop the habit of saving money, of committing themselves firmly to factory work in order to secure the future, or of showing any other signs of a new concern with the future.[85] Some of the women would quit after earning a sufficient amount of money to pay certain debts. Could their refusal to be enslaved to a "time-is-money" future indicate an alternate, and perhaps better, mode of actualization?

The latter statement provides a clue to the answer, which is that a future orientation and perspective are necessary for the actualizing individual, but we must not equate the future perspective that facilitates actualization with the typical perspective of capitalistic people. The Marxist image of the future, for example, includes human freedom from the tyranny of monied time and the consequent rehumanization of individuals and society. The image of the future in some Christian thought proceeds upon the premise that the love of money is

the root of all evil. That is, the actualizing individual is oriented
toward the future, but this future perspective is not one that implies
that the individual will be shaped and constrained by such externalities
as money and material possessions.

I agree with the notion that the phenomenal future is significant
for our self-actualization. An individual can exist while being oriented
to the past or present, but growth occurs only when the individual is
oriented to the future. In fact, some individuals sense so keenly their
need for a meaningful future, that they may seek gratification in the
collective future of the state when their personal future is lacking.[86]
This, of course, can legitimate and firmly establish political tyranny.

The importance of the future to our total well-being is also
demonstrated by the problems of adequate medical care for the
Spanish-speaking Americans mentioned above. The problems generated
by the present orientation of these people increase the likelihood of
debilitating physical and emotional illnesses. Furthermore, those
who are presently oriented are more likely to acquiesce to the status
quo, to accept social conditions as they are and strive to adjust,
cope, and maximize gratification in a capricious world. But the
actualizing individual strives to direct and to control, rather than to
merely adjust or cope. Directing and controlling require a future
orientation and perspective. To realize one's potential, to become a
fully functioning person, the individual must actively strive to exercise some control over the environment rather than allowing the
environment to become the master.

Thus, one way in which the phenomenal future can facilitate
actualization is by giving direction and autonomy to the process of
the individual's existence. A second way is through its effects upon
both disjunctive and conjunctive experiences and emotions; in brief,
an adequate image of the future minimizes the debilitating effects of
the disjunctive experience, and tends to generate and support the
conjunctive experience.

An example of the relationship between the future and disjunctive
experience is provided by Maurice L. Farber's early study of
prisoners.[87] Farber sought to discover the effects of prison life on
behavior, attitudes, and emotional responses; he found that the
experience of suffering was particularly influenced by the future time
perspective of the prisoner. Neither factors in the past nor the
immediate situation of prison life were decisive in suffering; the
crucial factor was the future outlook concerning release from prison.
One might have expected that the prisoner's level of ambition or the
kind of work he was required to do in the prison would bear upon his
sense of suffering. But neither these factors nor others dealing
with similar matters were significantly correlated with suffering.
Rather, the disjunctive experience of suffering was a function of the

psychological future time perspective. A sense of the injustice of the time served and the perceived indefiniteness of the time of release were two of the most highly significant factors in suffering.

Uncertainty with respect to the future is, then, a disjunctive experience that tends to generate disjunctive emotions. On the other hand, conjunctive experiences and emotions are also related to the phenomenal future. In particular, morale has been linked with the phenomenal future. Kurt Lewin pointed out that the Zionists in Germany were able to maintain a high degree of morale and cope with the situation presented by the rise of Hitler to power much better than the majority of Jews. Further, this high morale and greater ability to handle the dangerous situation was a function of a distinctive time perspective. In contrast to the majority of Jews, who refused to believe that the pogroms of czarist Russia would ever occur in Germany, the Zionists considered pogroms a possibility and incorporated that possibility into a future orientation and perspective. According to Lewin, instead of passivity in the face of a perilous situation, "the Zionists with a long-range and realistic time perspective showed initiative and organized planning."[88] In the midst of a precarious present, therefore, they maintained a high level of morale.

Lewin also suggests that different time perspectives are inherent in autocratic and democratic groups, a factor affecting the morale of group members. The autocratic group involves a submission to the will of the leader, so that the future of the members is in the leader's power and under his or her direction. In the democratic group, on the other hand, the members share in the mapping out of the future; their future perspective includes a measure of self-direction and, probably, a clearer image. Understandably, the work morale of democratic groups may remain high even when the leader is absent, while the morale of the autocratic group may collapse.[89]

Thus, we all face disjunctive and conjunctive experiences, but whether a particular experience is conjunctive or disjunctive depends on the temporal orientation and temporal perspective used to define the situation and not merely on the situation itself. Whether the Nazi threat was dealt with in an actualizing or self-destructive way depended upon the manner in which the threat was temporally defined. This is not to say, of course, that any situation can be used for actualizing nor that the Nazi threat was employed in a manner that had no debilitating effects. But the Zionists did maximize the actualizing potentialities within that situation because of their temporal orientation and perspective. We need not forget that different situations and diverse social structures admit of differential possibilities for individual self-actualization in order to remember that, given a particular situation or a particular social structure, actualization potential is a function of temporality.

A third and last way in which the phenomenal future bears upon the process of actualization is in its provision of the contradiction that is necessary for human growth. While a good part of social psychology has stressed the drive toward consistency and/or tension reduction in humans, others have pointed to the contradictions and inconsistencies that characterize the individual. "We are all seething with contradictions," writes psychiatrist Paul Tournier.[90] And social psychologist Kenneth J. Gergen points out that inconsistency in concepts of the self "may be perfectly natural and widespread."[91] Furthermore, such contradictions can be stimuli for growth rather than indicators of problems. As Maslow states, it is "useful to think of growth or lack of it as the resultant of a dialectic between growth-fostering forces and growth-discouraging forces (regression, fear, pains of growth, ignorance, etc.)."[92]

The particular contradiction set forth here is between the image of the future and the reality and image of the present. The actualizing individual grows through efforts to resolve the contradictions between future image and present existence. The image of the future provides the actualizing individual with both motivation and direction. It is possible to live in the mode that Kierkegaard described as a series of instants, but it is not possible to engage in actualization while living in that mode. We are temporal creatures; our existence is a process. If that existence is also to be an actualizing one, its processual nature must be affirmed; there must be an optimal structuring of the temporal system within which the individual functions; there must be an optimal congruence between the temporality of the social milieu and the movements of the individual's mental, physical, and emotional states; and, finally, the individual must incorporate an appropriate image of the future into his or her phenomenal reality. The latter will give direction and a degree of autonomy to the process of individual existence, minimize the disjunctive and facilitate the conjunctive experiences and emotions, and serve as a driving mechanism for growth because of its contradiction with the individual's present.

NOTES

1. Blaise Pascal, Pensees, trans. W. F. Trotter (New York: The Modern Library, 1941), p. 143.
2. Information in this paragraph is drawn from Morton Deutsch and Robert M. Kraus, Theories in Social Psychology (New York: Basic Books, 1965), pp. 4-5.
3. G W. F. Hegel, The Phenomenology of Mind, trans. J. B. Baillie (New York: Harper Torchbooks, 1967), pp. 80-81.

4. M. Merleau-Ponty, Phenomenology of Perception (New York: Humanities Press, 1962), p. 411. See also Edmund Husserl, The Phenomenology of the Internal Time-Consciousness (Bloomington: University of Indiana Press, 1964) and Philip Merlan, "Time Consciousness in Husserl and Heidegger," Philosophy and Phenomenological Research 8 (1947): 23-54.

5. Charles Hartshorne, "Introduction: The Development of Process Philosophy," in Philosophers of Process, ed. Douglas Browning (New York: Random House, 1965), p. xi. Cf. the statement of Whitehead, Process and Reality, p. 106: "The enduring personality is the historic route of living occasions which are severally dominant in the body at successive instants."

6. Ibid., p. xii.

7. Whitehead, Process and Reality, p. 106.

8. Ibid., p. 179.

9. Norman L. Munn, Psychology, 5th ed. (Boston: Houghton Mifflin, 1966), p. 376.

10. J. A. Michon, "Time Experience and Memory Processes," in The Study of Time II, ed. J. T. Fraser and N. Lawrence (New York: Springer-Verlag, 1975), p. 303.

11. See Robert E. Ornstein, On the Experience of Time (Baltimore: Penguin Books, 1969)

12. George Herbert Mead, Mind, Self, and Society, ed. Charles W. Morris (Chicago: University of Chicago Press, 1934), p. 140.

13. See Gay Gaer Luce, Body Time: Physiological Rhythms and Social Stress (New York: Pantheon Books, 1971), and Wallerstein and Roberts, "All Together on the Bio-Curve," pp. 8-15.

14. Freud, Collected Papers, pp. 13-21.

15. Wallace and Rabin, "Temporal Experience," pp. 214-15.

16. Benjamin Whorf, Language, Thought, and Reality (New York: John Wiley, 1956), pp. 134-59, 207-19.

17. Meerloo, "The Time Sense in Psychiatry," p. 247.

18. Arnoldo Momigliano, "Time in Ancient Historiography," in History and the Concept of Time, ed. George H. Nadel (Middletown, Conn.: Wesleyan University Press, 1966), p. 6.

19. Leach, Rethinking Anthropology, p. 125.

20. Jean Piaget, "Time Perception in Children," in The Voices of Time, ed. J. T. Fraser (New York: George Braziller, 1966), pp. 202-16.

21. Ibid., p. 202.

22. Gustav Jahoda, "Children's Concepts of Time and History," Educational Review 15 (February 1963): 95.

23. David Zern, "The Influence of Certain Child-Rearing Factors Upon the Development of a Structured and Salient Sense of

Time," Genetic Psychology Monographs 81 (May 1970): 197-254.

24. Ibid., p. 199.

25. J. R. Seeley, R. A. Sim, and W. E. Loosley, Crestwood Heights (New York: John Wiley, 1956), p. 66.

26. Fraisse, The Psychology of Time, p. 185.

27. Julius A. Roth, Timetables: Structuring the Passage of Time in Hospital Treatment and Other Careers (New York: Bobbs-Merrill, 1963).

28. Thompson, "Time, Work-Discipline," pp. 85-86.

29. Ibid., p. 82.

30. Weber, The Protestant Ethic, p. 158.

31. Quoted by M. W. Flinn, "Social Theory and the Industrial Revolution," in Social Theory and Economic Change, ed. Tom Burns and S. B. Saul (London: Tavistock Publications, 1967), pp. 17-18.

32. Thompson, "Time, Work-Discipline," p. 91.

33. Catherine Beecher, A Treatise on Domestic Economy (New York: Schocken Books, 1977), p. 171.

34. G. W. Stacy, "The Improvement of Time," The Practical Christian, January 6, 1844, p. 1.

35. Reported by Lawrence Wright, Clockwork Man (London: Elek Books, 1968), p. 211.

36. Leonard Nadler, "Helping the Hard-Core Adjust to the World of Work," Harvard Business Review 48 (March/April 1970): 123.

37. See Thomas J. Cottle, "The Circles Test: An Investigation of Perceptions of Temporal Relatedness and Dominance," Journal of Projective Techniques and Personality Assessment 31 (1967): 58-71, and "Future Orientations and Avoidance: Speculations on the Time of Achievement and Social Roles," Sociological Quarterly 10 (Fall 1969): 419-37. In the latter, he reports that women who become future oriented are more intelligent. That is, women who develop a future orientation in our society are "special" in some way.

38. Margaret Hennig and Anne Jardim, "Women Executives in the Old-Boy Network," Psychology Today, January 1977, p. 76.

39. Meyerhoff, Time in Literature, p. 114.

40. Robert H. Lauer, "The Middle Class Looks at Poverty," Urban and Social Change Review 5 (Fall 1971): 8-10.

41. Seeley, Sim, and Loosley, Crestwood Heights, pp. 65 f.

42. Robert Jay Lifton, "Individual Patterns in Historical Change: Imagery of Japanese Youth," in Comparative Perspectives on Social Change, ed. S. N Eisenstadt (Boston: Little, Brown, 1968), pp. 160-75.

43. Jerome M. Sattler, "Counselor Competence, Interest and Time Perspective: A Follow-up Note," Counselor Education and Supervision 6 (1967): 185-86.

44. See Hall, The Silent Language, pp. 160-64.
45. See Jean Piaget, The Psychology of Intelligence, trans. Malcolm Percy and D. E. Berlyne (Paterson, N.J.: Littlefield, Adams, 1963); and The Child's Conception of the World, trans. Joan and Andrew Tomlinson (Paterson, N.J.: Littlefield, Adams, 1963).
46. James, The Principles of Psychology, 1, p. 609.
47. Ibid., p. 624.
48. Information in this paragraph is from J. E. Orme, Time, Experience and Behavior (London: Iliffe Books, 1969), p. 12.
49. Mark Zborowski, "Cultural Components in Responses to Pain," Journal of Social Issues 8 (1952): 16-30.
50. Lyle Saunders, Cultural Differences and Medical Care (New York: Russell Sage Foundation, 1954), p. 119.
51. Ibid., p. 121.
52. Jerome Platt and Robert E. Taylor, "Homesickness, Future Time Perspective, and the Self Concept," Journal of Individual Psychology 23 (1967): 94-97.
53. Alan H. Roberts and Robert S. Herrman, "Dogmatism, Time Perspective, and Anomie," Journal of Individual Psychology 16 (1960): 67-72.
54. Milton Rokeach, The Open and Closed Mind (New York: Basic Books, 1960), pp. 51-53.
55. Fraisse, The Psychology of Time, p. 186.
56. Robert H. Barndt and Donald M. Johnson, "Time Orientation in Delinquents," Journal of Abnormal and Social Psychology 51 (1955): 343-45; Anthony Davids, Catherine Kidder, and Melvyn Reich, "Time Orientation in Male and Female Juvenile Delinquents," Journal of Abnormal and Social Psychology 64 (1962): 239-40.
57. Roger Lee Kroth, "A Study of Three Aspects of Time Among Normal and Delinquent School Age Mates in Costa Rica and the United States," Ph.D. diss., University of Kansas, 1968.
58. P. Roos and R. Albers, "Performance of Alcoholics and Normals on a Measure of Temporal Orientation," Journal of Clinical Psychology 21 (1965): 34-36.
59. Reginald G. Smart, "Future Time Perspectives in Alcoholics and Social Drinkers," Journal of Abnormal Psychology 73 (1968): 81-83.
60. Wallace and Rabin, "Temporal Experience," pp. 223-24, 229; Orme, Time, Experience and Behavior, p. 24.
61. Adolfo E. Rizzo, "The Time Moratorium" Adolescence 2 (1967-68): 469-80.
62. Radhakamal Mukerjee, "Time, Technics, and Society, Sociology and Social Research 27 (1943): 255-66.
63. Ibid., p. 259.
64. For a detailed discussion of various problems with shift

work, see Paul E. Mott, Floyd C. Mann, Quin McLoughlin, and Donald P. Warwick, Shift Work (Ann Arbor: The University of Michigan Press, 1965), and James Walker, The Human Aspects of Shiftwork (London: Institute of Personnel Management, 1978).

65. Robert H. Lauer, "The Scientific Legitimation of Fallacy: Neutralizing Social Change Theory," American Sociological Review 36 (October 1971): 884.

66. For more details on the study, the rationale for the measures used, and the results, see Robert H. Lauer, "Rate of Change and Stress: A Test of the 'Future Shock' Thesis," Social Forces 52 (June 1974): 510-16.

67. For a fuller theoretical explanation, along with supporting historical evidence, see Lauer and Lauer, "The Experience of Change," pp. 520-45.

68. Kurt Goldstein, "The So-Called Drives," in The Self: Explorations in Personal Growth, ed. Clark E. Moustakas (New York: Harper & Brothers, 1956), p. 17.

69. Peter M. Litchfield and Jerome M. Sattler, "An Hypothesis: The Existential Notion of Intentional Time as a Dimension of Psychological Health," Journal of Genetic Psychology 79 (1968): 257-70.

70. Ibid., p. 269.

71. See, for example, Gardell, "Technology, Alienation," and de Grazia, Of Time, Work, and Leisure, p. 57.

72. Stanley Cohen and Laurie Taylor, "The Experience of Time in Long-Term Imprisonment," New Society, December 31, 1970, p. 1159.

73. Doob, Patterning of Time, p. 170.

74. John P. Robinson and Philip E. Converse, "Social Change Reflected in the Use of Time," in The Human Meaning of Social Change, ed. Angus Campbell and Philip E. Converse (New York: Russell Sage Foundation, 1972), p. 65n.

75. Jack W. Brehm, Responses to Loss of Freedom: A Theory of Psychological Reactance (Morristown, N.J.: General Learning Press, 1972), p. 21.

76. Robert H. Smith, "Cultural Differences in the Life Cycle and the Concept of Time," in Aging and Leisure: A Research Perspective into the Meaningful Use of Time, ed. Robert W. Kleemeier (New York: Oxford University Press, 1961), p. 99.

77. John Cohen, Psychological Time in Health and Disease (Springfield, Ill.: Charles C. Thomas, 1967), p. 7.

78. Ibid., pp. 6-9, passim.; Gay Gaer Luce, Body Time.

79. Philip Hilts, "The Clock Within," Science 80, December 1980, p. 62. The animal studies mentioned in this paragraph come from this article.

80. John R. Platt, The Step to Man (New York: Wiley, 1966).

81. Lawrence K. Frank, Society as the Patient: Essays on Culture and Personality (New Brunswick, N.J.: Rutgers University Press, 1949), p. 355.

82. Ibid., p. 356.

83. Cohen, Humanistic Psychology, p. 111.

84. Abraham Maslow, Toward a Psychology of Being, 2d ed. (New York: Van Nostrand Reinhold, 1968), p. 214.

85. Ritzenthaler, "The Impact of Small Industry," p. 147.

86. Erich Fromm, Escape From Freedom (New York: Farrer & Rinehart, 1941).

87. Maurice L. Farber, "Suffering and Time-Perspective of the Prisoner," Studies in Topological and Vector Psychology 20 (1944).

88. Kurt Lewin, Resolving Social Conflicts (New York: Harper & Row, 1948), p. 104.

89. Ibid., pp. 116-18. Lewin also posited a relationship between time perspective and such qualities as persistency and level of aspiration. Both of these qualities depend upon a valued goal and an optimistic outlook for the future. See pp. 107-13.

90. Paul Tournier, The Meaning of Persons (New York: Harper & Row, 1957), p. 46.

91. Kenneth J. Gergen, The Concept of Self (New York: Holt, Rinehart and Winston, 1971), p. 22.

92. Maslow, Toward a Psychology of Being, p. 204.

4

SOCIAL TIME AND HUMAN INTERACTION

An understanding and analysis of human interaction is basic to our knowledge of social life. An emphasis on interaction means that humans are viewed in a distinctive manner. Thus, the individual is not the mere product of impinging stimuli or the reflection of a transcendent and overwhelming cultural system or the result of internal and ineluctable biological drives. Rather, what the individual is depends upon interaction with others. And the interaction, in turn, is both a creator of, and a function of, social time. Temporal symbols emerge out of both interaction and influence interaction. The relationships between interaction and social time, therefore, are of prime importance. In this chapter, we will look at the notion of interaction as a process, at the way in which social time affects interaction in general, and at the way in which social time relates to three particular kinds of interaction—status, power, and conflict relationships.

INTERACTION AS PROCESS

The processual nature of interaction has been particularly emphasized by symbolic interactionists.[1] Even the concept of "role," which has often been treated in a more or less static fashion, becomes dynamic in Ralph H. Turner's notion of "role-making."[2] Turner argued that we continually modify roles through our interaction with others. We do not merely assume or play out roles but make them. Similarly, Herbert Blumer stressed the processual nature of interaction in his notion that human group life is "a continuing matter of fitting developing lines of conduct to one another."[3]

In other words, interaction is a creative process in its own right and is not merely the outcome of preexisting factors such as the interactants' personalities or attitudes. An individual comes into an interaction situation with certain interests and with a definition of the situation that is based on previous experience. The individual initiates a particular line of action that is congruent with those interests and definition of the situation. However, the definition and the behavior both tend to alter during interaction, and they tend to alter for all participants. Thus, there are reciprocal effects, which means ongoing socialization of each participant by other participants.

This is not to say that interaction is totally fluid. Symbolic interactionists recognize that there are certain relatively stable and recurrent types of interaction. But in any case, interactional processes may be conceptualized in terms of social time, for all interaction has a particular duration, sequence, and so forth. And all interaction embodies certain temporal meanings.

INTERACTION IN SOCIAL TIME

We have already noted that social time arises out of interaction. There is no kind of time that is "natural" to humans. Rather, time is the result of the structure and functioning of the social order. Once a particular temporality emerges, however, it tends to persist and to influence subsequent interaction. Various groups construct systems of social time with diverse meanings and with, therefore, diverse consequences for social interaction.

Perhaps the most fundamental difference in the meaning of time is that between those groups in which time is measured predominantly by social events and those in which the clock is predominant over social life. In the former, one knows the time by the activities of the group. In the latter, one schedules activities by the clock. Social time is basically qualitative for the former; in the latter, it is basically quantitative. For the former, time has significance only in terms of the activities that are taking place. For the latter, time is money, a scarce commodity, and all activities take place in the shadow of the clock. The bulk of human history has occurred in the context of the former. Alexander Szalai claims:

> Nowadays, in the age of timetables and schedules, it sounds almost funny to learn when reading Herodotus that this great traveler and well-informed man of his age never met the concept of "hour" in his world and could not even find the right word for it. In his time, and even much later, human activity served much

more as a measure of time and not the other way around.[4]

The two kinds of social time are, of course, ideal-typical. Few groups or societies could be characterized as bound exclusively by the clock or as wholly independent of the constraints of some system of temporality. But whatever its nature in a particular society, social time has implications for interaction. This may be illustrated by considering the impact of social time on interaction in two different social settings. Bali has had an intricate system of temporality, though clock time has been of little significance, while the United States has had a social time in which the clock is paramount.

The Balinese have had, according to Clifford Geertz, a "detemporalizing" conception of time.[5] Their social time includes a calendar with a complex system of periodicity. Geertz calls it a "permutational" calendar, for it contains ten different cycles of day names ranging in length from ten days to one day. Thus, every day is the conjunction of ten different cycles, although only the five-, six-, and seven-day cycles are of primary importance. The manner in which these three cycles intersect is quite important in determining social activity. Particular combinations of days from all three cycles occur every 210 days. Combinations of days from any two of the cycles occur every 30 days (five- and six-day cycles), every 35 days (five- and seven-day cycles), and every 42 days (six- and seven-day cycles). To determine the significance of a day for practical and religious purposes, one needs to identify it in terms of the cycles. For instance, Boda-Klion is in the 35-day set and is the conjunction of Boda in the seven-day cycle with Klion in the five-day cycle. They combine to form rainan, the day on which small offerings are to be placed at different places to feed the gods.

This complex system is used for various religious and practical purposes. It identifies nearly all of the holidays and temple celebrations, and it also guides the individual in daily activities. According to Geertz, "There are good and bad days on which to build a house, launch a business enterprise, change residence, go on a trip, harvest crops, sharpen cock spurs, hold a puppet show, or (in the old days) start a war, or conclude a peace."[6]

By its very nature, the system also "detemporalizes" time, for the days that are identified are parts of endless cycles, without any significance to their sequence. Each day is a discrete period of time for which there are appropriate and inappropriate activities, but there is no progression to an end, no climax to the process. This same characteristic—the emphasis on the present rather than on progression—is found in interaction patterns. Balinese social activities have traditionally been characterized by the absence of climax. The activities "do not build, or are not permitted to build, toward definite consummations."[7] Quarrels between people rarely come to a head Issues are seldom brought to a sharp focus and resolved. Even artistic performances simply come to a halt without having reached any climax or traveled in any particular direction. Balinese events, like the calendar, are discrete affairs. The orientation of the events is to the present. Recurring social activities, devoid of the climactic, are a logical reflection of Balinese social time, with its orientation to the present and its complex system of periodicity.

In contrast, in the United States time is money. Time is a scarce commodity of great value, and interaction generally is characterized by extreme attentiveness to the time involved. This finds expression in a variety of ways. Interaction will be controlled in accordance with some notion of the appropriate amount of time for that particular situation. For example, in everyday interaction we distinguish between the amount of our time that can be rightly consumed by strangers and that which can be given to friends and relations. As Andrew J. Weigert has pointed out, interaction time is a measure of the meaning of the relationship between two people.[8] If two casual acquaintances happen to meet somewhere, they will likely take only a few minutes to exchange recognition and perhaps a pleasantry or two. The interaction time for such a meeting is clearly limited.

> The strength of the temporal boundaries is felt if one of the casual acquaintances attempts to transform the meeting into a lengthy encounter by launching into a detailed recounting of everything which has happened since the last time they met. Such an extension beyond the appropriate interaction time violates the expectations governing the usual meaning of a chance public meeting among acquaintances. The violator . . . may even be defined as insensitive or boorish.[9]

On the other hand, if two good friends happened to meet and one attempted to limit interaction time as though the friend were a casual acquaintance, we would again have a case of violation of a temporal norm. The violator would be expected to account for his or her terseness, and if no explanation were forthcoming the friendship could be strained.

Thus, interaction will be evaluated in terms of time consumption. The nature of the relationship between two people is reflected in interaction time. With the exception of friends and lovers (and not always then), people tend to minimize the duration of any particular interaction in our society. There are, of course, some kinds of interaction that cannot be, or that cannot easily be, manipulated. But where there is the option, the tendency will be to minimize duration (since time equals money, this minimizes the cost).

For those who have some problems in organizing their lives around the norm of minimal duration for any particular interaction, there is an abundance of literature available for guidance. There are articles, books, and even seminars that teach us how to maximize each minute, and a good deal of the advice bears upon our interaction patterns. Thus, one expert tells businesspeople that telephone calls and unexpected visitors are among the leading time wasters. What, then, should one do if a fellow worker drops in and asks if you "have a minute?" The worker who values time will not simply say yes to such a question but will say something like, "That depends. What is it you would like to discuss? Could we do it sometime later or over lunch? I'm right in the middle of an important project now."[10] That response may indeed conserve your time, but it is also likely to say to others that you are a person who does not have time to care about your fellow workers' needs or concerns; you are not the kind of person to whom one can easily talk.

In other words, much of the advice given by the time-efficiency experts can depersonalize interaction. The individual who follows the advice may have far more hours in which to do things and far fewer friendships and intimate relationships. What other outcome could be expected if you take the advice seriously and learn the skills of nonverbal communication so that you can let others know you are a busy person? Or if you avoid using pleasantries in meetings because they consume precious moments? Or if you ask those people around you who most affect the way you spend your time to help you make better use of your time in the future (which may be saying to them, "Please don't bother me as much as you have been doing in the past")? This is not to say that some people cannot profit from becoming more efficient, but those who intend to literally follow the advice of the experts might well ask what profit it would be to gain an hour and lose a friend.

The tendency to minimize duration applies to both productive and nonproductive interaction and to both instrumental and expressive interaction. Productive interaction means that which involves the individual's income. Obviously, the less time expended in any particular interaction, the more one "gets done" and the more productive one is likely to be. A salesman will spend as much—and as little—time as necessary with a particular customer in order to cement a sale and a relationship conducive to future sales. An abundance of literature and sales managers will inform the salesman that any additional time spent with the customer is foolish. Perhaps the most time-obsessed role in the United States is, appropriately enough, that of the business executive. Peter F. Drucker has called the executive a "captive" because everyone can "move in on his time, and everybody does."[11] The executive's time, says Drucker, is continually preempted by matters that are important to others, so that executives have little or no time of their own. Nevertheless, they will attempt to minimize each particular interaction in accordance with good management practice. As one management consultant states, as much as one-third of the average person's life may be wasted in "trivia." The executive can lose time to such trivia as "telephone conversations discussing nonessential, personal matters in an effort to gain rapport" and long "bull sessions" with subordinate members of the organization.[12] In other words, every effort should be made to minimize the duration of any particular interaction, for there is no commodity more scarce than time.

Even nonproductive, expressive interaction is affected by the obsession with clock time. Bruno Bettelheim has remarked that dating and mating patterns reflect the abundance of money and the scarcity of time:

> In other societies it was well known that the greatest attention one could show the courted person was to devote time and attention to him or her. In our society . . . money must often make up for time; a boy's car or the money he can spend on his date now replaces the time and attention spent in being with her.[13]

Because time is more scarce than money, money may be used to reduce interaction time. Money may "buy" time from interaction. Thus, time-pressured parents may buy things for their children in lieu of interacting with them. Children may be shipped off to a private school, or provided with various toys or hobbies with which to occupy themselves. In his study of Washington, D.C., Chapin secured information on the duration of weekday activities of heads of households and found an inverse relationship between income level and duration of family activities. As income level rises, there is a temporal reallocation that includes less time for family interaction.[14]

I have suggested above that one consequence of minimizing the time spent in particular interactions is a loss of intimacy. Is this necessarily true? Can we have the quality of intimacy in spite of the lack of duration? I would argue that, in general, we cannot. Intimacy requires duration of a twofold sort—duration in particular interaction episodes (at least, in some of those episodes) and duration of the relationship. The latter has been forcefully argued by William Kilpatrick, who claims that one of the shortcomings of the encounter group movement is that it attempts to create intimacy without one of the prime requisites of intimacy—an ongoing, durable relationship.

> Unfortunately, the two most beguiling promises the Human Potential Movement holds out—intimacy and community—are undermined by its emphasis on the present. For once you have cut out past and future, you have removed the basis for human relationships, which is commitment over time, and you are left with the capacity only for intimacy and community of the most transitory nature.[15]

Relationships become significant, Kilpatrick asserts, when they give meaning to our lives, and that occurs after months and years of building bonds of trust and commitment. He quotes a woman who spent a year in various encounter groups and concluded that "history" is an integral part of any meaningful friendship. Small groups simply cannot hasten a process that requires one or more years for its development. There are no shortcuts to intimacy.

The link between duration and intimacy is important to recognize because it appears that many observers sense a lack of intimacy in modern life. The decline of primary relationships and consequent enlargement of the sphere of secondary relationships has often been attributed to something inherent in modern society, such as the anonymity of urban, industrial life. But is it true that urban, industrial living as such demands impersonal relationships? I would argue that it is the growing affluence and the social time dominated by the clock that are associated with urban industrialism and that lead to the proliferation of secondary relationships. As Staffan Burenstam Linder points out, we have a preference for larger groups—banquets, conventions, cocktail parties, and such. These groups provide a very efficient use of the time available for socializing. According to Linder, "One devotes oneself to the simultaneous consumption of food and people. . . . Efforts to economize one's time in this way lead in due course to one's having numerous acquaintances and no friends."[16]

Linder has provided numerous other examples of the way in which the time for particular interactions is minimized in his description of the "harried leisure class." He argues that economic growth per se results in an increase in the scarcity of time. As people become increasingly affluent, they have increasing alternatives with respect to time use. The demands on time, therefore, increase enormously, but the supply remains the same. As a result, affluence brings a harried rather than a utopian existence.

The tendency for economic growth to result in a new temporality, and, consequently, new kinds of interaction, is illustrated by the changes that occurred in a Danish maritime village as it became a suburb of Copenhagen. The village's annual cycle of life was totally altered:

> The long quiet winter, that formerly gave every man a change of pace, is now replaced by regular, and short, winter and summer vacations. With all of these changes has gone the intimate communality of Dragorian men. No longer do they congregate at the harbor in the evenings, or exchange visits in the winter. The sea has ceased to bind them in a shared maritime interest. Each goes his own way. The dispersion into the urban network of work-a-day jobs reflects itself in the community as a concentration of each individual on his own home and his own private circle of friends.[17]

Thus, interaction under the tyranny of the clock is not unique to the United States, nor is it confined to modern times. Ricardo J. Quinones has shown that a sense of urgency and the need to maximize the use of time developed during the Renaissance: "For the men of the Renaissance, time is a great discovery—the antagonist against which they plan and plot and war, and over which they hope to triumph."[18] The advice of one fourteenth-century Florentine, for example, sounds almost contemporary: "who sleeps too much loses time," "always work toward and pursue gain," "think that time passed can never be regained," and "be diligent and provident in all your affairs, and keep from laziness as from the Devil himself or from any other enemy if you want to arrive at success."[19] Such ideas developed in the context of the growing commercialization and urbanization of the late Middle Ages and early Renaissance.

Such historical examples suggest that Linder is correct in linking the sense of time scarcity with economic growth. Societies with otherwise widely divergent ideologies and cultures have developed a compulsion about the use of time during periods of economic growth. If the wasting of time was "the deadliest of sins" in the ideology of the Protestant ethic, it was no less of an infraction in the ideology of the Soviet Union during the 1920s. There was a massive effort to inculcate methodical work habits during the Soviet drive toward rapid economic development. Small groups were organized to promote the proper use of time. Members of the Time League were required to keep a daily record of their activities and to report any instances they observed of wasting time. A leaflet published by the Time League sounds, in fact, like the work of a zealous advocate of the Protestant ethic:

> Measure your time, control it!
> Do everything on time! exactly, on the minute!
> Save time, make time count, work fast!
> Divide your time correctly, time for work and time for leisure![20]

It is not only duration but all of the elements of the temporal pattern that are affected by our emphasis on clock time. In another example, David Kantor and William Lehr have pointed out the significance of timing in modern family interaction.[21] Their analysis proceeds on the assumption that all family interactions involve "access": "Every waking minute, but particularly those minutes we spend with our families, each of us is engaged in seeking, permitting, denying, or being denied access to one thing or another."[22] We seek access to those things that will enable us to reach the goals that are common to all of us—intimacy, power (in the sense of being able to make our own decisions and get the things we want), and a meaningful existence. Whether or not we gain such desirable goals depends upon the way in which we and our families regulate our space, time, and energy. One of the problems of time is what Kantor and Lehr call "clocking," which involves daily cycles of activities: "If people are out of phase with one another, they may not even be able to be home together at the same time, much less make love or fight with one another."[23] Obviously, this is a problem of timing or synchronization of activities. Though Kantor and Lehr do not link timing problems with the dominance of the clock, it does not require much imagination to take that step, for the more we feel constrained to minimize the duration of interaction episodes, and the more our lives are closely regulated by the clock, the greater will be our difficulty in synchronizing our own schedule with that of someone else in order to maintain a fulfilling relationship. And when the synchronization involves not merely one other person, but three or more people in a family, the difficulties may become monumental.

In sum, the social time of any group tends to structure interaction in particular ways. This is dramatically illustrated by the obsession with clock time that characterizes periods of economic growth. The social time that emerges with economic development results in a general tendency to minimize the duration of any particular interaction, and to control and evaluate all interaction in accordance with time consumption. Moreover, timing and the other elements of the temporal pattern will be affected, so that both the forms and various problems of interaction will reflect the dominance of the clock.

SOCIAL TIME AND STATUS RELATIONSHIPS

Because temporality in the United States stresses the scarcity of time, to infringe upon another's time is to expropriate a valued possession. As Eviatar Zerubavel has pointed out, "it has become generally accepted that every person has a basic right to be socially inaccessible at certain times."[24] But the right of inaccessibility is not quite the same for everyone, for as a scarce resource time has intrinsic status implications. The temporal features of interaction, including the nature of one's right to inaccessibility, will express status relationships and, in turn, legitimate those relationships.

In this sense, temporal characteristics are similar to other facets of interaction such as space and clothing. There are certain cultural differences in the appropriate spatial relationships and clothing of interactants, but there are also status differences within any culture. Thus, the high-status individual occupies the "better" spatial positions (head of the table), the approach to a person seated at a desk will depend upon the status of each, and the distance between two interactants of similar status will tend to be less than that between two of dissimilar status.[25] With respect to clothing, Gregory P. Stone has detailed the way in which people believe that there is appropriate and inappropriate attire for various statuses. For instance, a truck driver said that he would feel "out of my class" in dress clothes, a woman who worked in a restaurant said that she and furs would not mix because it would be as if one were trying to "overdo, and make people think they're higher than they are," and a small shop operator said that going "too far" in dress would make it appear that he was stepping out of his class.[26] In all societies at all times, people have used clothing to indicate status and to legitimate status differences.[27]

Similarly, there are temporal characteristics to interaction that derive from status relationships. Certain kinds of temporal behavior express status differences. And to the extent that interactants accept such behavior as legitimate, those status differences will be perpetuated. Thus, interactants who strive to maintain a particular status relationship must not only watch their spatial relations, gestures, language, clothing, and so forth, but must also watch the time. Since time is a scarce resource, the time of the high-status individual is more important than that of the low-status individual. Specifically, there is evidence that status differences are expressed in three kinds of temporal behavior: group participation time, waiting time, and discretionary time. In each case, there are norms concerning the appropriate behavior for individuals in different statuses.

With respect to group participation time, various studies of small groups show that lower-status members defer to higher-status members, allowing the latter a disproportionate amount of group time for speaking. For example, in a study of the process of jury deliberations, high-status members (as measured by occupation) participated more in the discussion than did low-status members. The high-status members talked more and had more influence on the others.[28] This disproportionate consumption of time by high-status members has been noted in other studies. It reflects the fact that the use of time involves group norms. As Josephine Klein notes in the context of her discussion about small-group behavior, it appears as though

> each member has in mind a standard time which he feels entitled to fill, so that when he feels he has spoken too much, or too little, in the first half-hour of the meeting, he will modify his volubility during the second half in order to average on the whole his self-appointed allowance of communication.[29]

Thus, interaction between individuals of disparate statuses is circumscribed by norms concerning participation time in small groups. Those with high status are accorded a greater portion of the group's time than those of low status, just as high-status individuals generally have a disproportionate share of valued, scarce commodities.

With respect to waiting time, it is well known that low-status individuals are required to wait for high-status individuals. In fact, an individual might require another to wait precisely to remind the individual of their relative statuses. A classic example is the medieval pope, Gregory VII, who is said to have required the Holy Roman emperor, Henry IV, to stand for three days and nights barefoot in the snow and ice before he would see him. The pope used waiting time to assert the superiority of his own status over that of the emperor (who had challenged the pope's authority). A more contemporary example is an incident involving President Truman.[30] Truman once kept the president of the Chase Manhattan Bank waiting for 30 minutes because, he stated, "When I was a United States senator and headed the war investigation committee, I had to go to New York to see this fella Aldrich. Even though I had an appointment he had me cool my heels for an hour and a half. So just relax, He's got a little while to go yet." Waiting time was used to remind the bank president of the altered statuses of the two men.

Another aspect to waiting is the fact that low-status individuals may have to wait longer for the same services than higher status individuals have to wait. In his study of access to medical care, Barry Schwartz found that blacks generally waited longer than whites for medical service.[31] A national sample was queried, among other things, on the length of time each respondent had to wait to see a doctor once in the doctor's office. Results were tabulated in terms of the proportion of the respondents who had to wait 30 minutes or more once in the office (status was measured by income). Schwartz found that the proportion who had to wait 30 or more minutes was 36 percent for high-status whites, 50 percent for high-status blacks, 51 percent for low-status whites, and 69 percent for low-status blacks.

Finally, high-status individuals generally have more discretionary use of their time. Consider the differences between men and women in our society. Women generally have a lower status than men. As a consequence, Nancy M. Henley has argued that whether in a work organization or in the home, the time of women is relatively unimportant.[32] A mother may be overworked, but her time is still considered to be at the disposal of the members of her family. "Mother's time, like mother's space, can always be interrupted." The woman is less likely to have a "night out" with friends than is the man. Women's time is also more constricted; they have less discretionary use of time both in the sense of having their time regarded as more violable and in the sense of having a more temporally bounded existence. For instance, dormitory hours at colleges have tended to be more restrictive and more strongly enforced for women than for men. Women have also been less free to go out at night alone than have men. Our differential temporal norms for the sexes reflect the higher status of males over females.

The relationship between discretionary time and status is also illustrated abundantly in organizations. Among other things, there will be, for people of various statuses, differing expectations about punctuality. Cohen notes that it was possible at one time to identify the grade of British Civil Service officials by the time of their arrival at work.[33] A 1969 study of British industry showed a number of temporal differences between white-collar and blue-collar groups. The white-collar workers tended to have a longer paid vacation time. They were also more likely to be paid while taking time off for domestic purposes. And only 8 percent of clerical workers were penalized (by loss of pay) for lateness, while 90 percent of blue-collar workers were penalized.[34]

Similarly, a study of time use in a factory showed differing expectations depending upon the status of the workers.[35] Technically, the workday began at 8:00 A.M., and bells signaled the lunch period and quitting time. But unlike other workers, management and staff personnel were not required to punch in, and typically arrived somewhat later than the other workers. On the other hand, when the other workers would prepare for lunchtime by stopping a bit early to wash or use the rest room or go to the supply room, management regarded their behavior as illicit, a waste of time. Clearly, the higher-status personnel allowed themselves the prerogative of a greater amount of discretion in the use of their time than they granted to lower-status workers.

In any particular organization the higher-status member will tend to have the greatest discretion in time use.[36] Ross A. Webber, in fact, has arranged managers and executives in a hierarchical order, ranging from least to greatest discretionary control over time: service managers, staff specialists, operating supervisors, sales managers, functional control managers, and general executives.[37] How does this correlate with what was said previously about the executive being a temporal captive? Actually, the executive's time has a greater number of demands made upon it, but an executive has more discretion in responding to those demands than does the service manager, for example. Webber notes that behavior varies more among general executives than any of the other positions: "Demands are ambiguous, so incumbents vary widely in behavior. Explicit short-range demands are relatively rare—for example, these men apparently make fewer decisions (although more important and more difficult) than service managers or operating supervisors."[38] In other words, the lower-level managers have much more explicit demands, although they are not bombarded with as many, or as important, demands. The greater ambiguity of the executive's task, combined with the temporal deference to high-status individuals, leaves the executive with greater temporal discretion than that possessed by those in lower-status positions.

One additional point is suggested by the above discussion. If temporal behavior expresses and legitimates status differences, then that behavior can be employed to alter one's status. "Temporal strategies," as Moore calls them,[39] can be used to exploit the status symbolism of time and gain new status for an individual. According to Erving Goffman, the individual who pursues a temporal strategy makes interaction

> less a scene of mutual considerationness than an arena in which a contest or match is held. The purpose of the game is to prevent everyone's line from an inexcusable contradiction, while scoring as many points as possible against one's adversaries and making as many gains as possible for oneself.[40]

An individual may "score points" by being sufficiently late to create an impression of busyness and importance, but not too late to generate suspicion or antagonism. In newly formed groups, as Peter M. Blau points out, there is competition for status and that competition initially involves participation time.[41] The individual must consume enough time to establish a particular status in the group; too little or too much time at the outset is likely to be counterproductive. Thus, contends Blau, in the newly formed group time "is a generalized means in the competition for a variety of social rewards, equivalent in this respect to profitable sales in economic competition. . . ."[42]

SOCIAL TIME AND POWER RELATIONSHIPS

As Ernest Gellner has stated, when dealing with the concept of power, it is well to speak of a particular power, to speak of the ability to "control the decision over this or that alternative."[43] By power relationships, then, I mean those in which one of the interactants is more likely than the other (or others) to decide between alternatives.

In the ongoing struggle for power—the struggle between individuals and groups to control decisions over alternatives—social time enters as both a goal and a resource. As a goal, social time, or some aspect of it, is the focus of struggle. That is, there is a struggle to alter or to retain a particular system of social time in the context of power differentials. This is likely to occur whenever some individuals or groups define the existing temporality as detrimental to their well-being. For instance, the rapid and unvarying tempo of an assembly line may be stifling to workers, who will struggle to create a rhythm of work more conducive to their well-being.

As a resource, on the other hand, social time validates or invalidates existing power arrangements. As in the case of status, the temporal characteristics of interaction express power differentials. Indeed, the very meaning of "waiting time" is that one of the interactants is more powerful and of higher status than the other. To the extent that such characteristics are accepted, power relationships are legitimated. Those who accept the existing temporality are likely to accept the existing power structure.

In ancient societies, perhaps the most important symbol of social time for exercising power was the calendar. In many societies, those who understood something of the workings of the solar system, at least something of its periodicity, developed into a priestly caste. They had charge of the calendar, and were accorded the status and power of the gods themselves.

In a pilot study designed to explore some of the meanings of social time in the United States, I found that students who accepted the legitimacy of the phrase, "time is money," were less approving

of institutional change and of using militant means to effect change
than were those who rejected the legitimacy of the phrase. There
was a correlation of -0.529 between the evaluation (as measured by
the semantic differential) of "time is money" and an index of commitment to radical change. The higher the evaluation of the former, the
lower the score on the latter.[44] Thus, the study supported the hypothesis that acceptance of the legitmacy of a system of social time is
likely to involve acceptance of the existing power structure as well.

In any struggle for power, however, there will be contradictory
meanings of time. Those who accept the existing temporality will
accept the existing power arrangements, while those who advocate a
contradictory temporality will reject the power structure. One of the
most important aspects of temporality in a power struggle regards
the allocation of time—the relative duration considered appropriate
for various activities. According to Schwartz, to exercise power is
to control both the budget and the schedule: "What is at stake in the
first instance is the amount of resources to which different parts of
a system are entitled; in the second, it is the priority of their entitle-
ments. Far from being a coincidental by-product of power, then,
control of time comes into view as one of its essential properties."[45]

Marx recognized the relationship between the exercise of power
and the control of time in his discussions of surplus value and the
tendency of capitalism to consume an increasing amount of the
workers' time. According to the theory of surplus value, any commodity has a worth that is approximately proportional to the amount
of human labor required to produce it. In capitalist society, the time
expended by the worker in producing a commodity has greater worth
than the wages received in compensation for the work. In other words,
the worker is exploited because a certain amount of uncompensated
time has been given to the employer. The value represented by this
time is "surplus" and is the source of capitalist profits. There is,
moreover, a tendency for an increasing amount of the workers' time
to be expropriated. Marx claimed that with respect to any single
working day, there is a twofold process: "(1) to lengthen it up to the
limits of natural possibility; (2) to shorten the necessary part of it
more and more. . . ."[46] The tendency for the workers' time to be
monopolized by the employers is critical, for it is in free time that
people develop their capacities. "Free time—which is both idle time
and time for higher activity—has naturally transformed its possessor
into a different subject. . . ."[47] The individual whose time is consumed by work becomes an instrument, a thing. That individual will
remain powerless and will continue to support a system of exploitation
in which a few are affluent at the expense of the many. Thus, Marx
correctly saw the importance of the control of time in the distribution
and use of power (the empirical validity of his analysis is not at issue
here).

In addition to labor-management struggles, the sphere of religion has been marked by power struggles over the allocation of time. In part, the struggle has been between religious and secular authorities, as each group sought to control the calendar. We pointed out in Chapter 2 that the temporal symbols of the calendar function as mechanisms of social control. Historically, religious authorities have asserted and legitimated their power by determining the calendar. The significance of shaping the calendar has not escaped the secular authorities, however, and from time to time they have challenged the religious control of the calendar.

An interesting case of this struggle has been described by Zerubavel.[48] In 1793, the National Convention established a "revolutionary calendar" in France. The new calendar, which lasted until 1805, effected a number of basic changes. First, the Christian era gave way to the new Republican era, with year one being 1792 of the Christian era. Second, the first day of each new year became September 22 of the old calendar. Third, each month was given 30 days, with five extra days at the end of the year (similar to the ancient Egyptian calendar). Fourth, months were divided into three ten-day cycles instead of seven-day weeks. Fifth, days were divided into units of ten rather than twenty-four. Finally, a whole new set of temporal symbols replaced the old concepts.

As Zerubavel points out, this massive change reflected the efforts of the revolutionaries to "gain social control by imposing a new rhythm of collective life" through a "total symbolic transformation of the standard temporal reference framework."[49] For various reasons, the experimental calendar ultimately failed, but the incident underscores the significance of temporal symbols in power struggles.

There has also been a struggle within the sphere of religion over the allocation of time of followers. Religious leaders have struggled to maintain a certain level of religious activity as an appropriate allocation of the individual's time. Church members are reminded about how little time they actually give to God. One religious magazine commented on a study that showed how many years a person living to the age of 70 would spend on various activities. "But," said the article, "there is no time indicated as to how much of the 70 years a Christian will spend in church." The writer estimated that only 9 1/2 months would be spent at church in 70 years, and concluded that it is "very revealing that in a lifetime we manage to give God and His church just about the smallest part of our time. One of our most priceless gifts from God is time. Share it with Him."[50] A Catholic pamphlet also estimated the amount of time allocated in 70 years to various activities—23 years sleeping, 11 years working, 6 years eating, and so forth. But only one-half year would be spent worshipping God. The pamphlet concludes: "Take three minutes a day for prayerful reflection. More if you can. Start right away. Now is the time. It's your life. Be sure it's headed in the right direction."[51] In the struggle with secular tendencies, then, the struggle to control the nature of social life and the kind of activities engaged in by individuals, Christian leaders have given religious meaning to the allocation of time.

Another important aspect of temporality in power struggles is the image of the future. Power struggles often involve contradictory perspectives on the future. If people can be persuaded to reject the future perspective implicit in the existing social order and accept an alternative perspective, they will act to alter the power structure. In other words, a utopian vision, the image of a different future, is an essential component of activism. As Moore has argued, utopias that are taken seriously shape present behavior and become self-fulfilling to some extent.[52] In addition to his point about the control of time, Marx created an alternative image of the future. His image has been influential in third world countries, where it has been accepted (often with modifications) and used to assault traditional power structures.

Finally, an important weapon in power struggles is the duration of the temporal pattern. As Frank P. Sherwood succinctly states, "he who has power is he who has capability to disrupt the fulfillment of a deadline. . . ."[53] In his study of a research and development organization, Sherwood found a number of instances where members of a department would demonstrate their power by deliberately delaying their part of a project. In any situation in which time is money—that is, in which clock time is a scarce and valued commodity—temporal strategies will be an important part of the struggle for power.

SOCIAL TIME AND CONFLICT RELATIONSHIPS

Power and conflict relationships form overlapping categories, for a power struggle is conflict. But not all power relationships involve conflict—there may be an exercise of power that is accepted as legitimate by all parties concerned. And not all conflict involves a power struggle—there may be conflict between equals or conflict over goals other than power. Therefore, we need to treat the two separately while recognizing that very often they are linked empirically.

As with power relationships, social time enters into conflict both as a goal and as a resource. In addition, social time can be a source of conflict, particularly where people interact who come from groups with disparate systems of social time. As a goal there may be conflict over some aspect of social time. For example, there may be conflict over the meaning of time, particularly as that meaning bears upon the legitimacy of certain kinds of behavior. Thus, the

Middle Ages in Europe were marked by a conflict between clergymen and businessmen over the meaning of time and the implications of that meaning for business activities.[54] The clergy argued that the profits of the merchants were bonds upon time and that time belongs only to God. One fourteenth-century cleric wrote that usury was against the "universal laws of Nature," for it was the sale of time and time belongs to all people equally. But bells were beginning to be used to call out the hours of work and commercial dealings, rather than to merely call men to prayer. Time was becoming secularized and rationalized. The merchants triumphed in the conflict. Time ultimately became money, with economic rather than religious activities as the main content of the inevitable temporal flow.

Social time is still, to some extent, the focus of conflict between religious and secular forces. And there is still conflict between labor and management over the appropriate temporality for workers. However, time is also a resource in conflict over other matters. Groups draw upon diverse images of the future in efforts to direct the course of societal change, and proclaim an image of the societal past that has been shaped to support group interests and group activities. Waiting time and schedule disruption are temporal strategies useful in many kinds of conflict. Timing may be crucial in war and in business competition. Tempo (slowdowns and speedups) may be used in labor-management conflict. The point is that social life is temporal. Temporality, therefore, inevitably becomes a part of social conflict as a resource.

Finally, social time may be the source of the conflict. It is the source in the sense that conflict arises at the point of intersection of diverse systems of social time. At one level, this may involve the differing systems of two individuals. For example, William Foote Whyte noted that work-flow coordination can be a tricky affair at times.[55] He observed a process in which one worker had to take bits brought to him by another worker and affix them to a heavy piece of material. If the bit gatherer worked a little faster, the other worker would have less lifting of the heavy material. But the bit gatherer insisted that he was working as quickly as he cared to and that the other worker would not make him increase his tempo. The outcome was a fight between the two. They had to work together but were, unfortunately, temporally incompatible. Temporal incompatibility has also been identified as a source of trouble in marriage.[56] So-called internal clocks differ from one individual to another Some people are "night owls" and others are "early birds." If a "night owl" and "early bird" get married, the outcome can be considerable stress and conflict. At the least, the couple will have more adjustment problems than those who are temporally compatible.

At another level, conflict arises because people belong to groups

with diverse systems of social time. The diverse systems may be
due to cultural differences or to inherent structural constraints. An
example of a structural constraint is found in the differing time
orientations of various units in a work organization.[57] The production
unit may have an orientation toward the near future, while marketing
must take a somewhat longer view and research and development must
look far into the future. These divergent orientations result in differing kinds of priorities for the units and differing modes of operation. The result can be conflict. As Charles Perrow sums up the
matter, the different units will disagree about matters such as the
allocation of resources or the priority given to various problems.
The structure of the units will reflect the differing temporal orientations. Production, with a short-range orientation, will be more
bureaucratic than research, which is likely to require a democratic
organization with a good deal of informal interaction. He claims,
"It may be difficult for members of these two departments to work
together, or even to communicate information easily, because of
their different 'styles.'"[58]

The other source of diversity, sociocultural background, may
be illustrated by conflict between people from different societies and
between those in different groups within the same society. Conflict
may arise merely out of a misunderstanding about the social time in
which interaction is occurring. That is, people from different groups
may assume that the social time of all participants is the same when,
in fact, diverse systems are interacting. This is particularly likely
to occur when people from different nations interact. In a study of
culture and stress, James P. Spradley and Mark Phillips asked a
sample of returned Peace Corps volunteers to evaluate 33 different
"cultural readjustment items" in terms of the amount of readjustment
they would require. The Peace Corps members ranked the language
spoken as the item requiring most adjustment, but the next two items
were both temporal matters—"the general pace of life" and "how
punctual most people are."[59] Similarly, Edward T. Hall and William
Foote Whyte identified five dimensions of time that are likely to result
in interpersonal conflict unless cultural differences are recognized
and dealt with: appointment time, discussion time, acquaintance
time, visiting time, and time schedules.[60] For example, in Latin
America one should expect to wait hours even when one has an appointment. Appointment time does not have the same meaning there as it
does in the United States. One U.S. diplomat experienced a feeling
of insult when he wrongly assumed that arrival time meant the same
to people of another country as it meant to him. He was unaware of
the fact that in some countries an individual "keeps" an appointment
by arriving as much as 50 minutes late.[61]

Similarly, discussion time is not, as it is in the United States, a mere means to an end. Rather, discussion is part of the joy of living. The Latin American is not concerned with reserving a specific segment of time for someone else, nor with rigidly separating business and pleasure. Hall and White claim, "He runs it all together and wants to make something of a social event out of what you, in your culture, regard as strictly business."[62] Acquaintance time refers to the fact that one might have to see a businessman a number of times before actually discussing business—a certain duration of the relationship is necessary before business is considered appropriate. Visiting time refers to the question of which interactant can appropriately set the time for a visit, while time schedules refer to the degree a culture temporally structures interaction.

In other words, there are considerable cultural differences in temporal patterns, and a failure to recognize and deal with these differences can result in interpersonal conflict. But conflict can also arise from the fact that interaction occurs in the context of incompatible social times, as illustrated in the example of conflict between the Micmac Indians and the Canadian authorities.[63] Two major periods of social time characterize the Restigouche Band of the Micmac—diffuse time and compact time. The latter is represented by the time when intense social activity occurs: catching and preserving fish during the salmon runs, accompanied by rituals, feasting, arrangement of marriages, inter-Band visiting, and so forth. Diffuse time, on the other hand, refers to the period that comprises the remainder of the year and is characterized by a dispersal of extended-family groups, hunting, and a struggle for survival.

This pattern conflicts with that of the Canadian government. Major policy decisions of the government are made during the diffuse time of the Micmac, so that the latter are not able to secure Band-wide consensus and thus synchronize their own decision making with the government deadline for the submission of budget requests.

Conflict is also generated by the Micmac custom of participation in the annual potato harvest in Maine, which falls between compact and diffuse time. Although the economic gains are minimal, the harvest functions both as a way of preserving values and as an emotional release. But this conflicts with both school authorities (school children are taken to Maine during the school year) and with governmental authorities (men who fail to report to the local unemployment office every two weeks face the loss of benefits for two or more months). Various sanctions have been employed against the Micmac in an effort to deter their participation, but the conflict continues (or at least was continuing at the time Philip K. Bock wrote about the situation). The conflict continues because of the incompatibility of the social time of the Micmac and of the Canadian institutional authorities.

Perhaps the most common kind of conflict arising from incompatible systems of social time, however, is that between members of different social classes. As noted in Chapter 2, a number of studies have shown that the lower class is characterized by a social time that is different from that of the middle class. In general, lower-class individuals are less future oriented, less punctual, and less regular in maintaining a schedule. For instance, Orville G. Brim, Jr. and Raymond Forer found that middle-class children are more likely than lower-class children to engage in long-range planning.[64] Martin Deutsch and his associates reported that lower-class, first-grade children had more difficulty with test items dealing with time judgments than did their middle-class peers. Moreover, the lower-class children were given assignments in their homes that were "motoric in character, have a short time span, and are more likely to relate to very concrete objects or services for people."[65] O'Rand and Ellis conclude that lower-class youth are more restricted in extensity and less likely to display sequence in their events, while middle-class youth have a more ordered temporality, a greater orientation to the future, and a greater capacity for organizing future behavior.[66]

What happens when individuals from these two different systems of social time interact? We would expect conflict to occur, most frequently in the context of organizations, which are generally run by middle-class individuals. There has not been a great deal of study of such interaction, but some evidence exists that conflict does arise directly out of the differing systems of social time. For instance, Raymond Prince has argued that the poor are not capable of engaging in insight therapy because of personality factors, and one such factor is the characteristic temporality of the poor:

> Insight therapy is a long, slow process, stretching over months or years, and therapeutic results are often slow to appear. Insight here means insight into the fact that present anxieties, hostilities, and disappointments are disproportionate because of childhood experience. In attaining insight, then, one must be preoccupied with the past so that it will yield up its secrets. Lower SES patients are unable or unwilling to wait for such results; nor are they interested in the past.[67]

Similarly, Alan L. Grey, in commenting on the inadequate psychotherapeutic care of the poor, numbers among the problems the tendency of lower-class patients to ignore hospital rules. In one study, hospital vocational advisors pointed out that while half of their middle-class patients were very regular in attendance, none of their lower-class patients were regular. The lower-class patients paid no heed to the temporal rules of the organization.[68]

Does such conflict between patients and therapists mean that the former are incapable of being helped by the latter, or does it mean that the therapists are operating within a temporality that is not intrinsically necessary for therapy? These are intriguing questions for which we have no answers at present.

It is not only in the context of therapy, however, that conflict occurs between individuals from differing social classes. In his study of a poverty-intervention organization that was structured on the basis of "maximum feasible participation" by the poor, Louis A. Zurcher, Jr. noted that there were significant differences in future orientation between two groups comprising the poverty board. The Target Neighborhood Committee Officers (TNOs) were poor people from the community who scored lower on future orientation than the others who served on the board—officials of various kinds, businessmen, professionals, and community leaders (Non-TNOs). This difference in orientation found expression in conflict at various points. For instance, the Non-TNOs were more tolerant of program delays and more committed to long-range planning, while the TNOs insisted on immediate action and were vexed by bureaucratic delays. Heated debates marked board meetings over such issues, issues that arose out of the disparate temporalities of the two groups.[69]

The evidence is sparse, but it supports our contention that conflict arises at the point of intersection of diverse systems of social time. There is, however, a need for a systematic exploration of the social time of various groups and the way in which intergroup conflict relates to the diverse systems of time.

NOTES

1. The processual nature of interaction as argued by symbolic interactionists is fully explicated in Robert H. Lauer and Warren Handel, Social Psychology: The Theory and Application of Symbolic Interactionism (Boston: Houghton Mifflin, 1977).

2. Ralph H. Turner, "Role-Taking: Process Versus Conformity," in Human Behavior and Social Processes, ed. Arnold M. Rose (Boston: Houghton Mifflin, 1962), pp. 20-40.

3. Herbert Blumer, "Sociological Implications of the Thought of George Herbert Mead," American Journal of Sociology 71 (March 1966):538.

4. Alexander Szalai, "Differential Evaluation of Time Budgets

for Comparison Purposes," in <u>Comparing Nations: The Use of Quantitative Data in Cross-National Research</u>, ed. Richard L. Merritt and Stein Rokkan (New Haven: Yale University Press, 1966), p. 241.

5. Clifford Geertz, <u>The Interpretation of Cultures</u> (New York: Basic Books, 1973), pp. 389-411.

6. Ibid., p. 396.

7. Ibid., p. 403.

8. Andrew J. Weigert, <u>Sociology of Everyday Life</u> (New York: Longman, 1981), pp. 200-1.

9. Ibid., p. 200.

10. See "How To Make the Most of Your Time," <u>U.S. News & World Report</u>, December 3, 1973. The various items of advice discussed here are found in several publications, including Paul L. Rice, "Making Minutes Count," <u>Business Horizons</u> 16 (December 1973):15-22; Alan Lakein, "The ABC's of Saving Time," <u>Readers' Digest</u>, April 1975, pp. 67-69; and Susan C. Thomson, "How To Get Ahead of Time," <u>St. Louis Post-Dispatch</u>, November 15, 1977, pp. 3F-12F.

11. Peter F. Drucker, <u>The Effective Executive</u> (New York: Harper & Row, 1966), p. 10.

12. Reported in the <u>Omaha World-Herald</u>, April 5, 1974, p. 45.

13. Bruno Bettelheim, "The Problem of Generations," in <u>The Challenge of Youth</u>, ed. Erik H. Erikson (Garden City: Anchor Books, 1965), p. 108.

14. Chapin, <u>Human Activity Patterns</u>, pp. 128-29.

15. William Kilpatrick, <u>Identity & Intimacy</u> (New York: Delta Books, 1975), p. 70.

16. Staffan Burenstam Linder, <u>The Harried Leisure Class</u> (New York: Columbia University Press, 1970), p. 70.

17. Robert T. Anderson and Barbara Gallatin Anderson, <u>The Vanishing Village: A Danish Maritime Community</u> (Seattle: University of Washington Press, 1964), p. 43.

18. Ricardo J. Quinones, <u>The Renaissance Discovery of Time</u> (Cambridge, Mass.: Harvard University Press, 1972), p. 3.

19. Ibid., pp. 9-10.

20. Reinhard Bendix, <u>Nation-Building and Citizenship</u> (New York: Anchor Books, 1969), p. 188.

21. David Kantor and William Lehr, <u>Inside the Family</u> (San Francisco: Jossey-Bass, 1975).

22. Ibid., p. 37.

23. Ibid., p. 82.

24. Eviatar Zerubavel, "Private Time and Public Time: The Temporal Structure of Social Accessibility and Professional Commitments," <u>Social Forces</u> 58 (September 1979): 38-58.

25. See Robert Sommer, Personal Space: The Behavioral Basis of Design (Englewood Cliffs: Prentice-Hall, 1969).

26. Gregory P. Stone, "The Circumstance and Situation of Social Status," in Social Psychology through Symbolic Interaction, ed. Gregory P. Stone and Harvey A. Farberman (Waltham, Mass.: Ginn-Blaisdell, 1970), p. 250.

27. See Jeanette C. Lauer and Robert H. Lauer, Fashion Power: The Meaning of Fashion in American Society (Englewood Cliffs: Prentice-Hall, 1981), pp. 56 ff.

28. Fred L. Strodtbeck, Rita M. James, and Charles Hawkins, "Social Status in Jury Deliberations," in Readings in Social Psychology, 3d ed., ed. Eleanor E. Maccoby, Theodore M. Newcomb, and Eugene L. Hartley (New York: Holt, Rinehart and Winston, 1958), pp. 379-88.

29. Josephine Klein, The Study of Groups (London: Routledge & Kegan Paul, 1956), pp. 166-67.

30. Reported in Barry Schwartz, "Waiting, Exchange, and Power: The Distribution of Time in Social Systems," American Journal of Sociology 79 (January 1974): 862.

31. Barry Schwartz, "Time, Patience, and Black People: A Study of Temporal Access to Medical Care," Sociological Focus 11 (January 1978): 11-20.

32. Nancy M. Henley, Body Politics: Power, Sex, and Nonverbal Communication (Englewood Cliffs: Prentice-Hall, 1977), p. 52.

33. Cohen, Psychological Time, p. 67.

34. Reported in Frank Parkin, Class Inequality & Political Order (New York: Praeger, 1971), p. 25.

35. See David R. Maines, "Social Organization and Social Structure in Symbolic Interactionist Thought," Annual Review of Sociology 3 (1977): 235-59.

36. For an example from the medical field see Zerubavel, "Private Time and Public Time."

37. Ross A. Webber, Time and Management (New York: Van Nostrand Reinhold, 1972), p. 38.

38. Ibid.

39. Moore, Man, Time, and Society, p. 52.

40. Erving Goffman, Interaction Ritual (Garden City: Anchor Books, 1967), p. 24.

41. Peter M. Blau, Exchange and Power in Social Life (New York: John Wiley & Sons, 1964), p. 125.

42. Ibid.

43. Ernest Gellner, Thought and Change (Chicago: The University of Chicago Press, 1964), p. 67.

44. This study is reported more fully in Robert H. Lauer, "Social Time and Social Change," Ph.D. diss., Washington University, 1970.

45. Schwartz, "Waiting, Exchange, and Power," p. 869.

46. Karl Marx, Grundrisse, trans. Martin Nicolaus (New York: Vintage Books, 1973), p. 399.

47. Ibid., p. 712.

48. Eviatar Zerubavel, "The French Republican Calendar: A Case Study in the Sociology of Time," American Sociological Review 42 (December 1977): 868-77.

49. Ibid., pp. 870-71.

50. Sunday Digest, May 1, 1966.

51. Christopher News Notes, February 1974.

52. Moore, Order and Change, p. 300.

53. Frank P. Sherwood, "The Clock and the Specialized R and D Society," in The Research Society, ed. Evelyn Glatt and Maynard W. Shelly (New York: Gordon and Breach, 1968), p. 77.

54. Jacques Le Goff, "Church Time and Merchant Time in the Middle Ages," Social Science Information 9 (August 1970): 151-68.

55. William Foote Whyte, Organizational Behavior: Theory and Application (Homewood, Ill.: Irwin-Dorsey, 1969), p. 256.

56. See "Temporal Incompatibility," Human Behavior, December 1978, p. 60.

57. Charles Perrow, Organizational Analysis: A Sociological View (Belmont, Calif.: Brooks/Cole, 1970), p. 69.

58. Ibid.

59. James P. Spradley and Mark Phillips, "Culture and Stress: A Quantitative Analysis," American Anthropologist 74 (June 1972): 524.

60. Edward T. Hall and William Foote Whyte, "Intercultural Communication: A Guide to Men of Action," Human Organization 19 (Spring 1960): 7-9.

61. Hall, The Silent Language, pp. 136-37.

62. Hall and Whyte, "Intercultural Communication," p. 8.

63. Philip K. Bock, "Social Time and Institutional Conflict," Human Organization 25 (Summer 1966): 96-102.

64. Orville G. Brim, Jr., and Raymond Forer, "A Note on the Relation of Values and Social Structure to Life Planning," Sociometry 19 (March 1956): 54-60.

65. Martin Deutsch and Associates, The Disadvantaged Child (New York: Basic Books, 1967), pp. 49-50.

66. O'Rand and Ellis, "Social Class and Social Time Perspective," pp. 53-62.

67. Raymond Prince, "Psychotherapy and the Chronically Poor," in Culture Change, Mental Health, and Poverty, ed. Joseph

C. Finney (New York: Simon and Schuster, 1969), p. 23.

68. Alan L. Grey, "Social Class and Psychiatric Patients: A Study in Composite Character," in <u>Class and Personality in Society</u>, ed. Alan L. Grey (New York: Atherton Press, 1969), p. 143.

69. Louis A. Zurcher, Jr., "The Poverty Board: Some Consequences of 'Maximum Feasible Participation,'" in <u>Planned Social Intervention</u>, ed. Louis A. Zurcher, Jr., and Charles M. Bonjean (Scranton: Chandler, 1970), pp. 307-9.

5

SOCIAL TIME AND SOCIAL CHANGE

Social time is a useful tool in explaining the kind of change that occurs in any social unit, for the kind of change will vary in accordance with the social time that characterizes that unit. Over three decades ago, Karl Mannheim stressed the importance of differing conceptions of time for the direction of social change when he delineated various "utopian mentalities":

> The innermost structure of the mentality of a group can never be as clearly grasped as when we attempt to understand its conception of time in the light of its hopes, yearnings, and purposes. On the basis of these purposes and expectations, a given mentality orders not merely future events, but also the past.[1]

There are four forms of the utopian mentality: the orgiastic chiliasm of the Anabaptists, the liberal-humanitarian idea, the conservative idea, and the socialist-communist utopia.[2] The chiliastic experience is one of "absolute presentness," an effort to transform the existing order through the "breach" of the present. The liberal-humanitarian idea also arises out of conflict with the existing order, but is oriented toward the future. The "idea" is a future goal toward which the social order is evolving. The future assumes supreme importance in this viewpoint, while the past is of minimal importance. In the conservative mentality, the past assumes supreme importance. The conservative experience involves the "discovery of time as the creator of value." Duration is nonexistent for the chiliastic mentality and is significant only in the sense of generating progress for the liberal-humanitarian mentality, but it is of prime significance for the conservative mentality, in which all being "has a positive and nominal value merely because it has come into existence slowly and gradually."[3]

Finally, the socialist-communist experience is similar to the liberal-humanitarian in its emphasis on the future, but makes the point in the future at which desired goals will be realized much more specific, namely, the breakdown of capitalism. The liberal-humanitarian idea is one of direct and linear movement toward a distant goal; the socialist-communist mentality distinguishes between the near and the remote, defining the process with greater specificity. Adam Schaff, in accordance with this line of reasoning, notes that there is in all revolutionary movements a "desire to shorten historical perspectives."[4] Reformers generally exhibit an impatience. But the desire to shorten the time may also reflect an implicit or explicit understanding of the consequences of a long-range development. According to Schaff, "The difference in time alone means that events turn out differently from what was originally anticipated, since with the passage of time they develop under changed conditions."[5]

It is not only the temporal orientation and perspective but the temporal pattern that is related to social change. This chapter will explore some of the relationships by looking at two phenomena that involve change—planning and modernization. These two phenomena overlap to the extent that modernization involves planned change, but they are also discrete topics for investigation. I will then examine in some detail a particular historical instance of change and show how two different systems of social time affected the kinds of change that occurred. By the end of the chapter, we will see a number of ways in which social time relates to change at all levels, from the individual to the societal.

SOCIAL TIME AND PLANNING

Planning is a rational activity. It is an attempt to create a particular future through a programmed set of behaviors. At the societal level, Otis L. Graham, Jr. points out, planning assumes that intervention into the social process must be "anticipatory rather than characterized by ad hoc solutions and timing dictated by crisis."[6] We can apply the same argument to lower levels, including the individual. When the individual engages in planning, he or she acts rationally in order to anticipate and create a particular future, rather than to wait for external events to demand a response and to time that response.

Strong arguments for planning are made by futurists and others who perceive the tempo of change as very rapid and argue, on that basis, that rational planning is essential for human well-being in the future. The only alternative to planning is societal drift or, worse, societal chaos. An early statement of this point of view came from researchers working out of the Lewinian school who began their work on planned change with a statement of their orientation:

> The modern world is, above everything else, a world of rapid change. This is something upon which observers in every field of thought and knowledge are agreed. . . . It means that the achievement and maintenance of our mutual well-being is becoming progressively more important and more difficult for us as individuals and as groups. It means that if we are to maintain our health and a creative relationship with the world around us, we must be actively engaged in change efforts directed toward ourselves and toward our material, social, and spiritual environments.[7]

One of the interesting developments in the United States is that, in spite of continuing dire warnings about the dangers of planning, political conservatives have begun in recent times to consider the utility of planning.[8] Planning has always been considered a positive form of action at the individual and organizational levels; increasingly, individuals of diverse perspectives view some form of planning as a positive action at the societal level.

How, then, does social time relate to planning? In the first place, the temporal pattern will crucially affect the success or failure of any planned change. Futurists constantly warn us that the tempo of change today is so rapid that we must plan for a considerable time ahead, otherwise, our plans will be worthless shreds of paper left quivering in the dust of tempestuous change. Tempo, in other words, must be considered when decisions are made concerning the extent of the future to be covered by the planning.

Timing is also crucial to planning. Along with budgetary, reporting, and evaluation considerations, timing is one of the critical elements of effective planning.[9] Efforts to bring about planned change in preindustrial societies have demonstrated again and again that an innovation is more likely to be accepted if it is synchronized with existing activities. As Conrad M. Arensberg and Arthur H. Niehoff state:

> A well-conceived project can fail simply because the right time was not chosen to initiate it. The change agent should become aware of the daily, seasonal, and periodic work patterns of the people and utilize them in starting and continuing his own projects.[10]

The temporal pattern is crucial not only to the success or failure of planned change, but also to the creation of viable plans. Temporality affects the entire planning process, from the initial phase of generating plans through the implementation phase to the final phase of goal achievement (or failure). For example, the initial phase demands creativity. According to C. West Churchman, "Good planners are continuously asking the most searching, radical, and ridiculous questions."[11] In an organization, such questions can lead to the creative formulation of plans most readily in the context of certain kinds of organizational periodicity.

This point has been stressed by Herbert A. Shephard in his study of innovation in organizations. Some industries, he notes, have natural periodicities that are either seasonal or traditional (for example, model change): "These rhythms permit an opportunity for alternation of periods of action, involvement, experience, discipline with periods of evaluation, revitalization, reflection, and planning."[12] Where such rhythm does not "naturally" exist, it must be created, for innovative organizations exhibit such periodicity.

A second way in which periodicity affects the rate of innovation is through structuring the kind of interaction that stimulates creative work. Shephard notes two ways in which this can be achieved.[13] One is to have two groups work on the same problem simultaneously with periodic intergroup communication. A second involves the creation of a "modified project form of organization." This organizational form is one in which ad hoc units are created for each task, units that contain the requisite skills for meeting the challenge of the task. In this way, organizational members are periodically regouped and confronted by novel challenges and creative planning may be maximized.

Obviously, planning relates to the temporal orientation and perspective as well as to the pattern of any social unit. Planning assumes a future orientation. Churchman goes so far as to say that "whenever planning begins to look as though it is following tried and true procedures that have worked in the past, then planning is in danger of becoming useless."[14] According to how the term is used here, planning has no intrinsic respect for tradition. The orientation is to the future; anything in the past has value only to the extent that it facilitates adaption to the future. This future orientation distinguishes planning from the "foresight" of peasant societies. As Thomas J. Cottle and Stephen L. Klineberg point out, members of peasant societies engage in coordinating and planning activities, but "when members of 'traditional' societies are asked their reasons for current practices, they usually refer in explanation to the past rather than to the future."[15] Planning or foresight in such a society means to follow the traditionally approved way, to be faithful to the past, and not to explore the new nor to conceive of a future that diverges from the past.

The greater the orientation to the past, then, the less will be the commitment to planned change (or, alternatively, the greater the future orientation, the greater the commitment to social planning is likely to be). We will see detailed support for this hypothesis at the societal level when we examine the case of China and Japan in the nineteenth century. An interesting example of this relationship between orientation and planning at the individual level is provided by Evon Z. Vogt's study of the Navajo use of automobiles. As noted before, the Navajo lack a future orientation. This involves a lack of planning, in terms of certain important maintenance practices. For instance, the Indians often did not put antifreeze into their radiators until cold weather had already caused an engine block to crack. In 1951, Vogt found, one-third of the cars of the Ramah Navajo had cracked engine blocks because of a failure to plan for the future, the winter, by filling the radiator with antifreeze.[16]

Planned change requires not only a future orientation, but a particular image of the future that gives direction to the change. We have pointed out the importance of the temporal perspective in directing change in the discussion of Polak's work and of the images of the future that are being constructed in Third World countries. Here, we will look at an example at the individual level. Individuals plan various aspects of their lives in order to achieve certain kinds of future states, particularly with respect to family life and careers. We would expect those who lack a future orientation and perspective to minimize any planning. It is, therefore, not surprising that those in the lower socioeconomic strata, whom we have shown to be more present oriented than future oriented, do little or no planning. In her study of working-class families, Lillian Breslow Rubin noted the differences between the middle-class and working-class boy:

> For the child—especially a boy—born into a professional middle-class home, the sky's the limit; his dreams are relatively unfettered by constraints.... For most working-class boys, the experience is just the reverse. Born into a family where daily survival is problematic, he sees only the frantic scramble to meet today's needs, to pay tomorrow's rent. Beyond that, it's hard for parents to see. In such circumstances, of what can children dream?... looking either backward or forward makes little sense; planning for the future seems incongruous. Consequently, work life generally is not planned; it just happens.[17]

Rubin quotes a truck driver who acknowledged that he did not "think about tomorrow," nor plan for tomorrow, nor, for that matter, know how to plan. Without a future orientation and an image of the future, planning has no foundation. This is not to say, of course, that those who exist in a predominantly present or past temporality are incapable of developing a future temporality. Again, temporality develops out of the social context in which one exists, and the social context of those in the lower strata teaches them in numerous, unmistakable ways that it is best to get what one can while one can. When the future is perceived to offer uncertainty at worst, the rational course of action is to live for the present.

SOCIAL TIME AND MODERNIZATION

Chapter 2 noted that particular kinds of temporality develop in, and are functional for, particular social contexts, that any society is likely to have diverse systems of social time, and that conflict results at the point of intersection of these diverse systems. These propositions are well-illustrated by the phenomenon of modernization, which may be defined as "a general process involving economic growth along with social and cultural development."[18] Generally, modernization has involved industrialization, though a society may modernize through some other means of economic growth. Since modernization is being avidly pursued by societies throughout the world, we need to examine the significance of temporality for the process.

First, since social processes have characteristic forms of temporality, we would expect a contradiction between the social time of traditional societies and that required of a modernizing society.[19] Traditional societies tend to be oriented to the past and to have a temporal pattern that is incongruous with the development of modern institutions. Some empirical evidence for this assertion will be given below. Here I want to point out that what was said prior about planning is applicable to modernization since planning is an integral part of the modernizing process. Thus, the temporality necessary for modernization includes a future orientation and perspective and a temporal pattern that facilitates the administrative tasks (such as coordination and scheduling) of development.[20]

A future orientation and perspective is necessary, among other things, to gain the commitment of people to modernization. Furthermore, entrepreneurial activity is associated with a futurist temporality. As David C. McClelland's studies have shown, those who lead a society in economic development are characterized by a high need for achievement combined with a future orientation:

> . . . if people with high n Achievement are to make good entrepreneurs, they should "think ahead" more. In fact they do. They tell stories that deal more often with the remote future . . . they think more in terms of anticipatory tenses . . . they tend to anticipate a future event before it occurs.[21]

Future-oriented individuals, according to McClelland, also are better able to tolerate frustration and to strive toward longer range goals "even when that means foregoing immediate pleasures."[22] Since modernization generally involves the foregoing of short-term indulgence in order to ensure long-term capital formation, it is important that people accept a somewhat Spartan mode of life in the service of future development (Spartan in the light of what would be immediately possible at a particular stage of economic growth).

The kind of social time we are discussing is not characteristic of traditional societies. It is important to note here, however, that the underdeveloped peoples of the world, such as those in the lower socioeconomic strata of the United States, are living in a social time that is functional for them. As Cottle and Klineberg point out, the "fatalism and resignation" of the poor in Third World nations reflects "a relatively accurate assessment of the actual limitations on action that exist in a real world of structured inequality" rather than any inherent inability to function within a different temporality.[23] At the same time, the traditional temporality must change if modernization is to occur.

As a society begins to modernize, there is likely to be conflict because of the contradiction between the traditional and the modern systems of social time.[24] We have already seen an example of this in the agony of the English worker as he was socialized into the temporality demanded by factory work. In that case, the conflict was resolved in favor of a modern temporality. In other cases, the conflict has been resolved by a rejection of modernization—people cannot have it both ways, so that, claims Rudolf Rezsohazy, "without a change in the value attributed to time, without forecasting, accuracy and control over time, there is no possibility of development."[25] Finally, there are cases where people have only partially accepted a modern temporality, so that development has been a difficult and slow process. Some examples will clarify these statements.

Although the pressure to modernize is great, some people have refused to alter their traditional ways for the sake of economic growth. Melville J. Herskovits has described how the people of the Upper Volta River in French West Africa refused to turn their part-time manufacture of iron implements into a full-time operation.[26] The people were primarily agriculturalists, earning only a part of their living by selling their iron products and operating their forges mainly during the agricultural off-season. Yet, there was an obvious market at hand. Why, then, asked Herskovits, did they not exploit the market by entrepreneurial activities, developing full-time specialization, training others, and so forth?

A part of the answer involves the rhythm of work that characterized the area. That rhythm, typical of the tropics, was seasonal, with a daily break around ten in the morning and one in midafternoon. The seasonal and daily work rhythms of the agriculturalist are contrary to those of the industrial laborer. Furthermore, the discipline of the African was self-imposed, while the discipline of the industrial worker is externally imposed. A radical change in the temporal pattern of work would have been required of the kind that subjected Western workers to such stress during the transition to an industrial pattern. The Africans were unwilling to accept the stress even though it would have meant economic grain. They rejected the change that could have been economically profitable in order to maintain a traditional rhythm of work.

The impact of a traditional orientation and perspective on development has been shown in A. A. Pepelasis' study of Greece from the early part of the nineteenth century through the 1950s.[27] According to Pepelasis, the economic backwardness of Greece reflected its orientation to the past and its Byzantine image of the past. The effort to mold the modern nation in accordance with the principles of the Byzantine past affected the educational and legal systems and the use to which foreign capital was put. Economic development was seriously hampered by the temporality and the resulting institutional processes.

A final example is provided by Kleber Nascimento's study of administrative reform in Brazil.[28] Although reform efforts had continued for over 30 years at the time of the study, there were few positive results. Nascimento investigated the problem by surveying a sample of 115 Brazilian and 137 U.S. public executives to get their differing perspectives on time and authority. He found that the Brazilians tended to report a lower tempo of work than the Americans; the Brazilians were less concerned about punctuality than the Americans; the Brazilians reported a shorter work week than the Americans; and the Brazilians tended to engage in decision making in the light of past precedents, while the Americans relied upon the future implications of their decisions. Nascimento concluded that the temporality of the Brazilians was "antagonistic" to that which would be "required by the strategy of change that has guided the attempts to reform that bureaucracy."[29]

There are diverse paths to modernization, but not a limitless number of paths. Certain temporal demands are inexorable, so that the traditional temporality will either change or the modernizing efforts will falter or fail. This is not to say that a traditional temporality must be totally altered. In fact, astute leaders can use some aspects of the traditional temporality to advantage. The contradiction between the traditional and the modern is never complete. Some facets of tradition can be utilized to facilitate change.[30] At the least, a sensitive awareness of tradition can enable leaders to minimize the stress of change.

For instance, in his study of Cantel, an Indian community in the western highlands of Guatemala, Manning Nash has shown how the adjustment to change can be facilitated by attending to timing.[31] Although industrialization has typically been a traumatic process for many people, Nash found in Cantel a "successful" move from a farming technology of the simplest kind to the operation of the largest textile mill in Central America. The inhabitants of Cantel are not noted for their innovative initiative. For example, they do not grow their own vegetables, even though it is quite possible. Packets of seeds in one store in the Pueblo "only grow dustier and dustier."

It might be expected that the attempt to erect a mill in this context would meet with significant resistance. Yet the Cantelense are flexible with respect to innovations, and the factory has been incorporated into the community with relatively little distress. In fact, argues Nash, the experience of Cantel shows that factories may be brought into peasant societies without the traumatic consequences normally associated with the process of industrialization. How did the Cantelense make the smooth transition?

Among other factors that might explain the Cantelense experience, the one that is of interest here regards the synchronization of factory activities with existing community activities. A religious-civic hierarchical system is the basis of Cantel's social structure. Through this hierarchy, all Cantelense are "interrelated in terms of prestige and public service." Every male is expected to serve in the hierarchy, usually beginning his service around the age of 15 or 17, and continuing in various civil and religious posts until at least the age of 65. The various offices involved a loss of both time and income, but participation was crucial to the operation of the social system.

The factory was integrated into this system. When a man's turn came for serving in some office, he was given time off from the factory. Certain offices required work only on alternate weeks; men who served in these offices were only expected to work on alternate weeks in the factory. When one man was elected _alcalde_, a two-year full-time job in the hierarchy, it was agreed that he would be rehired at the factory at the end of his term of office without loss of tenure. Thus, the rhythm of the factory was modified to allow the workers to continue their civic obligations. The workers were also given extended holidays during the two most important festivals and could work overtime in order to minimize any loss of income during the holidays.[32]

Like all social processes, modernization has certain temporal demands. In general, there is a contradiction between the demands of most traditional temporality and a modern temporality. The contradiction is not complete; some facets of the traditional temporality may prove useful in modernizing efforts. But if changes are not made in the traditional temporality, modernization will be impeded and may be completely stifled. Our case study will provide further evidence for the significance of social time in modernization.

A CASE STUDY:
NINETEENTH-CENTURY CHINA AND JAPAN

The similarity of the challenge and the strikingly different responses of China and Japan to the Western incursion in the nineteenth century has been detailed by a number of authors. Scholars from a variety of disciplines have been intrigued by the very different patterns of development of the two nations and have offered a variety of reasons for the differences.

In essence, the story of Japan is one of success, while the story of China is one of failure. Both nations were required to accept unequal treaties that impaired their sovereignty and threatened their economic independence.[33] Subsequent estimates of China's response to this situation generally characterize that response as inept and inappropriate. The Japanese response was quite the opposite. Japan caught up with the West, overcoming the obstacles of language and culture to confront the West as an equal. It was "an almost incredible feat."[34]

While the Chinese inability to change to the same extent as Japan may be understandable, their actual response was so inappropriate (from the point of view of the well-being of the Chinese people and nation) that it also requires explanation. This section will discuss briefly the rationale for, and problems of, the historical method, provide an overview of the challenges and responses and of various explanations offered for the responses (all of which provide the background necessary to fully appreciate the significance of social time in the situation), and describe the social time characteristic of China and Japan and show how the two systems affected the differing responses.

The Use of Historical Materials

Sociology was born as a historical discipline. Auguste Comte asserted that sociologists should use the historical method and also demonstrated the wrong way to use it. According to Nicholas B. Timasheff, "He used predominantly what he called the historical method, which in actuality was mainly an arrangement of selected historical facts in the light of his view of social evolution."[35] Since Comte's time, sociologists have taken diverse approaches to the use of historical materials, from those who insist upon an essentially nonhistorical discipline to those who, states Lucien Goldman, argue that a "concrete science of human reality . . . can only be a historical sociology or a sociological history."[36] An intermediate position was articulated by Weber, who said that all of our interpretations should be verified by the "concrete course of events," which generally means "comparing the largest possible number of historical or contemporary processes which, while otherwise similar, differ in the one decisive point of their relation to the particular motive or factor the role of which is being investigated."[37]

As a step toward verifying some of the relationships we have discussed, I selected the case of China and Japan in their nineteenth-century confrontation with the West. The selection was made purely on the basis of interest in the two societies and their varied responses. There are, of course, problems in the use of any historical materials.[38] One must be sensitive to errors, falsification, and bias in the documents. This demands that one attempt to know the authors of the documents and to be familiar with other sources of information dealing with the same phenomenon or situation. The researcher must also be sensitive to his or her own biases, including selective inattention to those materials contrary to the hypothesis. There may be problems of insufficient information, gaps in the evidence, or an inappropriate selection of materials.

Historical materials are not immutable "facts" that are simply waiting somewhere for someone to make use of them. As one historian has stated, we can only view the past through the perspective of the present:

> The historian is of his own age, and is bound to it by the conditions of human existence. . . . My first answer therefore to the question, What is History?, is that it is a continuous process of interaction between the historian and his facts, an unending dialogue between the present and the past.[39]

Every method, of course, has some problems that are unique and some that are shared with other methods. And there are various ways of dealing with the problems of any method. In the case to be discussed below, my confidence in the results of the research rests on a number of things. First, the results are congruent with other conclusions in this book, conclusions developed out of the study of numerous pieces of empirical research. Second, the descriptions of the two systems of social time are based upon numerous observers, both contemporaries and later interpreters, and both Oriental and Western. In other words, there is corroboration from numerous, diverse, and independent sources. Finally, a number of historians read the materials and affirmed their accuracy.

Challenge and Response

The history of nineteenth-century relationships between the West and the Orient is a story of a determined effort by the former to fully exploit the economic opportunities that were perceived to lie in the latter. Prior to the Opium War, the West had engaged in trade with China within the Canton system, a relationship that assumed the superiority of China (at least, the Chinese established a system that reflected their own conviction that they were superior to other peoples). The Chinese knew little about the West, and the ruling class utilized the theory of tributary relations in establishing trade relations. According to this theory, foreign nations desiring to trade with the Middle Kingdom, the center of civilization, were expected to enroll as tributaries, accept investiture, send representatives who would perform the kowtow before the Emperor, and so forth. But by the end of the eighteenth century, a network of problems developed with respect to diplomatic equality, trade taxation, and legal procedures.[40]

Furthermore, China was experiencing growing economic distress, a situation attributed to the opium trade. This, combined with British demands for equal diplomatic relations, led the Chinese to blockade British merchants at Canton and destroy their opium. The Opium War (1939-42) resulted and ended in military humiliation for China and the establishment of a series of unequal treaties that gradually forced the opening of the entirety of China to the West. The West, then, entered China through the treaty ports, which became the focal points of the challenge presented to China. That challenge was a diverse one, involving the military, political, economic, and sociocultural areas of life. Moreover, the influences that were brought to bear were inevitably subversive of the old order.[41]

Japan was also confronted by the Western demand for trade relations. But the approach to Japan was not as violent. In addition, the Japanese profited by a time lag, for they knew about the Western encroachments in India, the Philippines, and China, and were determined to preserve Japanese independence. The Harris Treaty of 1858 opened Japan. It was similar to the treaties established with China, but was negotiated under considerably different conditions. Japan's isolation, which had persisted through most of the Tokugawa era (1600-1868) and had caused Japan to fall behind the West in scientific and industrial development, now ended. Like China, Japan had to respond to the challenge of the West.

Political developments within both nations had significance for their responses. In Japan, forces had been impinging upon the Tokugawa regime for some time, forces challenging the legitimacy of the government. The foreign challenge was used to hasten the demise of that government. The powerful Satsuma and Choshu clans rallied behind a "keep-the-foreigners-out" banner, placing the shogun in an untenable position. The shogun was not able to satisfy the internal opposition nor could he cope with the external threat. The samurai of the powerful "outer daimyo" secured his end and established an imperial government—the so-called Meiji restoration of 1868. The Meiji government acted with dispatch.

Early in 1869, the samurai who had seized power for themselves and the emperor began to tear apart the feudal system. It was a system that had given their own class a superordinate position in the society, but it had to be dismantled and replaced with a system that would facilitate the modernization of the nation. Centralized control was established, and the government implemented an aggressive, innovative policy of reform, seeking to maintain Japanese independence through economic development, military superiority, and Westernization of vital facets of Japanese life.[42]

China, on the other hand, displayed an inability or unwillingness to replace its inert, passive, bureaucratic Manchu government. The government had lost much of its popular support; rebellion was rampant. The Taiping Rebellion (1850-64) violently shook China, threatening to establish a revolutionary new order. This was perceived by the West to be a threat, and by the late 1850s both Britain and France had aligned themselves with the Manchu Dynasty.[43] The revolution failed, therefore, and in the 1860s a concerted effort was made to restore the Manchu government to a position of international strength through a process of "self-strengthening." Self-strengthening involved a reaffirmation of the ancient Confucian principles. Reforms were sought, but within the orthodox Confucian framework. The intellectual leadership was in the hands of scholar-officials who were, according to Ssu-Yu Teng and John K. Fairbank, "steeped in the teachings of loyalty and ethical government."[44]

An example of this approach is provided in a letter of Tseng Kuo-fan, a leader of the Restoration movement. He says that while relationships with foreigners ("barbarian affairs") are difficult, "the basic principles are no more than the four words of Confucius: chung, hsin, tu, and ching—faithfulness, sincerity, earnestness, and respectfulness."[45]

Within this framework of self-strengthening through the application of Confucian principles, law and order were restored, rebellions were crushed, and the examination system was strengthened. But commerce and industry were still viewed with disfavor, and modern machinery was disdained. With foreign domination continuing to grow, however, another effort at reform was made in 1898. K'ang Yu-wei and others led the movement, issuing over 40 reform edicts (which were justified by a reinterpretation of Confucian classics). However, the empress dowager rescinded the imperial decrees. Effective reform was stifled within the political framework, and the way was paved for future radical revolution. Confucian principles were not capable of generating needed change, and young Chinese, states Joseph Levenson, "came to a paradoxical conclusion: to preserve the Chinese spirit, they must change the spirit as well as the tools of their Chinese civilization."[46]

In the face of increasing Western exploitation and continuing inability to cope with the West, xenophobia intensified in China, cresting in the Boxer Rebellion of 1900. In Japan, however, hostility to the West was minimal by comparison. Most Japanese at least admired the technological achievements of the West; some were even convinced that Japan must follow the Western way of development in detail. The Japanese, then, were generally prepared to borrow from the West in order to modernize. The Meiji government took the initial risks in establishing such major industries as railroads, shipyards, steel, and so forth. Eventually, some of the industries were turned over to private enterprise. The Japanese strengthened their economy by modernizing their currency, creating a national banking system, and revising the tax system. A considerable amount of capital also came from the merchant class, so that modernization did not depend upon foreign loans.

Numerous other changes were implemented by the Meiji government in order to facilitate modernization. The traditional privileges of the samurai were abolished. Many of the samurai became successful entrepreneurs or assumed positions of leadership in the government. Legal reforms were introduced. A drive for universal education was begun.

As a result, by the close of the century Japan had become a modern nation. Within a few short decades, Japan had emerged as a military power and gained recognition of equality from the West, which previously saw all of Asia as barbarian.[47] Marion J. Levy, Jr.

claims the Japanese achievement was "as close to being one of lifting oneself by one's bootstraps" as the modern world has ever beheld.[48] The Japanese began the trek near to bankruptcy and used virtually no foreign capital. Furthermore, they accomplished the feat with very little bloodshed and minimal internal disintegration. It is little wonder that observers generally agree that the Japanese experience was one of the most remarkable transformations of history.

China, on the other hand, was still mired in tradition. By 1914, the forces for change finally became too great to be resisted and the Manchu dynasty was overthrown. But the precarious republic would soon decline into warlordism. Meanwhile, in the same year of 1914, Japan had reached the stage of economic take-off, and is today in the mass-consumption stage. Thus, both the initial response and the subsequent course of development have been radically different. We shall now probe into explanatory factors.

Explanations of the Differential Responses

As might be expected, the explanatory factors offered for the developments outlined above are myriad in number and diverse in nature. We will take note of the more important explanations, categorizing them according to their major emphasis. In other words, the analysis offered by any one author will fall into two or more of the categories, but there will be an emphasis on one as the most significant.

A number of authors offer explanations in terms of the contrast between the two nations, while others focus on one or the other of the two nations and try to explain a single development. Before looking at these explanations, it will be of value to note some factors that were not operative and cannot account for the differential patterns of development.

The Protestant ethic, which includes diligence, is often thought to lead to economic development. But the Chinese did not lack diligence. While it is true that a kind of Protestant ethic pervaded Tokugawa Japan, including the usual admonitions to work hard, and so forth,[49] the Chinese were no less noted for their own willingness to work with great diligence. Chinese tradition stressed the virtue of ch'in (diligence). Ancient rulers were praised for diligence and frugality, and an ancient saying noted that people's welfare depended on their diligence.[50] Foreign observers pointed out that this stress of diligence was not merely an ideal. Arthur H. Smith noted the intense effort expended in preparing for and taking the examinations, and also called attention to the fact that the Chinese farmer was no less diligent: "Doubtless this is more or less true of farming everywhere, but the Chinese farmer is industrious with an industry which it would be difficult to surpass."[51] Furthermore, what is true of farmers is "true with still greater emphasis of the mere labourer."[52] Another U.S. observer, William Barclay Parsons, saw great potential for development in China because "the people are by nature peaceful, law-abiding, industrious, frugal, hard-working, and patient. . . ."[53]

Nor was there a lack of certain other characteristics commonly associated with modernization. Chinese historical writing, Etienne Balazs points out, was essentially produced by officials for other officials. In his analysis of the contents of the monographs, Balazs found that from about 90 B.C. until A.D. 1927 there was "a displacement of attention from the irrational to the rational, from the ritual to the functional, from the speculative to the factual—in short, emerging secularization, rationalization, bureaucratization."[54] An analysis of encyclopedias produced between A.D. 801 and 1242 showed a similar trend. This, of course, is in accordance with the view that Chinese civilization has generally been secular, rational, and bureaucratic.

As the above makes clear, then, there were in China a number of factors already present that are typically believed to be essential prerequisites and/or concomitants of modernization. In other words, an observer armed with contemporary knowledge around the middle of the nineteenth century would have undoubtedly predicted an outcome the reverse of that which occurred. In addition, William W. Lockwood points out certain other characteristics that support this.[55] Japan, for example, was at a great disadvantage in natural resources in comparison with China. Japanese farmlands were overcrowded, and other than coal and copper there were few minerals. The geographic location, although a factor in making the Western challenge a somewhat less abrasive and more manageable one for Japan, was economically undesirable—Japan was on the economic edge of the world.

The various social and political characteristics of the two nations would also have led to the conclusion that China would win the modernization race. A feudal social order prevailed in Japan; European development occurred by breaking the bondage of feudalism. And while the Tokugawa shogunate united the country for 250 years, Lockwood contends that it "failed to create the moral basis of unity so long characteristic of China."[56] As the Tokugawa government approached its end, there was a danger of the nation falling into the chaos of regional separatism. And, finally, the "traditional skills and habits of domination over an unfree people" that characterized the ruling class "were dubious ascents for modernization."[57]

In China, on the other hand, there existed to a degree unknown elsewhere in Asia a tradition of egalitarianism of social mobility, of the right of transference of private property, of "this-worldly" concern, pragmatism and materialism, learning, humanistic politics, and so forth. It is little wonder that scholars have assiduously attempted to discern explanatory factors for the subsequent course of events.

Let us turn to an examination of the kinds of explanations that have been offered. Some are essentially elitist. They find the most significant factor to be an elite group, although they may be cognizant of other factors that were necessary. Lockwood, for example, explains the Japanese development in terms of elements that favored the emergence of an elite able to cope with the challenge of the West and willing to opt for modernization as the mode of response.[58]

Lockwood investigated various sociocultural factors that gave rise to such an elite. William Burke also posits an elitist explanation of Japanese development, combined with the typical Japanese adaptive reaction to novel challenges. Where a "creative entrepreneurship was strong," the combination of that leadership with the "typical adaptive response" was sufficient to transform Japan into a modern economy.[59]

The Chinese failure to develop has been explained in socioeconomic terms as rooted in a lack of growth of foreign trade and a lack of development of autonomous cities.[60] A variety of institutional, physical, and economic factors operated to preclude the economic stimuli that were present in the treaty ports from spreading into the rest of China.[61]

Most explanations offer a variety of sociocultural factors that worked together to inhibit Chinese development and stimulate Japanese change. Ping-ti Ho offers a number of reasons why the Chinese economy failed to develop into a capitalistic type, including the failure to reinvest money on the part of merchants, the absence of primogeniture combined with other mechanisms that tended toward leveling, the Confucian value on learning rather than on technology, and the state control of the economy.[62] Douglas H. Mendel, Jr. identifies, in contrast, basic factors that resulted in Japanese economic development, including Japan's "insular advantage," the samurai ethic (the Japanese equivalent of the Protestant ethic), and various aspects of the modus operandi of the lower samurai who led the early development that facilitated acceptance of change by a circumspect blending of the new and the old.[63]

Levy sums up the sociocultural approach in his thesis that it was not differences in the Western approach to the two nations, but differences in the social structures into which the new forces of the West were introduced that account for the subsequent developments.[64] The significance of the factors that these various scholars have identified cannot be denied.[65] At the same time, I would suggest an additional factor that was operative and has not yet been explored, namely, the differential social time that characterized the two societies. The temporal orientation and temporal perspective of China and Japan were strikingly different and facilitated the course of development that each nation followed.

Chinese Temporality and Change

Before we look at the details of the two systems of social time, we should recall the proposition that all societies are likely to have diverse systems of social time. The systems described below, therefore, represent those that were dominant in the two societies. They do not necessarily represent the exact system of any individual nor should they be understood as the only type found within the society. However, the evidence supports the argument that the types discussed were predominant, and that societal decision making was carried on within the framework of the dominant types.

In analyzing Chinese temporality, it becomes immediately evident that Chinese temporality differed from that which characterizes the modern West. The Chinese did not confront time with the Western obsession to maximize activity in a minimum of time. The Chinese, therefore, have not normally fought for those things that might be obtained through diplomacy, negotiations, or simply waiting for the opportune moment. That "moment" might be in the distant future. Helmut G. Callis claims, "a half a century to wait is not too long according to Chinese concepts of time."[66]

An interesting example of this patience in the face of the temporal process is found in Commissioner Lin's responses to an English appeal for more time when China tried to cut off the flow of opium. The English requested a moratorium on penalties of five months for opium coming from India and ten months for ships coming from England (the death penalty was to be imposed on both sellers and smokers of opium). The Chinese response was to extend the time limit to six months (from India) and one year (from England)![67]

U.S. observers in nineteenth-century China also noted this different attitude toward time. Entitling a chapter in his book as "The Disregard of Time," Arthur H. Smith said that the Chinese are free from "that feeling which to us has become a second nature, that time is money, and under ordinary circumstances is to be improved to its final second. . . ."[68] He also spoke of the "interminable Chinese feasts," which the Chinese found "but too short" yet are "the terror and despair of all foreigners who have experienced them."[69]

Parsons, in discussing Chinese boats, observed that the Chinese view of time was a factor in boat maintenance:

A new sail is scarcely ever seen, and many of them are
so dilapidated as to cause wonder at their being set at
all. But a Chinese never considers time as of value;
he feels no incentive to keep his source of motive power
in repair, but goes on using it as it is until it can be
no longer hoisted.[70]

Finally, another observer wrote that the Chinese manner of keeping appointments included a "broad margin for waiting," so that meeting an appointment within one or two hours was considered "punctuality which is the politeness of princes."[71]

Thus, a first characteristic of Chinese temporality was an absence of the coerciveness of clock time that prevails in much of the West. A second aspect was the slow tempo of change (which will be dealt with more below). The slow tempo is meant to emphasize a fundamental assertion of the theory of social time—reality is process. The slowness of change may obscure the fact of process and lead to an acceptance of persistence as the basic reality. However, as illustrated, this in part depends upon the level of analysis. Balazs reminds us that Hegel sensed the persistent character of China's social structure and was correct, for no matter what is said about change in China, the duration of empire, the imperial institutions, and Confucianism are all extremely impressive.[72] Nevertheless, the Hegelian idea of "a China stagnating in immobility" is an easy matter to refute, according to Balazs, "for with each advance in knowledge it can be seen more and more clearly that China's history was full of upheavals, abrupt transitions, and gradual changes."[73] Despite a superficial impression of sameness, a more detailed analysis reveals continuing change in China.

Third, Chinese temporality was cyclic. A prominent belief of Taoism and Neo-Taoism, Confucianism and neo-Confucianism, and Buddhism is that the universe is in a "constant state of flux."[74] This state of flux is not, however, like that of Heraclitus but follows a regular pattern that is of two types: perpetual oscillation between two poles or "cyclical movement within a closed circuit." Either way the pattern of change lacks the linearity common to Western thought, for the process always returns to its point of origin rather than culminating in some new locus.[75]

Because of the cyclical nature of the temporal process, Chinese historians have provided world history with neither a beginning nor an end. Time is a series of cycles based upon planetary motions, and may therefore be thought of as "extending indefinitely into the past and future for as long as the planets themselves exist."[76] Mingled with the cyclical view, however, is another that sees the past as a golden age and all history since that time as a process of deterioration. Some thinkers have reconciled these two views by asserting that history is cyclical and that we are living in the downswing of a cycle.[77]

The cyclical view of time is also reflected in the tendency of Chinese philosophy to clearly differentiate between the "three worlds" of past, present, and future.[78] The scholar Yen Fu saw in this aspect of Chinese temporality a significant difference with the West, a difference that, in part, accounted for Western superiority in material benefits. He pointed out that the Chinese neglect the present in their fondness for antiquity. By contrast, the Western men whom Yen Fu observed were striving in the present in order to transcend the past. In China, both order and disorder and prosperity and decline are expected to occur in regular cycles. Teng and Fairbank claim this cyclic pattern is, in fact, the "natural course of heavenly conduct of human affairs," whereas in the West progress is expected to be daily and endless so "that when things are well governed, they will not be in disorder again. . . ."[79]

A fourth characteristic of Chinese temporality is its strong orientation to and clear image of the past. The Chinese veneration of the past is well known. Antiquity was exalted, while the present and future were considered to be "degraded and corrupted."[80] This strong orientation to the past was manifested in numerous ways. For one thing, the Chinese often stressed precedents rather than abstract principles.[81] Intellectual controversies were waged on the basis of conformity or deviation from the past, which had unquestionable authority. For example, critics would charge that a certain mode of thinking was wrong not because it failed to meet present needs, but because it had deviated from past truths.[82]

Like the other characteristics mentioned, this one also caught the attention of foreigners. Parsons declared that no dictator ever ruled with greater power than "Precedent in China" and that the Chinese tend to regard the future "as merely an opportunity to relive the past."[83]

This orientation to the past included a temporal perspective with a clear image. Mencius had been specific in his delineation of the ideal, offering detailed descriptions of the feudal system "that had characterized those glorious reigns of the past."[84] This meant that the Chinese golden age was quite different from the Western myth of Eden. The latter may have provided innocence and peace, but not a viable social structure. The Chinese image of the past was potentially replicable in the present. Unlike the early Christians, the Chinese could do more than decry a lost innocence; they could work to preserve and restore the past. It may well be that the myth of Eden facilitated the rise of the belief in progress in the West, since Eden was obviously of no practical, mundane use. The Chinese golden era, on the other hand, could not be replaced without denying the values of the whole Confucian system. To substitute an image of the future that included progress for the image of the past that included Confucian ideals would amount to an abrogation of the essence of China.

The effects of these various characteristics of Chinese temporality may be seen in the nature of the change that took place. First, the tempo of change was extraordinarily slow. For example, changes occurred in the periodicity of the work schedule of the officials.[85] In the Han dynasty, officials were permitted one day off in every five days. In the Liang dynasty in Nanking and the T'ang dynasty through the Yuan dynasty, regular holidays fell once in every ten-day period. By Ming and Ch'ing times, there were no provisions for holidays. The period of time comprised by the changed just mentioned is over 2,000 years!

Thus, the emphasis in China is on duration and on order and stability. In an extreme view, there is no change at all:

> Abandoned and incorrigible people say: Ancient and present times are different in nature; the seasons for their order and disorder differ. . . . Past and present are the same. Things that are the same in kind, though extended over a long period, continue to have the self-same principles.[86]

More commonly, however, the Chinese viewed the order of society as fixed, and history was not thought to be temporally directed toward any goal. The purpose of society, states John T. Marcus, was "to try to arrest decay."[87]

Thus, the Chinese did not deny change, but they did deny that change was impelled by the future. Change was perceived to be and constrained to be of a very specific kind: relative rather than absolute, slow rather than rapid, predetermined rather than directed, and in accord with an ideal past rather than an ideal future. This view of change has its roots in antiquity. The recurrent, fixed nature of change finds expression in the <u>Kuan-Tzu</u>, an ancient politico-philosophical work. The following quotation has been dated from somewhere around the first century B.C.:

> Heaven does not change its constant activities. Covering all things, regulating cold and heat, setting in motion the sun and moon, maintaining the orderly sequence of the stars and planets—such are the constant activities of Heaven. . . . when constant activities function, there is order; when they are neglected, there is disorder.

> Heaven has never changed its name of maintaining
> order.[88]

This fixed, narrow range within which change occurs is, says Helmut Wilhelm, implicit in the very word for change: "The concept I as such connotes not only the dynamic aspect of life, but also what is firm, reliable and irrevocable in the system of coordinates it covers."[89]

Therefore, history is movement, change, rather than atemporal uniformity. The change exhibited by history is not capricious; rather, according to Derk Bodde, change follows a "fixed and therefore knowable pattern."[90] The reality that is flux is not amorphous, but fixed and predictable. And Chinese historians reflected this view in their writings. They pressed their ancient legends and records into an a priori philosophical system so that Chinese history indicated a clear and reasonable image of the past and an equally clear and predictable image of the future.[91] The latter, of course, was a replication of the past rather than something novel.

This temporality finds expression in the whole of Chinese culture. The emphasis on order and stability, as opposed to motion and change, was seen by the U.S. engineer Parsons in Chinese engineering progress, which was

> along static rather than dynamic lines—that is, they
> have learned how to construct bridges, erect pagodas,
> and concentrate their forces to build a wall fifteen
> hundred miles long, but not how to construct a machine,
> or to do any of the things the basal principle of which is
> movement.[92]

In the language, we have already noted the connotations of the word for change. Hajime Nakamura further points out that the Chinese language is well suited for expressing bodies and shapes, but is "poor in verbs expressing change and transformation."[93]

Kurt Singer examined Chinese writing, art, poetry, and various other aspects of Chinese culture and found a decided characteristic pervading all, namely, an emphasis on the spatial rather than the temporal.[94] For example, Chinese calligraphy may be called a "dancing" rather than a "running" script. Singer states that Chinese writing provides the eye with "the sense of perfect equipoise," and seems to reflect a "belief in a cosmic law which units opposites in a rhythmical sequence of alternating states, aspects, patterns of universal life."[95] In Chinese art he claims there is always "an element of a spatial whole the parts of which coexist in a subtle state of balancing and supporting one another."[96] In other words, an equilibrium pervades Chinese culture—an order and stability that does not deny motion but rather gives that motion a fixed pattern and subjugates it to the overall equilibrium.

It is not surprising, then, that when the Chinese tried to direct the social process, they responded in ways that clearly reflect their particular temporality. Since the basic pattern of change was predetermined rather than constructed, and in accordance with an image of the past rather than an image of the future, the Chinese typically sought to guide development into the modern era in an inept and inappropriate way. In the Sino-Japanese War of 1894-95, this became apparent when the Chinese were utterly humiliated by the Japanese forces. The Chinese navy was far superior on paper, with over twice as many ships as the Japanese. But the Japanese were trained by the British and carried superior armaments. The Chinese forces were hampered by corruption, inefficiency, and a lack of planning—in sum, by entering into war against a modernizing nation in a past-oriented fashion.

Prior to the war it was evident that the Chinese were seeking to meet the Western challenge in a way that was destined to fail. Despite a considerable amount of poverty, the Ch'ing dynasty was marked by significant wealth and productivity. Commercial progress had occurred in China as well as in other parts of the world. But China could do no more than expand the existing system—she was "unable to create a new economy" in the way that eighteenth-century England and Europe had done.[97]

Although reformers recognized the increasingly intense need for change if China were to keep pace with the Western world, they were bound by their own past. Tseng Kuo-fan, a leader in the self-strengthening movement, did not comprehend modern economic development. The attempt to strengthen China by the adoption of Western technology was therefore marked by efforts that have been described as "limited and circumspect," justified on the basis of current defense needs or immediate profit, and "supported by the rationalization that Western techniques . . . had originally come from China and had been merely developed further in the West."[98]

Likewise, Chang Chi-tung, a liberal official who sought reforms, was a conservative scholar. While insisting that it was necessary to study Western knowledge, he also asserted that Chinese knowledge was necessary as a foundation, so that scholars should still "master the classics first."[99] The classics, the Chinese past, must still have priority in guiding change. Even K'ang Yu-wei, as noted above, sought to justify basic reforms by reference to Confucian thought. K'ang interpreted Confucian writings in order to justify basic changes, but his "vision of the future still strongly reflects the past."[100]

In sum, attempts to guide the social process during the

nineteenth century were wholly inadequate, for China maintained an iron faith in the past and insisted that the past would guide present behavior. This faith precluded a realistic understanding of the West and of the seriousness of the challenge presented by the West.[101]

As we would expect, then, more radical change or attempts at radical change typically displayed elements that departed from the Confucian tradition. The peasant revolts that had occurred periodically throughout China's history were marked by strong Taoist thought in ideology.[102] The rise of nationalism during the latter part of the Ch'ing dynasty involved a disowning of the past; problems of China were finally traced not to deviance from the past, but to the tyranny of the past over the present and the future. The tradition that had been viewed as a savior took on the appearance of a tyrant.[103]

Gradually, the Confucian exaltation of the past was rejected. Under Western pressure, Marcus asserts, a new attitude involving "expectation of progress and consequently of a linear conception of time" developed in China.[104] The peasants shifted from a position of resignation to one of expectation of progress. The beneficiaries of this change were the Communists, who, states Marcus, "stepped into a ready-made psychological environment" and utilized the new sense of historical evolution that the West had taught the Chinese but "which it seemed itself unable to fulfill."[105] The work and writings of Mao provided China with a clear image of the future that finally broke the shackles of the past and enabled the nation to come to terms with the realities of its situation. Thus, the shift in temporal orientation and temporal perspective enabled the radical change to occur.

Japanese Temporality and Change

The Japanese, like the Chinese, have not been tyrannized by clock time.[106] In Japan, both work and leisure patterns tend to be somewhat amorphous. It is not necessary to adhere to a strict schedule in eating meals. Keeping appointments is a casual affair, and prearrangements are not deemed essential since schedules are presumed to be flexible enough to allow anyone "to adjust his activities to any emergency which may arise."[107] Industrialization has not completely changed this pattern.

But the Japanese may not have been quite as casual as this would indicate. Robert N. Bellah has shown that the Japanese equivalent of the Protestant ethic included admonitions to maximize the proper use of time to avoid wasting time.[108] The Chinese also stressed diligence and proper use of time. While the extent to which the Chinese and Japanese differed in their view of the coerciveness of time is problematic, both peoples lacked the kind of coerciveness associated with the West.

Beyond this, the Chinese and Japanese temporality are strikingly different. Whereas the tempo of change in China was slow, it was rather rapid in Japan prior to the Meiji restoration. Various social changes that had been occurring since about 1700 led the Japanese to assert that they lived in a time of rapid change and to recognize that this created problems.[109] Among those changes were various fiscal and monetary problems (including a shortage of currency), the increased social status of the merchants and consequent diminished status of some of the samurai, and a rapid increase in educational opportunities during the latter part of the eighteenth century. Despite the feudal system and the overall stability of the Tokugawa era, change was not only occurring but was rapid—at least in comparison with China.

A third aspect of Japanese temporality is that reality is viewed as process and that process is linear rather than cyclic as with the Chinese. Dōgen, who introduced the Sōtō Zen sect into Japan in the thirteenth century, held that absolute reality is nothing other than fluidity, impermanence. In his philosophy of time, the "ever-changing, incessant temporal flux is identified with ultimate being itself."[110]

The three major religious traditions in Japan have been the Buddhist, the Confucian, and the Shinto. The first two were modified by the Japanese in accordance with their own perspective. The latter, a distinctively Japanese product, has a linear view of history. Bellah states, "To Shinto Japanese history could be seen as the unfolding of the will of the gods, and religious ends might be fulfilled in time and history as the destiny of the Japanese people."[111]

A medieval Shinto writing, for example, points out that while the Chinese idea of creation was vague, the Japanese conceived of creation as proceeding from "the seed of the heavenly gods."[112] Since the creation itself, a "single undeviating line" has followed the first divine ancestor to the throne. Paul Thomas Welty contends that the Shinto religion is also concerned with natural processes of change: "Birth, growth, and life are blessings which should be sought from the gods and for which thanks should be given when obtained."[113]

The linear temporality and emphasis on growth and development in the Shinto religion pervades Japanese culture. An interesting illustration of this perspective is found in Nyozekan Hasegawa's definition of tradition:

> The importance of tradition in culture does not mean that the ways of life of the past should be carried on quite unaltered, nor would to do so be to preserve tradition in the proper sense. . . . Tradition's role lies not so much

> in the preservation of the cultural properties of the
> past in their original form as in giving shape to con-
> temporary culture; not, in the retention of things as
> they were, but in the way certain national qualities
> inherent in them live on in the contemporary culture.[114]

Clearly, this is a radically different view of the role of the past than we have encountered in Chinese thought.

Concomitantly with their emphasis on linear temporality, the Japanese have stressed existential time rather than metaphysical time. Hasegawa calls Japanese civilization a "civilization of everyday life."[115] The emphasis is on the existential situation. Although Buddhist thought has greatly influenced Japan, that thought was modified and shaped into a peculiarly Japanese form. Thus, as Ruth Benedict points out, the Buddhist ideas of transmigration and nirvana have been unable to take root in Japan.[116] Nirvana is "here and now in the midst of time," and can be seen in the pine tree or a wild bird. As a result, the Japanese accept and welcome the fluidity, the lack of permanence, in the world. For them there is no changeless Absolute; rather, "the phenomenal world itself" is the Absolute and there is no ultimate reality that is above or beyond the phenomenal world.[117]

A final characteristic of Japanese temporality is that it is future oriented rather than past oriented; the Japanese, unlike the Chinese, have limited images of the past but have developed clearly defined images of the future. Filial piety in Japan does not follow the Chinese pattern of including centuries of ancestors. The Japanese venerate only recent ancestors; they do not maintain a grave when the ancestor is no longer remembered. Piety is valued only for those "remembered in the flesh."[118]

Another example of the way in which the Japanese orientation to the past is limited to the near past is in the use of tradition by officials and leaders. Each generation since the Meiji restoration, notes Herbert Passin, has sought its "tradition" not in the remote past but in the immediate past so that tradition itself is in a state of continual flux.[119]

During the early years of the Meiji government, there was a tendency to disown the past completely and focus on the future alone. A German doctor who came to teach in Tokyo in 1876 wrote that the Japanese whom he met were obsessed with the future to the extent of appearing both impatient and ashamed of their past. In response to a question about Japanese history, the doctor was told by one informant: "We have no history. Our history begins today."[120]

Faced with the Western challenge, the Japanese responded by coming to terms with their own temporal location. There were, argues Kenneth B. Pyle, two divergent answers to the need of the new generation for historical orientation.[121] One response involved a perception of the Meiji restoration as Japan's embarkation upon the path trodden by the advanced Western nations. Modernization, in this view, was a fixed, universal pattern of change; progress necessarily meant following that pattern, and Japan was not immersed in it.

The second answer viewed progress as compatible with diverse cultural patterns, so that the Japanese need not sacrifice their own uniqueness in order to modernize. Clearly, both answers involved a definite image of the future—a modernized Japan—and minimal bonds with the past. Japan's development would not, as China's, be constrained by an idealized past. Rather, the past would be used to further the development of a modern nation. The past would be subjugated to the future, with the latter being the phenomenal reality directing present behavior. Japanese development was facilitated by the fact that the image of the future was both a consensual one and a specific one.

The Japanese propensity to be future oriented and to construct images of the future has been called their "goal-oriented" character, while the Chinese past orientation and perspective has been called a "status-oriented" character. These differences have been linked with the fact that, in the face of the Western challenge, "many Chinese tried to control the situation by playing traditional roles, while the Japanese generally reacted by seeking specific objectives."[122]

As with China, we find the social time characteristic of Japan being manifested throughout the culture. If the Chinese focus on spatial qualities rather than temporal, asserts Singer, in Japan it is not space that matters "but time, and continuous, spontaneous change."[123] Japanese history, according to Hasegawa, has not been marked by "national disaster or social collapse," but has "pursued a steady course of development."[124] Singer has compared Japanese and Chinese culture and found that the writing of the former reveals the "laws of absolute motion" in contrast with China's "perfect equipoise."[125] The same contrast is shown in art and poetry. In other words, just as Chinese culture is pervaded by the equilibrium maintained by its past orientation and perspective, Japanese culture is pervaded by movement that is maintained by its emphasis on change and development.

Therefore, when the Japanese were confronted with a challenge similar to the one imposed upon China, their response was quite different. Unlike the Chinese, the Japanese did not view the future as fixed and predetermined, nor as requiring conformity to the past. The Japanese attempted to <u>create</u> their future rather than to merely adapt to it. Levy has aptly summed up the differences:

The Chinese [believed] the structure of society would function to the best interests of everyone if it were set up in accord with the will of Heaven and left as much alone as possible, with occasional interference only to restore the Will of Heaven. The rulers of Japan, however, often seem to have been preoccupied by the possibilities of manipulating social structure for purposes of control.[126]

It is evident that the Japanese employed planning in their efforts to create the future. (The Chinese failure in this respect will be discussed in the next section) In accordance with their future temporality, however, the Japanese engaged in specific and long-range planning. An interesting example of this is the perspective of the Japanese peasant Ninomiya Sontoku (1787-1856), a quite successful farmer who implemented various agricultural improvements in the Kantō. He advocated "mutual aid and cooperation in farm communities" and insisted "on careful, long-term planning and budgeting."[127]

Finally, as mentioned previously, the Japanese utilized the past without being bound by it. The basic directives for present behavior came from the future; the past was utilized to provide symbolic legitimation for that behavior. In theory, for example, the Meiji restoration was a revival of the imperial rule of the past. Thus, a number of the ancient names of offices and of government organs were revived. This was only a semantic facade, a symbolic legitimation for the process of modernization.[128] In Japan, notes Levenson, modernization was "combined with myth-making about antiquity."[129] The "restoration" was by no means a reversion, but a utilization of symbolism out of the past in order to facilitate a process directed by an image of the future. The Japanese traditions that survived modernization were generally conducive to that modernization. Unlike the social order dictated by Confucian thought, or the caste system of India or tribalism of Africa, Japanese tradition proved no barrier to change. On the contrary, the future-minded Japanese found that tradition useful in the rapid transformation of their country.

The net effect of the Western challenge to Japan, then, was to give content to the Japanese image of the future, thereby increasing Japan's range of adaptive possibilities. The Japanese had traditionally been oriented to the future and had continually redefined the past in accordance with present exigencies. An interesting study supports these arguments using the method developed by Kluckhohn and Strodtbeck. W. Caudill and H. A. Scarr measured the temporal orientation of contemporary Japanese and found them to be future oriented with respect to technological matters and to have a mixture of present and future orientation with respect to social behavior.[130]

This agrees perfectly with my analysis and with the slogans that pervaded the Meiji era regarding the maintenance of Japanese culture along with the assimilation of Western knowledge.

Social Time and Social Control

People have always used symbols to express their experience of time and duration.[131] As noted earlier, we are symbolic creatures whose responses are a function of the way in which situations are defined. We create symbols of social time in order to gain control over the processes in which they are engaged and in order to legitimate and comprehend their responses. At the same time, the creation of those symbols introduces a mechanism of social control. By formulating processual symbols, people control processes. Consequently, the symbols of social time legitimate the processes and serve as mechanisms of control.

The legitimating function may be seen in systems of primitive time reckoning. For example, among the Malays of Sumatra there were three different methods of determining weeks—the Christian, the Islamite, and the native. Weeks were counted in terms of Sundays, Fridays, or market days, depending upon which of the three traditions was followed. Thus, various religious and economic processes that characterized the society were legitimated by the employment of diverse symbols of social time.[132] Similarly, Weber provided numerous illustrations of the legitimation of capitalism through making sacred the diligent use of time.[133]

Once a process is legitimate, of course, it follows that those engaged in it are controlled. It is in this sense that we may understand the very slow rate of change in primitive societies. The dominant temporal orientation of those societies was toward the past. The social process was conceptualized in terms of the past and legitimated by the extent to which it conformed to the past (as was the case in China during the nineteenth century). In the mythical concept of time, various facets of human existence were considered sacral through association with the mythical past. Existence was comprehensible to the mythical mind only in terms of that primordial past.[134]

This section is from my article, "Temporality and Social Change: The Case of 19th Century China and Japan," Sociological Quarterly 14 (Autumn 1973):451-64, by permission of Sociological Quarterly.

Although the historical materials do not yield much data, control in China is exemplified in the temporal organization of official life and in the calendar. As noted earlier, during the Ming and Ch'ing periods in China there were various changes in holidays, leaves, vacations, and so forth. According to Lien-sheng Yang, these changes do not reflect increasing benefits for workers, but "an increasing or continuous emphasis on one's duty to the emperor and to one's parents, with relatively less regard to other social relations."[135] The symbols of time, in other words, legitimated existing social processes. For example, leaves of absence were traditionally allowed for family and clan duties such as the marriage or death of a close relative. In the Ming and Ch'ing periods, however, many of the leaves were either omitted or contingent upon the permission of the emperor. The temporal organization of official life legitimated the existing order and enhanced the power of the emperor.

The calendar also legitimated the existing order. In China, the calendar was of far greater significance than a mere record of the passage of time. Joseph Needham asserts that in a predominantly agrarian society, the people must know "exactly what to do at particular times, and so it came about that the promulgation of the luni-solar calendar . . . was the numinous cosmic duty of the imperial ruler."[136] The calendars gave the dates of the solstices and equinoxes and provided considerable information regarding agricultural work; this information was particularly important in view of the fact that the luni-solar year was rarely in harmony with actual seasons. The calendars also had information that could be used for divination and geomancy. Since the calendar provided all this necessary information, the emperor was understandably the "master and regulator of Time."[137] To accept the calendar was to demonstrate submission to the emperor. Indeed, from ancient times there had been a tendency to make calendars more abstractly cosmological, less agricultural, and more political in content.[138] While continuing to provide important agricultural information, the calendars more and more tended to legitimate the existing order.

Furthermore, mundane activities had to be in accordance with the pattern determined by the heavens. Both the duty and virtue of man consisted of knowing and observing the way imposed upon the microcosm by the macrocosm.[139] The calendars provided the people with a knowledge of the macrocosmic path, a path that came to people via the emperor. The calendar, in sum, legitimated the social processes by identifying those processes with the way of heaven. In this regard, and in accordance with the Japanese temporality as outlined, it is significant that among the initial acts of the Meiji rulers of Japan was the adoption of the Western calendar.

In both China and Japan, temporal concepts and the temporal content of various other concepts served to control social processes in the directions indicated by this analysis. Learning in China was referred to as <u>Chi-ku</u>, which means "searching out the ancient ways," clearly denoting an orientation to the past.[140] For the Japanese, as noted previously, learning involved a use of the past to adapt to the exigencies of the present and create a new future.

The concept of history (<u>shih</u>) had been of paramount importance among Chinese scholars. However, strange as it may sound to Western ears, <u>shih</u> was traditionally concerned, claims Levenson, "not with process but with permanence, with the illustration of the fixed ideals of the Confucian moral universe."[141] In contrast with the Japanese idea of movement and impermanence, the Chinese emphasis fell on order and permanence, even in the domain of history. Moreover, the social time of Communist China is in pointed contrast to that of traditional China. The new temporality brought in by the Communists included the notion of progress, of development through stages. Therefore, in the People's Republic of China, states Levenson, "traditional Chinese civilization has not been renewed . . . but unravelled."[142] A new temporality controls the behavior of modern Chinese, a temporality that includes a vision of the future, an image of a new social order that brings to fruition the essence of China without being hamstrung by the past manifestations of that essence.

Finally, we may note that the notion of time itself was strikingly different in nineteenth-century China and Japan. Like premodern societies generally, nineteenth-century China saw time in terms of its content rather than seeing content in terms of its time. In other words, time was not something that had to be used with great diligence as was true in the West. In nineteenth-century China the people employed a variety of ways to express short periods of time: "the time it would take to drink a cup of tea," "the time it would take for an incense-stick to burn," "the time it would take to eat a bowl of rice," and so forth.[143] This reflects what Sorokin called the "purely local" clock; phrases such as "time of cock-crowing," "time of sending the cattle to pasture," and "the time necessary to cook rice," are quite common to the premodern society.[144]

In Japan, however, a different conception of time had already taken root in the Tokugawa era. The Japanese equivalent of the Protestant ethic was in full flower. Included among the regulations issued by the government and read periodically to the people were admonitions not to waste time. In Shin tracts, maxims such as "cheerfully do not neglect diligent activity morning and evening" were to be found. In Japan, time gave meaning to content, whereas in China content gave meaning to time.

SOCIAL TIME AND SOCIAL CHANGE / 143

CONCLUSION

This final section delineates how the data from nineteenth-century China and Japan support the basic theses of this book. Some specific hypotheses about social change and social time derive from the analysis.

In the first place, I have asserted that it does make a difference whether one views change or persistence as the basic reality. In China, persistence was viewed as the basic reality. The Chinese valued order, which was derived from the Mandate of Heaven, given to the emperor that he might, according to Nakamura, "organize a moral system and establish the social order."[145] Change in this content was severly limited in scope. Certain recurrent processes were legitimate and even inevitable. However, the absolute change, the incessant flux that was characteristic of Japanese thought was absent in China. Consequently, the Chinese resisted radical change, which would have been an anomaly in the Chinese world of order. The Japanese, in contrast, implemented rapid and radical changes; change was not viewed as deviance but as a necessity for the well-being of the people.

I have maintained that the symbols of social time arise out of particular social processes. In addition to the data already given, Marius B. Jansen provides support for this proposition in noting changes that occurred in the Japanese orientation as a result of the Western incursion.[146] Specifically, the Confucian scholars in Japan who had valued the tradition represented by China veered from their admiration of China because of that nation's humiliation by the West. As their admiration for China declined, their admiration for the West grew. The result was a shifting of orientation, with the past becoming even less important and the future even more important.

Similarly, we have seen support for the other propositions given in Chapter two. Clearly, the symbols of social time in China and Japan legitimated social processes and served as mechanisms of social control. We were able to conceptualize social processes in the two societies in terms of social time. Various contradictions were driving mechanisms of change in the two societies.

Finally, the varied data in this chapter may be used to state a number of conclusions and construct the following specific hypotheses about the relationships between social change and social time.

<u>Timing is crucial in planned change</u>. Though unintended, the Western challenge was well timed with respect to Japan but not to China. The challenge confronted Japan at a time when internal developments (such as the alienation of certain elements of the ruling elite) prepared the nation for radical change. In addition,

Japanese temporality was such that the changes could be synchronized with the course of development. This was not true in China.

The success of an attempted change is a function of the sequence of activities that comprise the implementation of that change. The Japanese systematically modernized their nation, giving due attention to the myriad of details and sequences necessary. The Chinese made the study of Confucian thought a prior element in their sequence. They could not modernize while still insisting that leaders first learn the classics and apply Confucian principles in directing change.

A curvilinear relationship exists between the tempo of change and experienced stress. The agonizingly slow tempo of change in China was accompanied by considerable unrest and finally culminated in the overthrow of the Manchu dynasty, the establishment of the republic, and the Communist revolution. In Japan, in contrast, the greatly accelerated tempo of change also resulted in significant psychological strain.

The greater the tempo of change, the greater the "gap" between the generations. Pyle argues that the increased tempo of change in Japan increased generational differences.[147] Despite the filial tradition, the younger generation tended to agree that there was little that adults could contribute to a time of rapid reform. A magazine published by young Japanese in the 1880s and 1890s declared that the elders of the society were useless and burdensome.

The stronger the orientation to the future, the greater the willingness to change. Obviously, the orientation to the future that prevailed in Japan resulted in that society having a far greater willingness and commitment to change than did the Chinese.

The greater the orientation to the future, the greater the value of activism. The Chinese orientation to the past was accompanied by a value of quietism, an emphasis on the "importance of quiescence as against movement."[148] In contrast, the Japanese placed a high value on activism. Even Japanese Confucians vigorously praised activism and attacked quietism of every kind.[149]

The greater the orientation to the future, the greater the tendency to democratization. Warren G. Bennis and Phillip E. Slater argue that a future orientation tends to generate certain "common attributes" independently of "differences in ideology and intent," and that at the present time those nations moving toward a future orientation are also tending to democratize.[150] Data from China and Japan support this hypothesis. Democratic tendencies appeared in the strongly future-oriented Meiji Japan. Some of the liberal democratic trends that entered Japanese life during the Meiji era have been called "the most surprising innovation" of that era because the Japanese lacked any precedent in either ideology or reality for representative government.[151]

The above hypotheses are meant to be illustrative, not exhaustive. They suggest that a proper consideration of social time will open up vast new areas of study and, hopefully, lead to numerous new insights about social processes. These insights will occur not only in the area of social change, but also, as we have seen, in organizational studies, analyses of human interaction, and various social psychological studies, for reality is process. Humans are temporal creatures. According to an old German saying, there is no movement without space and time, and there is no life without movement.

NOTES

1. Karl Mannheim, Ideology and Utopia, trans. Louis Wirth and Edward Shils (New York: Harcourt, Brace and World, 1936), p. 209.
2. Ibid., pp. 211-47.
3. Ibid., p. 235.
4. Adam Schaff, A Philosophy of Man (New York: Monthly Review Press, 1963), p. 94.
5. Ibid.
6. Otis L. Graham, Jr., Toward A Planned Society: From Roosevelt to Nixon (New York: Oxford University Press, 1976), p. xiii.
7. Ronald Lippitt, Jeanne Watson, and Bruce Westley, The Dynamics of Planned Change (New York: Harcourt, Brace & World, 1958), p. 3.
8. See Graham, Toward A Planned Society, for details of both liberal and conservative views on planning.
9. Neil W. Chamberlain, Enterprise and Environment: The Firm in Time and Place (New York: McGraw-Hill, 1968), pp. 161-66.
10. Conrad M. Arensberg and Arthur H. Niehoff, Introducing Social Change (Chicago: Aldine, 1964), p. 122.
11. C. West Churchman, The Systems Approach (New York: Delta Books, 1968), p. 164.
12. Herbert A. Shephard, "Innovation-Resisting and Innovation-Producing Organizations," in The Planning of Change, 2d ed., ed. Warren G. Bennis, Kenneth D. Benne, and Robert Chin (New York: Holt, Rinehart and Winston, 1969), p. 523.
13. Ibid.
14. Churchman, The Systems Approach, p. 164.
15. Thomas J. Cottle and Stephen L. Klineberg, The Present of Things Future (New York: The Free Press, 1974), p. 172.

16. Evon Z. Vogt, "The Automobile in Contemporary Navaho Culture," in A Reader in Culture Change, vol. 2, ed. Ivan Brady and Barry Isaad (New York: John Wiley, 1975), p. 45.

17. Lillian Breslow Rubin, Worlds of Pain (New York: Basic Books, 1976), pp. 38-39.

18. Robert H. Lauer, Perspectives on Social Change, 2d ed. (Boston: Allyn & Bacon, 1977), p. 302.

19. Peter Berger, Brigitte Berger, and Hansfriend Kellner, The Homeless Mind: Modernization and Consciousness (New York: Vintage Books, 1973), pp. 148-50.

20. The temporal problems of administration in a developing society are discussed in the various chapters in Dwight Waldo, ed., Temporal Dimensions of Development Administration (Durham, N.C.: Duke University Press, 1970).

21. David C. McClelland, The Achieving Society (New York: The Free Press, 1961), pp. 237-38.

22. Ibid., p. 328.

23. Cottle and Klineberg, The Present of Things Future, p. 181.

24. Berger, Berger, and Kellner, The Homeless Mind, p. 150.

25. Rudolf Rezsohazy, "The Concept of Social Time: Its Role in Development," International Social Science Journal 24 (1972):36.

26. Melville J. Herkovits, "The Problems of Adapting Societies to New Tasks," in Development and Society, ed. David E. Novack and Robert Lekachman (New York: St. Martin's Press, 1964), pp. 279-92.

27. A. A. Pepelasis, "The Image of the Past and Economic Backwardness," Human Organization 17 (Winter 1958-59):19-27.

28. Reported by Frank P. Sherwood, "Leadership, Organizations, and Time," in Temporal Dimensions of Development Administration, ed. Dwight Waldo (Durham, N.C.: Duke University Press, 1970), pp. 216-27.

29. Ibid., p. 226.

30. For examples, and for a more extended discussion of the relationships between traditionalism and modernization, see Lauer, Perspectives, pp. 322 ff.

31. Manning Nash, Machine Age Maya (Chicago: The University of Chicago Press, 1967).

32. Ibid., p. 130.

33. John K. Fairbank, Edwin O. Reischauer, and Albert M. Craig, East Asia: The Modern Transformation, vol. 2 (Boston: Houghton Mifflin, 1965), p. 313.

34. Ibid.

35. Nicholas S. Timasheff, Sociological Theory: Its Nature and Growth, rev. ed. (New York: Random House, 1957), p. 28.

36. Lucien Goldman, The Human Sciences and Philosophy (London: Grossman, 1969), p. 23. Cf. Mills' statement that "all sociology worthy of the name is 'historical sociology'" in C. Wright Mills, The Sociological Imagination (New York: Grove Press, 1969), p. 146.

37. Max Weber, The Theory of Social and Economic Organization, ed. and with an introduction by Talcott Parsons (New York: The Free Press, 1947), p. 97.

38. A good, concise discussion of the problems of historical research is found in David C. Pitt, Using Historical Sources in Anthropology and Sociology (New York: Holt, Rinehart and Winston, 1972), pp. 46-62.

39. Edward Hallett Carr, What Is History? (London: Macmillan, 1962), pp. 19, 24.

40. Ssu-Yu Teng and John K. Fairbank, China's Response to the West (New York: Atheneum, 1967), p. 18.

41. John K. Fairbank, Alexander Eckstein, and L. S. Yang, "Economic Change in Early Modern China: An Analytic Framework," Economic Development and Cultural Change 9 (October 1960):23.

42. Edwin O. Reischauer, Japan: Past and Present, 3d ed. rev. (Tokyo: Charles E. Tuttle, 1964), pp. 119 ff.

43. Franz Schurmann and Orville Schell, eds., Imperial China: The Decline of the Last Dynasty and the Origins of Modern China (New York: Vintage Books, 1967), p. 179.

44. Teng and Fairbank, China's Response, p. 49.

45. Ibid., p. 63.

46. Joseph Levenson, Confucian China and Its Modern Fate: A Trilogy, 3 vols. (Berkeley and Los Angeles: University of California Press, 1968), 1:80.

47. Reischauer, Japan, p. 134.

48. Marion J. Levy, Jr., "Contrasting Factors in the Modernization of China and Japan," Economic Development and Cultural Change 2 (1953):191.

49. Robert N. Bellah, Tokugawa Religion (New York: Free Press, 1957). See especially pp. 110-13, 186-87.

50. Lien-sheng Yang, "Schedules of Work and Rest in Imperial China," Harvard Journal of Asiatic Studies 18 (1955):320.

51. Arthur H. Smith, Chinese Characteristics (New York: Fleming H. Revell, 1894), pp. 29-30.

52. Ibid., p. 30.

53. William Barclay Parsons, An American Engineer in China (New York: McClure, Phillips, 1900), p. 136.

54. Etienne Balazs, Chinese Civilization and Bureaucracy, trans. H. M. Wright, ed. Arthur P. Wright (New Haven: Yale University Press, 1964), p. 138.

55. William W. Lockwood, "Japan's Response to the West: The Contrast with China," World Politics 9 (October 1956):37-54.
56. Ibid., p. 39.
57. Ibid., p. 40.
58. Ibid., p. 41.
59. William Burke, "Creative Response and Adaptive Response in Japanese Society," American Journal of Economics and Sociology 21 (January 1962):106. For yet another elitist approach, see Thomas C. Smith, "Japan's Aristocratic Revolution," in Class, Status, and Power, 2d ed., ed. Reinhard Bendix and Seymour Martin Lipset (New York: The Free Press, 1966), pp. 135-40.
60. Fairbank, Eckstein, and Yang, "Economic Change," p. 14.
61. Ibid., p. 24.
62. In Schurmann and Schell, Imperial China, pp. 76 ff.
63. Douglas H. Mendel, Jr., "Japan Today: Case Study of a Developing Nation," Trans-Action 3 (March-April 1966):15-21.
64. Levy, "Contrasting Factors," p. 161.
65. This is not to say that all these factors are equally valid or important in terms of the differential response. For example, we have identified a "Confucian ethic" that is, like the Samurai ethic, similar to the Protestant ethic. Such an ethic, then, does not explain the differential development.
66. Helmut G. Callis, China: Confucian and Communist (New York: Henry Holt, 1959), p. 37.
67. Teng and Fairbank, China's Response, p. 27.
68. Smith, Chinese Characteristics, p. 41.
69. Ibid., p. 43.
70. Parsons, An American Engineer, p. 229.
71. Adele Fields, A Corner of Cathay: Studies from Life Among the Chinese (New York: Macmillan, 1894), p. 119.
72. Balazs, Chinese Civilization, p. 15.
73. Ibid.
74. Derk Bodde, "Harmony and Conflict in Chinese Philosophy," in Studies in Chinese Thought, ed. Arthur F. Wright (Chicago: American Anthropological Association, 1953), p. 21.
75. Ibid.
76. William Theodore de Bary, Wing-tsit Chan, and Burton Watson, Sources of Chinese Tradition (New York: Columbia University Press, 1960), p. 221.
77. Bodde, "Harmony and Conflict," p. 27.
78. Hajime Nakamura, Ways of Thinking of Eastern Peoples, ed. Philip P. Wiener (Honolulu: East-West Center Press, 1964), p. 244.
79. Teng and Fairbank, China's Response, p. 151.
80. Nakamura, Ways of Thinking, p. 212.

81. Ibid., p. 206.
82. Levenson, Confucian China, 1:49.
83. Parsons, An American Engineer, pp. 130, 136.
84. de Bary, Chan, and Watson, Sources of Chinese Tradition, p. 101.
85. Yang, "Schedules of Work," pp. 303 ff.
86. Hsun Tzu, as quoted in Bodde, "Harmony and Conflict," p. 28.
87. John T. Marcus, "Time and the Sense of History: West and East," Comparative Studies in Society and History 3 (January 1961): 134.
88. W. Allyn Rickett, Kuan-Tzu: A Repository of Early Chinese Thought (Hong Kong: Hong Kong University Press, 1965), pp. 122-23.
89. Helmut Wilhelm, "The Concept of Time in the Book of Changes," in Man and Time, ed. Joseph Campbell (New York: Pantheon Books, 1957), p. 212.
90. Bodde, "Harmony and Conflict," p. 29. These two points about history were set forth by Mencius.
91. de Bary, Chan, and Watson, Sources of Chinese Tradition, p. 217.
92. Parsons, An American Engineer, p. 217.
93. Nakamura, Ways of Thinking, p. 177.
94. Kurt Singer, "Differences Between Chinese and Japanese Culture," Yale Review 27 (Summer 1938):787.
95. Ibid., p. 774.
96. Ibid., p. 777.
97. See Schurmann and Schell, Imperial China, p. 67.
98. Fairbank, Reischauer, and Craig, East Asia, p. 350.
99. Teng and Fairbank, China's Response, p. 169.
100. de Bary, Chan, and Watson, Sources of Chinese Tradition, p. 729.
101. Schurmann and Schell, Imperial China, p. 130.
102. Balazs, Chinese Civilization, p. 157.
103. Levenson, Confucian China, 1:99.
104. Marcus, "Time and the Sense of History," p. 138.
105. Ibid.
106. Robert J. Smith, "Cultural Differences in the Life Cycle and the Concept of Time," in Aging and Leisure: A Research Perspective into the Meaningful Use of Time, ed. Robert W. Kleemeier (New York: Oxford University Press, 1961), p. 99.
107. Ibid.
108. Bellah, Tokugawa Religion, pp. 111, 119.
109. Marius B. Jansen, ed., Changing Japanese Attitudes Toward Modernization (Princeton, N.J.: Princeton University Press, 1965), p. 53.

150 / TEMPORAL MAN

110. Nakamura, Ways of Thinking, p. 353.

111. Bellah, Tokugawa Religion, p. 63.

112. In Ryusaku Tsunoda, William Theodore de Bary, and Donald Keene, Sources of Japanese Tradition (New York: Columbia University Press, 1958), p. 279.

113. Paul Thomas Welty, The Asians: Their Heritage and Their Destiny, 3d ed. (Philadelphia: J.B. Lippincott, 1970), pp. 238-39.

114. Nyozekan Hasegawa, The Japanese Character, trans. John Bester (Tokyo: Kodansha International, 1965), pp. 101-2.

115. Ibid., p. 27.

116. Ruth Benedict, The Chrysanthemum and the Sword (Cleveland and New York: Meridian Books, 1967), pp. 237-38.

117. Hajime Nakamura, "Time in Indian and Japanese Thought," in The Voices of Time, ed. J. T. Fraser (New York: George Braziller, 1966), pp. 85-86.

118. Benedict, The Chrysanthemum and the Sword, p. 122.

119. Herbert Passin, "Modernization and the Japanese Intellectual: Some Comparative Observations," in Changing Japanese Attitudes Toward Modernization, ed. Marius B. Jansen (Princeton, N.J.: Princeton University Press, 1965), p. 475.

120. Quoted by Lockwood, "Japan's Response," p. 42.

121. Kenneth B. Pyle, The New Generation in Meiji Japan (Stanford: Stanford University Press, 1969), pp. 21-22.

122. Fairbank, Reischauer, and Craig, East Asia, pp. 181-82.

123. Singer, "Differences Between Chinese," p. 789.

124. Hasegawa, The Japanese Character, pp. 113-14.

125. Singer, "Differences Between Chinese," pp. 774-77.

126. Levy, "Contrasting Factors," p. 182.

127. Edwin O. Reischauer and John K. Fairbank, East Asia: The Great Tradition, vol. 1 (Boston: Houghton Mifflin, 1958), p. 661.

128. Reischauer, Japan, p. 122.

129. Levenson, Confucian China, 2:136.

130. W. Caudill and H. A. Scarr, "Japanese Value Orientations and Culture Change," Ethnology 1 (January 1962):71-72.

131. Meerloo, "The Time Sense in Psychiatry," p. 246.

132. Martin P. Nilsson, Primitive Time-Reckoning (Lund: G.W.K. Gleerup, 1920), pp. 358-59.

133. Weber, The Protestant Ethic.

134. Cassirer, The Philosophy of Symbolic Forms, p. 105.

135. Yang, "Schedules of Work," p. 307.

136. Joseph Needham, "Time and Knowledge in China and the West," in The Voices of Time, ed. J. T. Fraser (New York: George Braziller, 1966), p. 100.

137. Jacques Gernet, Daily Life in China: On the Eve of the Mongol Invasion, 1250-1276, trans. H. M. Wright (Stanford: Stanford University Press, 1962), p. 180.
138. Rickett, Kuan-Tzu, p. 188.
139. Cassirer, The Philosophy of Symbolic Forms, p. 115.
140. Nakamura, Ways of Thinking, p. 205.
141. Levenson, Confucian China, 1:91.
142. Ibid., 3:47.
143. J. Dyer Ball, Things Chinese, 4th ed. (New York: Charles Scribner's Sons, 1906), p. 713.
144. Sorokin, Sociocultural Causality, p. 169.
145. Nakamura, Ways of Thinking, p. 271.
146. Jansen, Changing Japanese Attitudes, pp. 56-63.
147. Pyle, The New Generation, pp. 6, 48-52.
148. Bodde, "Harmony and Conflict," p. 59.
149. Bellah, Tokugawa Religion, p. 77.
150. Warren G. Bennis and Philip E. Slater, The Temporary Society (New York: Harper & Row, 1968), p. 51.
151. Fairbank, Reischauer, and Craig, East Asia, p. 278.

BIBLIOGRAPHY

Albert, S. "Time, Memory, and Affect: Experimental Studies of the Subjective Past." In *The Study of Time III*, edited by J. T. Fraser, N. Lawrence, and D. Park, pp. 269-90. New York: Springer-Verlag, 1978.

Anderson, Robert T., and Barbara Gallatin Anderson. *The Vanishing Village: A Danish Maritime Community*. Seattle: University of Washington Press, 1964.

Ariotti, P. E. "The Concept of Time in Western Antiquity." In *The Study of Time II*, edited by J. T. Fraser and N. Lawrence, pp. 69-80. New York: Springer-Verlag, 1975.

Augenstine, Leroy G. "Evidence of Periodicities in Human Task Performance." In *Information Theory in Psychology*, edited by Henry Quastler, pp. 208-26. Glencoe, Ill.: Free Press, 1955.

Bailey, Marilyn L. "How Well Spent Is Your Time?" *Home Life*, 1971, pp. 50-51.

Balazs, Etienne. *Chinese Civilization and Bureaucracy*. Translated by H. M. Wright. Edited by Arthur P. Wright. New Haven: Yale University Press, 1964.

Ball, J. Dyer. *Things Chinese*. 4th ed. New York: Charles Scribner's Sons, 1906.

Barndt, Robert H., and Donald M. Johnson. "Time Orientation In Delinquents." *Journal of Abnormal and Social Psychology* 51 (1955): 343-45.

Becker, Gary S. *The Economic Approach To Human Behavior*. Chicago: University of Chicago Press, 1976.

Beecher, Catherine. *A Treatise On Domestic Economy*. New York: Schocken Books, 1977.

Bell, Wendell, and James A. Mau. "Images of the Future: Theory and Research Strategies." In *The Sociology of the Future*, edited by Wendell Bell and James A. Mau, pp. 6-44. New York: Russell Sage Foundation, 1971..

Bellah, Robert N. Tokugawa Religion. New York: Free Press, 1957.

Bendix, Reinhard. Nation-Building and Citizenship. New York: Anchor Books, 1969.

Benedict, Ruth. The Chrysanthemum and the Sword. Cleveland and New York: Meridian Books, 1967.

Benjamin, A. Cornelius. "Ideas of Time in the History of Philosophy." In The Voices of Time, edited by J. T. Fraser, pp. 3-30. New York: George Braziller, 1966.

Bennis, Warren G., and Philip E. Slater. The Temporary Society. New York: Harper & Row, 1968.

Berger, Peter, Brigitte Berger, and Hansfriend Kellner. The Homeless Mind: Modernization and Consciousness. New York: Vintage Books, 1973.

Berger, Peter, and Thomas Luckmann. The Social Construction of Reality. Garden City: Doubleday, 1966.

Bergson, Henri. Time and Free Will. Translated by F. L. Pogson. New York: Harper & Row, 1910.

Bettelheim, Bruno. "The Problem of Generations." In The Challenge of Youth, edited by Erik H. Erikson, pp. 76-109. Garden City: Doubleday, 1965.

Black, C. E. The Dynamics of Modernization. New York: Harper & Row, 1966.

Blau, Peter M. Exchange and Power in Social Life. New York: John Wiley & Sons, 1964.

Blumer, Herbert. "Sociological Implications of the Thought of George Herbert Mead." American Journal of Sociology 71 (March 1966): 535-44.

Boas, George. The Acceptance of Time. Berkeley: University of California Press, 1950.

Bock, Philip K. "Social Structure and Language Structure." Southwestern Journal of Anthropology 20 (Winter 1964): 393-403.

———. "Social Time and Institutional Conflict." Human Organization 25 (Summer 1966): 96-102.

Bodde, Derk. "Harmony and Conflict in Chinese Philosophy." In Studies In Chinese Thought, edited by Arthur F. Wright, pp. 19-80. Chicago: American Anthropological Association, 1953.

Brandon, S. G. F. "Time and the Destiny of Man." In The Voices of Time, edited by J. T. Fraser, pp. 140-57. New York: George Braziller, 1966.

Brehm, Jack W. Responses To Loss of Freedom: A Theory of Psychological Reactance. Morristown, N.J.: General Learning Press, 1972.

Brim, Orville G., Jr., and Raymond Forer. "A Note on the Relation of Values and Social Structure to Life Planning." Sociometry 19 (March 1956): 54-60.

Brown, Julia S., and Brian G. Gilmartin. "Sociology Today: Lacunae, Emphases, and Surfeits." The American Sociologist 4 (November 1969): 283-91.

Bull, C. Neil. "The Use of Time-Budgets to Monitor Social Relations." Paper read at the Midwest Sociological Society, March 1973.

Burke, William. "Creative Response and Adaptive Response in Japanese Society." American Journal of Economics and Sociology 21 (January 1962): 103-12.

Callis, Helmut G. China: Confucian and Communist. New York: Henry Holt, 1959.

Carr, Edward Hallett. What Is History? London: Macmillan, 1962.

Cassirer, Ernst. An Essay On Man. New York: Bantam Books, 1944.

———. The Philosophy of Symbolic Forms. Vol. 2. New Haven: Yale University Press, 1955.

Caudill, W., and H. A. Scarr. "Japanese Value Orientations and Culture Change." Ethnology 1 (January 1962): 53-91.

Chamberlain, Neil W. Enterprise and Environment: The Firm in Time and Place. New York: McGraw-Hill, 1968.

Chapin, F. Stuart, Jr. Human Activity Patterns in the City. New York: John Wiley, 1974.

Churchman, C. West. The Systems Approach. New York: Delta Books, 1968.

Cohen, John. Humanistic Psychology. New York: Collier Books, 1958.

———. Psychological Time in Health and Disease. Springfield, Ill.: Charles C. Thomas, 1967.

Cohen, Stanley, and Laurie Taylor. "The Experience of Time in Long-Term Imprisonment." New Society, December 31, 1970, p. 1159.

Cottle, Thomas J. "The Circles Test: An Investigation of Perceptions of Temporal Relatedness and Dominance." Journal of Projective Techniques and Personality Assessment 31 (1967): 58-71.

———. "Future Orientations and Avoidance: Speculations on the Time of Achievement and Social Roles." Sociological Quarterly 10 (Fall 1969): 419-37.

Cottle, Thomas J., and Stephen L. Klineberg. The Present of Things Future. New York: The Free Press, 1974.

Davids, Anthony, Catherine Kidder, and Melvyn Reich. "Time Orientation in Male and Female Juvenile Delinquents." Journal of Abnormal and Social Psychology 64 (1962): 239-40.

Davis, Flora. "Exploit Your Biological Rhythms." Woman's Day, April 24, 1978, pp. 103 ff.

de Bary, William Theodore, Wing-tsit Chan, and Burton Watson. Sources of Chinese Tradition. New York: Columbia University Press, 1960.

de Broglie, Louis. The Revolution In Physics. New York: Noonday Press, 1953.

de Grazia, Sebastian. Of Time, Work, and Leisure. Garden City: Anchor Books, 1962.

Deutsch, Martin, and Associates. The Disadvantaged Child. New York: Basic Books, 1967.

Deutsch, Morton, and Robert M. Kraus. Theories In Social Psychology. New York: Basic Books, 1965.

Dewey, Edward R. Cycles—Selected Writings. Pittsburgh: Foundation for the Study of Cycles, 1970.

Dillistone, F. W. Traditional Symbols and the Contemporary World. London: Epworth Press, 1973.

Doob, Leonard W. Patterning of Time. New Haven: Yale University Press, 1971.

Drucker, Peter F. The Effective Executive. New York: Harper & Row, 1966.

Durkheim, Emile. The Elementary Forms of the Religious Life. Translated by Joseph Ward Swain. New York: The Free Press, 1915.

Eliade, Mircea. The Myth of the Eternal Return. New York: Pantheon Books, 1954.

──────. "Time and Eternity in Indian Thought." In Man and Time, edited by Joseph Campbell, pp. 173-200. New York: Pantheon Books, 1957.

Evans-Pritchard, E. E. The Nuer. London: Oxford University Press, 1940.

Fairbank, John K., Edwin O. Reischauer, and Albert M. Craig. East Asia: The Modern Transformation. Vol. 2. Boston: Houghton Mifflin, 1965.

Farber, Maurice L. "Suffering and Time-Perspective of the Prisoner." University of Iowa Studies in Child Welfare 20 (1944): 153-227.

Farley, John. "Activities and Pastimes of Children and Youth: Age, Sex, and Parental Effects." Journal of Comparative Family Studies 10 (Autumn 1979): 385-410.

Feierabend, Ivo K., and Rosalind L. Feierabend. "Coerciveness and Change: Cross-National Trends." American Behavioral Scientist 15 (July/August 1972): 914-15.

Fields, Adele. A Corner of Cathay: Studies from Life Among the Chinese. New York: Macmillan, 1894.

Flinn, M. W. "Social Theory and the Industrial Revolution." In Social Theory and Economic Change, edited by Tom Burns and S. B. Saul, pp. 9-34. London: Tavistock, 1967.

Fraisse, Paul. The Psychology of Time. Translated by Jennifer Leith. New York: Harper & Row, 1963.

Frank, Lawrence K. Society As the Patient: Essays on Culture and Personality. New Brunswick: Rutgers University Press, 1949.

Fraser, J. T. Time As Conflict. Basel and Stuttgart: Birkhauser Verlag, 1978.

Freud, Sigmund. Collected Papers. Vol. 4. London: Hogarth Press, 1925.

Friedman, Bertha B. Foundations of the Measurement of Values. New York: Columbia University Press, 1946.

Fromm, Erich. Escape From Freedom. New York: Farrar & Rinehart, 1941.

Gale, Richard M. The Philosophy of Time. Garden City: Doubleday, 1967.

Gardell, Bertil. "Technology, Alienation and Mental Health: Summary of a Social Psychological Study of Technology and the Worker." Acta Sociologica 19 (1976): 83-93.

Geertz, Clifford. The Interpretation of Cultures. New York: Basic Books, 1973.

Gelles, Richard J., and Robert R. Faulkner. "Time and Television News Work: Task Temporalization in the Assembly of Unscheduled Events." Sociological Quarterly 19 (Winter 1978): 89-102.

Gellner, Ernest. Thought and Change. Chicago: The University of Chicago Press, 1964.

Gergen, Kenneth J. The Concept of Self. New York: Holt, Rinehart and Winston, 1971.

Gernet, Jacques. Daily Life in China: On the Eve of the Mongol Invasion, 1250-1276. Translated by H. M. Wright. Stanford: Stanford University Press, 1962.

Gioscia, Victor. "On Social Time." In The Future of Time, edited by Henri Yaker, Humphry Osmond, and Frances Cheek, pp. 73-141. Garden City: Doubleday, 1971.

Givens, Douglas R. An Analysis of Navajo Temporality. Washington, D.C.: University Press of America, 1977.

Goffman, Erving. Interaction Ritual. Garden City: Anchor Books, 1967.

Goldman, Lucien. The Human Sciences and Philosophy. London: Grossman, 1969.

Goldstein, Kurt. "The So-Called Drives." In The Self: Explorations in Personal Growth, edited by Clark E. Moustakas, pp. 1-17. New York: Harper & Brothers, 1956.

Graham, Otis L., Jr. Toward A Planned Society: From Roosevelt to Nixon. New York: Oxford University Press, 1976.

Green, H. B. "Temporal Stages in the Development of the Self." In The Study of Time II, edited by J. T. Fraser and N. Lawrence, pp. 1-19. New York: Springer-Verlag, 1975.

Grey, Alan L. "Social Class and Psychiatric Patient: A Study in Composite Character." In Class and Personality in Society, edited by Alan L. Grey, pp. 136-60. New York: Atherton Press, 1969.

Gurvitch, Georges. "Social Structure and the Multiplicity of Times." In Sociological Theory, Values, and Sociocultural Change, edited by Edward A. Tiryakian, pp. 171-84. New York: Harper & Row, 1963.

―――. The Spectrum of Social Time. Dordrecht, Holland: D. Reidel, 1964.

Hall, Edward T. The Silent Language. Garden City: Doubleday, 1959.

Hall, Edward T., and William Foote Whyte. "Intercultural Communication: A Guide to Men of Action." Human Organization 19 (Spring 1960): 7-9.

Hart, Hornell. "Social Theory and Social Change." In Symposium on Sociological Theory, edited by Llewellyn Gross, pp. 196-238. Evanston: Row, Peterson, 1959.

Hartshorne, Charles. "Introduction: The Development of Process Philosophy." In Philosophers of Process, edited by Douglas Browning, pp. v-xxii. New York: Random House, 1965.

Hasegawa, Nyozekan. The Japanese Character. Translated by John Bestor. Tokyo: Kodansha International, 1965.

Hawley, Amos H. Human Ecology. New York: The Ronald Press, 1950.

Hegel, G. W. F. The Phenomenology of Mind. Translated by J. B. Baillie. New York: Harper & Row, 1967.

Heirich, Max. "The Use of Time in the Study of Social Change." American Sociological Review 29 (June 1964): 386-97.

Henley, Nancy M. Body Politics: Power, Sex, and Nonverbal Communication. Englewood Cliffs: Prentice-Hall, 1977.

Hennig, Margaret, and Anne Jardim. "Women Executives in the Old-Boy Network." Psychology Today, January 1977, pp. 76-81.

Henry, Jules. "White People's Time, Colored People's Time." Trans-Action 2 (March/April 1965): 31-34.

Herskovits, Melville J. "The Problems of Adapting Societies to New Tasks." In Development and Society, edited by David E. Novack and Robert Lekachman, pp. 279-92. New York: St. Martin's Press, 1964.

Hilts, Philip. "The Clock Within." Science 80, December 1980, pp. 61-67.

Hitt, W. D. "Two Models of Man." American Psychologist 24 (1969): 651-58.

Hughes, W. Stuart. Consciousness and Society. New York: Random House, 1958.

Husserl, Edmund. The Phenomenology of the Internal Time-Consciousness. Bloomington: Indiana University Press, 1964.

Jahoda, Gustav. "Children's Concepts of Time and History." Educational Review 15 (February 1963):87-104.

James, William. The Principles of Psychology. Vol. 1. New York: Dover, 1890.

Jansen, Marius B. Changing Japanese Attitudes Toward Modernization. Princeton: Princeton University Press, 1965.

Kantor, David, and William Lehr. Inside the Family. San Francisco: Jossey-Bass, 1975.

Kaplan, Abraham. The Conduct of Inquiry. San Francisco: Chandler, 1964.

Ketchum, J. D. "Time, Values, and Social Organization." Canadian Journal of Psychology 5 (September 1951):97-109.

Kilpatrick, William. Identity and Intimacy. New York: Delta Books, 1975.

Klein, Josephine. The Study of Groups. London: Routledge & Kegan Paul, 1956.

Kluckhohn, Florence R., and Fred L. Strodtbeck. Variations in Value Orientations. Evanston, Ill.: Row, Peterson, 1961.

Knapp, Robert H., and John T. Garbutt. "Time Imagery and the Achievement Motive." Journal of Personality 26 (1958):426-34.

Kohn, Melvin L. Class and Conformity. Homewood, Ill.: Dorsey, 1969.

Kroth, Roger Lee. "A Study of Three Aspects of Time Among Normal and Delinquent School Age Mates in Costa Rica and the United States." Ph.D. dissertation, University of Kansas, 1968.

Krutch, Joseph Wood. The Modern Temper. New York: Harcourt, Brace, 1929.

Lakein, Alan. "The ABC's of Saving Time." Readers' Digest, April 1975, pp. 67-69.

Landau, L. D., and G. B. Rumer. What Is Relativity? New York: Basic Books, 1960.

Lauer, Jeanette C., and Robert H. Lauer. Fashion Power: The Meaning of Fashion in American Society. Englewood Cliffs: Prentice-Hall, 1981.

Lauer, Robert H. "The Middle Class Looks at Poverty." Urban and Social Change Review 5 (Fall 1971):8-10.

―――. Perspectives on Social Change. Boston: Allyn & Bacon, 1977.

―――. "Rate of Change and Stress: A Test of the 'Future Shock' Thesis." Social Forces 52 (June 1974):510-16.

―――. "The Scientific Legitimation of Fallacy: Neutralizing Social Change Theory." American Sociological Review 36 (October 1971): 881-89.

―――. "Social Time and Social Change." Ph.D. dissertation, Washington University, 1970.

―――. "Temporality and Social Change: The Case of 19th Century China and Japan." The Sociological Quarterly 14 (Autumn 1973): 451-64.

Lauer, Robert H., and Warren H. Handel. Social Psychology: The Theory and Application of Symbolic Interactionism. Boston: Houghton Mifflin, 1977.

Lauer, Robert H., and Jeanette C. Lauer. "The Experience of Change: Tempo and Stress." In Social Change: Explorations, Diagnoses and Conjectures, edited by George K. Zollschan and Walter Hirsch, pp. 520-45. Cambridge, Mass.: Schenkman, 1976.

Leach, E. R. Rethinking Anthropology. London: Athlone Press, 1961.

Lebhar, Godfrey. The Use of Time. 3d ed. New York: Chain Store, 1958.

Le Goff, Jacques. "Church Time and Merchant Time in the Middle Ages." Social Science Information 9 (August 1970): 151-68.

Lerner, Max. Ideas Are Weapons. New York: Viking Press, 1939.

Levenson, Joseph. Confucian China and Its Modern Fate: A Trilogy. 3 vols. Berkeley and Los Angeles: University of California Press, 1968.

Levy, Marion J., Jr. "Contrasting Factors in the Modernization of China and Japan." Economic Development and Cultural Change 2 (1953): 161-97.

Lewin, Kurt. Resolving Social Conflicts. New York: Harper & Row, 1948.

Lieber, Arnold L., and Carolyn R. Sherin. "Homicides and the Lunar Cycle: Toward a Theory of Lunar Influence on Human Emotional Disturbances." American Journal of Psychiatry 129 (July 1972): 69-74.

Lifton, Robert Jay. "Individual Patterns in Historical Change: Imagery of Japanese Youth." In Comparative Perspectives on Social Change, edited by S. N. Eisenstadt, pp. 160-75. Boston: Little, Brown, 1968.

Linder, Staffan Burenstam. The Harried Leisure Class. New York: Columbia University Press, 1970.

Lippitt, Ronald, Jeanne Watson, and Bruce Westley. The Dynamics of Planned Change. New York: Harcourt, Brace & World, 1958.

Litchfield, Peter M., and Jerome M. Sattler. "An Hypothesis: The Existential Notion of Intentional Time as a Dimension of Psychological Health." The Journal of Genetic Psychology 79 (1968): 257-70.

Lockwood, William W. "Japan's Response to the West: The Contrast with China." World Politics 9 (October 1956): 37-54.

Luce, Gay Gaer. Body Time: Physiological Rhythms and Social Stress. New York: Pantheon Books, 1971.

McClelland, David C. The Achieving Society. New York: Free Press, 1961.

MacIver, Robert. The Challenge of the Passing Years. New York: Simon and Schuster, 1962.

MacIver, Robert M., and Charles H. Page. Society: An Introductory Analysis. New York: Rinehart, 1937.

Maines, David R. "Social Organization and Social Structure in Symbolic Interactionist Thought." Annual Review of Sociology 3 (1977): 235-59.

Mannheim, Karl. Ideology and Utopia. Translated by Louis Wirth and Edward Shils. New York: Harcourt, Brace and World, 1936.

Marcus, John T. "Time and the Sense of History: West and East." Comparative Studies in Society and History 3 (January 1961): 123-39.

Marx, Karl. Grundrisse. Translated by Martin Nicolaus. New York: Vintage Books, 1973.

Maslow, Abraham. Toward a Psychology of Being. 2d ed. New York: Van Nostrand Reinhold, 1968.

Mead, George Herbert. Mind, Self, and Society. Chicago: University of Chicago Press, 1934.

Meade, Robert D. "Time On Their Hands." Personnel Journal 39 (1960): 130-32.

Meerloo, Joost A. M. "The Time Sense in Psychiatry." In The Voices of Time, edited by J. T. Fraser, pp. 235-52. New York: George Braziller, 1966.

Melbin, Murray. "City Rhythms." In The Study of Time III, edited by J. T. Fraser, N. Lawrence, and D. Park, pp. 444-65. New York: Springer-Verlag, 1978.

———. "Night As Frontier." American Sociological Review 43 (February 1978): 3-22.

Mendel, Douglas H., Jr. "Japan Today: Case Study of a Developing Nation." Trans-Action 3 (March-April 1966): 15-21.

Merlan, Philip. "Time Consciousness in Husserl and Heidegger." Philosophy and Phenomenological Research 8 (1947): 23-54.

Merleau-Ponty, M. *Phenomenology of Perception*. New York: Humanities Press, 1962.

Merton, Robert K. *Social Theory and Social Structure*. Glencoe, Ill.: Free Press, 1957.

Meyerhoff, Hans. *Time In Literature*. Berkeley and Los Angeles: University of California Press, 1955.

Michon, J. A. "Time Experience and Memory Processes." In *The Study of Time II*, edited by J. T. Fraser and N. Lawrence, pp. 302-13. New York: Springer-Verlag, 1975.

Mills, C. Wright. *The Sociological Imagination*. New York: Grove Press, 1969.

Momigliano, Arnoldo. "Time In Ancient Historiography." In *History and the Concept of Time*, edited by George H. Nadel, pp. 1-23. Middletown, Conn.: Wesleyan University Press, 1966.

Moore, Wilbert E. *Man, Time, and Society*. New York: John Wiley, 1963.

―――. *Order and Change: Essays in Comparative Sociology*. New York: John Wiley, 1967.

―――. *Social Change*. Englewood Cliffs: Prentice-Hall, 1963.

Mott, Paul E., Floyd C. Mann, Quin McLoughlin, and Donald P. Warwick. *Shift Work*. Ann Arbor: The University of Michigan Press, 1965.

Mukerjee, Radhakamal. "Time, Technics, and Society." *Sociology and Social Research* 27 (1943): 255-66.

Munn, Norman L. *Psychology*. 5th ed. Boston: Houghton Mifflin, 1966.

Nadler, Leonard. "Helping the Hard-Core Adjust to the World of Work." *Harvard Business Review* 48 (March/April 1970): 117-26.

Nakamura, Hajime. "Time in Indian and Japanese Thought." In *The Voices of Time*, edited by J. T. Fraser, pp. 77-91. New York: George Braziller, 1966.

———. Ways of Thinking of Eastern Peoples. Honolulu: East-West Center Press, 1964.

Namenwirth, J. Zvi. "Wheels of Time and the Interdependence of Value Change in America." Journal of Interdisciplinary History 3 (Spring 1973): 649-83.

Nash, Manning. Machine Age Maya. Chicago: The University of Chicago Press, 1967.

Needham, Joseph. "Time and Knowledge in China and the West." In The Voices of Time, edited by J. T. Fraser, pp. 92-135. New York: George Braziller, 1966.

Nelkin, Dorothy. "Unpredictability and Life Style in a Migrant Labor Camp." Social Problems 17 (Spring 1970): 472-87.

Nikhilananda, Swami. The Upanishads. Vol. 1. New York: Harper & Brothers, 1949.

Nilsson, Martin P. Primitive Time-Reckoning. Lund, Sweden: G. W. K. Gleerup, 1920.

O'Rand, Angela, and Robert A. Ellis. "Social Class and Social Time Perspective." Social Forces 53 (September 1974): 53-62.

Orme, J. E. Time, Experience and Behavior. London: Iliffe Books, 1969.

Ornstein, Robert E. On the Experience of Time. Baltimore: Penguin Books, 1969.

———. The Psychology of Consciousness. 2d ed. New York: Harcourt Brace Jovanovich, 1977.

Parkin, Frank. Class Inequality & Political Order. New York: Praeger, 1971.

Parkinson, C. Northcote. The Law of Delay. London: John Murray, 1970.

———. Parkinson's Law. New York: Ballantine Books, 1957.

Parsons, Talcott, and Edward A. Shils. Toward A General Theory of Action. New York: Harper & Row, 1951.

Parsons, William Barclay. *An American Engineer In China*. New York: McClure, Phillips, 1900.

Pascal, Blaise. *Pensees*. Translated by W. F. Trotter. New York: Random House, 1941.

Passin, Herbert. "Modernization and the Japanese Intellectual: Some Comparative Observations." In *Changing Japanese Attitudes Toward Modernization*, edited by Marius B. Jansen, pp. 447-87. Princeton: Princeton University Press, 1965.

Pepelasis, A. A. "The Image of the Past and Economic Backwardness." *Human Organization* 17 (Winter 1958-59):19-27.

Perrow, Charles. *Organizational Analysis: A Sociological View*. Belmont, Calif.: Brooks/Cole, 1970.

Piaget, Jean. *The Child's Conception of the World*. Translated by Joan and Andrew Tomlinson. Paterson, N.J.: Littlefield, Adams, 1963.

―――. *The Psychology of Intelligence*. Translated by Malcolm Percy and D. E. Berlyne. Paterson, N.J.: Littlefield, Adams, 1963.

―――. "Time Perception in Children." In *The Voices of Time*, edited by J. T. Fraser, pp. 202-16. New York: George Braziller, 1966.

Pitt, David C. *Using Historical Sources in Anthropology and Sociology*. New York: Holt, Rinehart and Winston, 1972.

Platt, Jerome, and Robert E. Taylor. "Homesickness, Future Time Perspective, and the Self Concept." *Journal of Individual Psychology* 23 (1967):94-97.

Platt, John R. *The Step to Man*. New York: John Wiley, 1966.

Polak, Fred L. *The Image of the Future*. Vols. 1 and 2. New York: Oceana Publications, 1961.

Prince, Raymond. "Psychotherapy and the Chronically Poor." In *Culture Change, Mental Health, and Poverty*, edited by Joseph C. Finney, pp. 20-41. New York: Simon and Schuster, 1969.

Pyle, Kenneth B. The New Generation in Meiji Japan. Stanford: Stanford University Press, 1969.

Quinones, Ricardo J. The Renaissance Discovery of Time. Cambridge, Mass.: Harvard University Press, 1972.

Reischauer, Edwin O. Japan: Past and Present. 3d ed. Tokyo: Charles E. Tuttle, 1964.

Reischauer, Edwin O., and John K. Fairbank. East Asia: The Great Tradition. Vol. 1. Boston: Houghton Mifflin, 1958.

Rezsohazy, Rudolf. "The Concept of Social Time: Its Role in Development. International Social Science Journal 24 (1972): 26-36.

Rice, Paul L. "Making Minutes Count." Business Horizons 16 (December 1973): 15-22.

Rickett, W. Allyn. Kuan-Tzu: A Repository of Early Chinese Thought. Hong Kong: Hong Kong University Press, 1965.

Ritzenthaler, Robert E. "The Impact of Small Industry on an Indian Community." American Anthropologist 55 (January-March 1953): 143-48.

Rizzo, Adolfo E. "The Time Moratorium." Adolescence 2 (1967-68): 469-80.

Roberts, Alan H., and Robert S. Herrman. "Dogmatism, Time Perspective, and Anomie." Journal of Individual Psychology 16 (1960): 67-72.

Robinson, John P. How Americans Use Time: A Social-Psychological Analysis of Everyday Behavior. New York: Praeger, 1977.

Robinson, John P., and Philip E. Converse. "Social Change Reflected in the Use of Time." In The Human Meaning of Social Change, edited by Angus Campbell and Philip E. Converse, pp. 17-86. New York: Russell Sage Foundation, 1972.

Robinson, John P., Philip E. Converse, and Alexander Szalai. "Everyday Life in Twelve Countries." In The Use of Time: Daily Activities of Urban and Suburban Populations in Twelve Countries, edited by Alexander Szalai, pp. 113-44. The Hague: Mouton, 1972.

Rokeach, Milton. The Open and Closed Mind. New York: Basic Books, 1960.

Roos, P., and R. Albers. "Performance of Alcoholics and Normals on a Measure of Temporal Orientation." Journal of Clinical Psychology 21 (1965): 34-36.

Roth, Julius A. Timetables: Structuring the Passage of Time in Hospital Treatment and Other Careers. New York: Bobbs-Merrill, 1963.

Rubin, Lillian Breslow. Worlds Of Pain. New York: Basic Books, 1976.

Rubin, Zick. "Seasonal Rhythms in Behavior." Psychology Today, December 1979, pp. 12-16.

Sackman, Harold. Computers, System Science, and Evolving Society. New York: John Wiley, 1967.

Sattler, Jerome M. "Counselor Competence, Interest and Time Perspective: A Follow-up Note." Counselor Education and Supervision 6 (1967): 185-86.

Saunders, Lyle. Cultural Differences and Medical Care. New York: Russell Sage Foundation, 1954.

Schaff, Adam. "Marxist Dialectics and the Principle of Contradiction." Journal of Philosophy 57 (March 31, 1960): 241-50.

———. A Philosophy of Man. New York: Monthly Review Press, 1963.

Schurmann, Franz, and Orville Schell. Imperial China: The Decline of the Last Dynasty and the Origins of Modern China. New York: Vintage Books, 1967.

Schwartz, Barry. "Time, Patience, and Black People: A Study of Temporal Access to Medical Care." Sociological Focus 11 (January 1978): 11-20.

———. "Waiting, Exchange, and Power: The Distribution of Time in Social Systems." American Journal of Sociology 79 (January 1974): 841-70.

Seeley, J. R., R. A. Sim, and W. E. Loosley. Crestwood Heights. John Wiley, 1956.

Shephard, Herbert A. "Innovation-Resisting and Innovation-Producing Organizations." In The Planning of Change, 2d ed., edited by Warren G. Bennis, Kenneth D. Benne, and Robert Chin, pp. 519-26. New York: Holt, Rinehart and Winston, 1969.

Sherwood, Frank P. "The Clock and the Specialized R and D Society." In The Research Society, edited by Evelyn Glatt and Maynard W. Shelly, pp. 67-82. New York: Gordon and Breach, 1968.

———. "Leadership, Organizations, and Time." In Temporal Dimensions of Development Administration, edited by Dwight Waldo, pp. 216-27. Durham, N.C.: Duke University Press, 1970.

Sigmund, Paul E. The Ideologies of the Developing Nations. New York: Praeger, 1967.

Singer, Kurt. "Differences Between Chinese and Japanese Culture." Yale Review 27 (Summer 1938): 772-89.

Smart, Reginald G. "Future Time Perspectives in Alcoholics and Social Drinkers." Journal of Abnormal Psychology 73 (1968): 81-83.

Smith, Arthur H. Chinese Characteristics. New York: Fleming H. Revell, 1894.

Smith, Robert H. "Cultural Differences in the Life Cycle and the Concept of Time." In Aging and Leisure: A Research Perspective into the Meaningful Use of Time, edited by Robert W. Kleemeier, pp. 83-112. New York: Oxford University Press, 1961.

Smith, Thomas C. "Japan's Aristocratic Revolution." In Class, Status and Power, 2d ed., edited by Reinhard Bendix and Seymour Martin Lipset, pp. 135-40. New York: The Free Press, 1966.

Sommer, Robert. Personal Space: The Behavioral Basis of Design. Englewood Cliffs: Prentice-Hall, 1969.

Sorokin, Pitirim A. Social and Cultural Dynamics. Vol. 2. New York: American Book, 1937.

———. Sociocultural Causality, Space, Time. New York: Russell and Russell, 1964.

Sorokin, Pitirim A., and Robert K. Merton. "Social Time: A Methodological and Functional Analysis." American Journal of Sociology 42 (March 1937):615-29.

Spradley, James P., and Mark Phillips. "Culture and Stress: A Quantitative Analysis." American Anthropologist 74 (June 1972): 518-29.

Stacy, G. W. "The Improvement of Time." The Practical Christian, January 6, 1844, p. 1.

Stoetzel, Jean. "The Contribution of Public Opinion Research Techniques to Social Anthropology." International Social Science Bulletin 5 (1953):494-503.

Stone, Gregory P. "The Circumstance and Situation of Social Status." In Social Psychology Through Symbolic Interaction, edited by Gregory P. Stone and Harvey A. Farberman, pp. 250-59. Waltham, Mass.: Ginn-Blaisdell, 1970.

Strauss, George. "Group Dynamics and Intergroup Relations." In Of Men and Machines, edited by Arthur O. Lewis, Jr., pp. 321-27. New York: E. P. Dutton, 1963.

Strodtbeck, Fred L., Rita M. James, and Charles Hawkins. "Social Status in Jury Deliberations." In Readings In Social Psychology, 3d ed., edited by Eleanor E. Maccoby, Theodore M. Newcomb, and Eugene L. Hartley, pp. 379-88. New York: Holt, Rinehart and Winston, 1958.

Swift, Jonathan. Gulliver's Travels. New York: Holt, Rinehart and Winston, 1961.

Szalai, Alexander. "Differential Evaluation of Time Budgets for Comparison Purposes." In Comparing Nations: The Use of Quantitative Data in Cross-National Research, edited by Richard L. Merritt and Stein Rokkan, pp. 239-58. New Haven: Yale University Press, 1966.

Tausky, Curt. Work Organizations. Itasca, Ill.: F. E. Peacock, 1970.

Teng, Ssu-Yu, and John K. Fairbank. China's Response to the West. New York: Atheneum, 1967.

Thompson, E. P. "Time, Work-Discipline, and Industrial Capitalism." Past and Present 38 (December 1967):56-97.

Timasheff, Nicholas S. Sociological Theory: Its Nature and Growth. New York: Random House, 1957.

Toffler, Alvin. Future Shock. New York: Random House, 1970.

Tournier, Paul. The Meaning of Persons. New York: Harper & Row, 1957.

Tsunoda, Ryusaku, William Theodore de Bary, and Donald Keene. Sources of Japanese Tradition. New York: Columbia University Press, 1958.

Turner, Ralph H. "Role-Taking: Process Versus Conformity." In Human Behavior and Social Processes, edited by Arnold M. Rose, pp. 20-40. Boston: Houghton Mifflin, 1962.

Varga, Karoly. "Leisure and Divorce: Marital Cohesion in the Time Budget." The New Hungarian Quarterly 11 (Winter 1970):137-50.

Veterans World Project. Wasted Men: The Reality of the Vietnam Veteran. Edwardsville, Ill.: Southern Illinois University Foundation, 1972.

Vogt, Evon Z. "The Automobile in Contemporary Navaho Culture." In A Reader in Culture Change, vol. 2, edited by Ivan Brady and Barry Isaad, pp. 41-46. New York: John Wiley, 1975.

Waldo, Dwight, ed. Temporal Dimensions of Development Administration. Durham, N.C.: Duke University Press, 1970.

Walker, James. The Human Aspects of Shiftwork. London: Institute of Personnel Management, 1978.

Wallace, Melvin, and Albert I. Rabin. "Temporal Experience." Psychological Bulletin 57 (1960):213-36.

Wallerstein, Immanuel. Africa: The Politics of Independence. New York: Vintage Books, 1961.

Wallerstein, Michael R., and Nancy Lee Roberts. "All Together On the Bio-Curve." Human Behavior, April 1973, pp. 8-15.

Webber, Ross A. Time and Management. New York: Van Nostrand Reinhold, 1972.

Weber, Max. The Protestant Ethic and the Spirit of Capitalism. Translated by Talcott Parsons. New York: Charles Scribner's Sons, 1958.

———. The Theory of Social and Economic Organization. Edited and with an introduction by Talcott Parsons. New York: The Free Press, 1947.

Weigert, Andrew J. Sociology of Everyday Life. New York: Longman, 1981.

Welty, Paul Thomas. The Asians: Their Heritage and Their Destiny. 3d ed., Philadelphia: J. B. Lippincott, 1970.

Wessman, Alden E., and Bernard S. Gorman. "The Emergence of Human Awareness and Concepts of Time." In The Personal Experience of Time, edited by Bernard S. Gorman and Alden E. Wessman, pp. 3-55. New York: Plenum Press, 1977.

Whitehead, Alfred North. Adventures of Ideas. New York: Mentor Books, 1933.

———. Process and Reality. New York: The Free Press, 1929.

———. Science and the Modern World. New York: Macmillan, 1925.

Whitrow, G. J. The Natural Philosophy of Time. New York: Harper & Row, 1961.

Whorf, Benjamin. Language, Thought, and Reality. New York: John Wiley, 1956.

Whyte, William Foote. Organizational Behavior: Theory and Application. Homewood, Ill.: Irwin-Dorsey, 1969.

Wilhelm, Helmut. "The Concept of Time in the Book of Changes." In Man and Time, edited by Joseph Campbell, pp. 212-32. New York: Pantheon, 1957.

Will, Frederick L. "Will the Future Be Like the Past?" In Logic and Language, edited by Anthony Flew, pp. 248-66. Garden City: Anchor Books, 1965.

Wright, Lawrence. Clockwork Man. London: Elek Books, 1968.

Yang, Lien-sheng. "Schedules of Work and Rest in Imperial China." Harvard Journal of Asiatic Studies 18 (1955): 301-25.

Zablocki, Benjamin. The Joyful Community. Baltimore: Penguin Books, 1971.

Zborowski, Mark. "Cultural Components in Responses to Pain." Journal of Social Issues 8 (1952): 16-30.

Zern, David. "The Influence of Certain Child-Rearing Factors Upon the Development of a Structured and Salient Sense of Time." Genetic Psychology Monographs 81 (May 1970): 197-254.

Zerubavel, Eviatar. "The French Republican Calendar: A Case Study in the Sociology of Time." American Sociological Review 42 (December 1977): 868-77.

———. Patterns of Time in Hospital Life. Chicago: University of Chicago Press, 1979.

———. "Private Time and Public Time: The Temporal Structure of Social Accessibility and Professional Commitments." Social Forces 58 (September 1979): 38-58.

Zurcher, Louis A., Jr. "The Poverty Board: Some Consequences of 'Maximum Feasible Participation.'" In Planned Social Intervention, edited by Louis A. Zurcher, Jr. and Charles M. Bonjean, pp. 300-19. Scranton, Pa.: Chandler, 1970.

NAME INDEX

Albert, S., 27
Arensberg, Conrad M., 113
Ariotti, P. E., 22
Augenstine, Leroy G., 30

Balazs, Etienne, 127, 130
Becker, Gary S., 4
Beecher, Catherine, 62
Bell, Wendell, 43
Bellah, Robert, 135
Benedict, Ruth, 137
Bennis, Warren G., 144
Bergson, Henri, 21
Bettelheim, Bruno, 91
Blau, Peter M., 99
Blumer, Herbert, 86
Boas, George, 16
Bock, Philip, 21
Brim, Orville G., Jr., 106
Burke, William, 128

Caudill, William, 138
Chapin, F. Stuart, Jr., 6, 91
Churchman, C. West, 115
Cohen, John, 77, 97
Cottle, Thomas J., 115, 118

de Grazia, Sebastian, 1
Drucker, Peter F., 91
Durkheim, Emile, 26, 27

Eliade, Mircea, 16, 27
Ellis, Robert A., 44-45, 106

Farber, Maurice L., 78
Faulkner, Robert R., 24
Forer, Raymond, 106
Fraisse, Paul, 10, 39
Frank, Lawrence K., 76, 77
Fraser, J. T., 6

Freud, Sigmund, 12
Friedman, Bertha B., 35

Geertz, Clifford, 88
Gelles, Richard J., 24
Gellner, Ernest, 99
Goffman, Erving, 99
Graham, Otis, L., 113
Grey, Alan L., 106
Gurvitch, Georges, 13, 14

Hall, Edward, 104
Hasegawa, Nyozekan, 136, 138
Hawley, Amos H., 28, 35
Hegel, G. W. F., 17, 130
Heirich, Max, 32
Henley, Nancy M., 97
Herskovits, Melville J., 118
Husserl, Edmund, 54

James, William, 33, 67
Jansen, Marius B., 143

Kantor, David, 94
Kaplan, Abraham, 27
Kilpatrick, William, 91, 92
Klein, Josephine, 96
Klineberg, Stephen L., 115, 118
Kluckhohn, Florence R., 36, 138
Knapp, Robert H., 16

Leach, E. R., 22, 59
Lehr, William, 94
Levy, Marion J., Jr., 128, 138-39
Lewin, Kurt, 79
Lifton, Robert Jay, 65, 66
Linder, Staffan Burenstam, 92, 93
Lockwood, William W., 127, 128

McClelland, David C., 117

MacIver, Robert, 41
Mannheim, Karl, 112
Marx, Karl, 100
Maslow, Abraham, 77, 80
Mau, James A., 43
Mead, George Herbert, 56
Meerloo, Joost A. M., 12
Melbin, Murray, 25
Mendel, Douglas H., Jr., 128
Merton, Robert K., 34
Momigliano, Arnoldo, 58
Moore, Wilbert E., 13, 14, 15, 28, 41, 98, 102
Mukerjee, Radhakamal, 72

Nakamura, Hajime, 133
Nash, Manning, 120
Nelkin, Dorothy, 29
Niehoff, Arthur H., 113

O'Rand, Angela, 43, 106
Ornstein, Robert E., 11

Page, Charles H., 41
Parkinson, C. Northcote, 33, 34
Parsons, William Barclay, 127, 129, 131, 133
Pascal, Blaise, 52
Passin, Herbert, 137
Pepelasis, A. A., 119
Perrow, Charles, 104
Phillips, Mark, 104
Piaget, Jean, 57, 59, 67
Polak, Fred L., 38, 116
Pyle, Kenneth B., 138, 144

Quinones, Ricardo J., 93

Robinson, John P., 5
Rubin, Lillian Breslow, 116, 117

Sattler, Jerome M., 66
Scarr, H. A., 138
Schaff, Adam, 113
Schwartz, Barry, 96, 100
Shephard, Herbert A., 115
Sherwood, Frank P., 102
Singer, Kurt, 133, 138
Smith, Arthur H., 126, 129
Sorokin, Pitirim A., 13, 22
Spradley, James P., 104
Stone, Gregory P., 95
Strodtbeck, Fred L., 36, 138
Swift, Jonathan, 23
Szalai, Alexander, 87

Toffler, Alvin, 32, 72

Vogt, Evon, 116

Webber, Ross A., 98
Weber, Max, 61, 122
Weigert, Andrew J., 89
Whitehead, Alfred North, 15, 27, 39, 54
Whorf, Benjamin, 58
Whyte, William Foote, 103, 104
Wilhelm, Helmut, 133

Zborowski, Mark, 68
Zern, David, 59
Zerubavel, Eviatar, 25, 95, 101
Zurcher, Louis A., Jr., 107

SUBJECT INDEX

achievement, 16, 118-19
actualizing individual, 73-80
anxiety: existential, 16; relationship to perceived rate of change, 72-73
Aristotle: reality of time, 7; time and motion, 58, 59

Balinese time, 88-89
black Americans: colored people's time, 44; waiting time of, 96-97

calendar, 59; Anglican, 44; Balinese, 88; Mayan, 44; means of power, 99, 101; mechanism of social control, 141; revolutionary calendar of France, 101
capitalism, 60-62, 100-1, 113
change, 112-45; Chinese concept of, 133; as loss, 16; rapid, and anxiety or stress, 73, 144; and the self, 54-56; versus permanence, 8-9
chronarchy, 62
circadian rhythms, 10
clock (see time, clock)
clocking, 94
conflict, 35, 102-7; because of diverse systems of social time, 45, 105-6, 118-19; between labor and management, 61, 100, 103-4; between social classes, 106-7; and meaning of time, 103
cycles and cyclic phenomena, 29, 42, 56-57, 130-31 (see also periodicity)

decision-making, 75, 119
definition of the situation, 68-70, 79-80
Delay, Law of, 34
development, economic, 122-27
dialectic, 41-42, 73, 80
disorganization, psychic, 27
disorientation, temporal, 70-73; of alcoholics, 71; and emotional disturbances, 71-72; and shift work, 72
dogmatism, 70
duration, 33-34, 43, 112, 132; cultural differences, 105; and interpersonal relationships, 89-93; and status, 96-97

economic growth, 92-93, 119
economics, 4-5, 122-29
efficiency, 90-91
executive behavior, 98
existentialism, 17

family: interaction in, 94; problems, 33; and temporal socialization, 59-60
future: creation of, 15; phenomenal, 77-80; study of, 15
future orientation, 35-37, 112; and activism, 144; of actualizing individuals, 76-80; of alcoholics, 71; and behavior, 38-39; and change, 37, 144; class differences in, 44-45; of delinquents, 71; and democratization, 144; in Japanese temporality, 77; and need achievement, 118; and planning, 115; of prisoners, 78

future perspective, 38-39, 71, 75-80, 102, 115, 116, 117
future shock, 32, 72

groups: differing temporality of, 79-80, 87, 103, 104; encounter, 91-92; participation time in, 95-96, 98; and power struggles, 99-100; and temporal definitions, 68-70

Hindu philosophy of time, 9
history: as change, 38-39; 133; Chinese view of, 133, 142; sociological use of, 122-23; "terror of," 16
hospital, temporal order of, 25
human potential movement, 92

internal clocks, 103
intimacy, 91-92, 94

Kachin time, 22
Khasi time, 23

linguistic explanation of time, 58

memory, 10, 56
modernization, 39, 117-29; in China, 123-29; and conflict, 118-21; and future orientation, 117-18; in Japan, 123-29, 138, 139
morale, 79
movement, 41-43; at the individual level, 53-57; in Japanese temporality, 138

Navajo time, 36
night as frontier, 25-26
Nuer time, 22

organizations, 57-58; duration and Parkinson's laws in, 33-34; innovation in, 114-15; periodicity in, 29-30; status and time use in, 97-98; tempo in, 31; time orientations, 104
orientation, future (see future orientation)
orientation, temporal (see temporal orientation)
orientation, spatial (see spatial orientation)
pain and temporal orientation, 68-69
past orientation, 35-36; Chinese, 131-32; and economic development, 134-35; of neurotics, 70; and planned change, 116; of traditional societies, 117
periodicity, 2, 10, 13, 28-31, 40; in organizations, 30, 114-15; relationship to health, 75; rhythms of social life, 28-29; and task performance, 30-31; and transcendental needs, 29; of work, 30-31, 119
philosophical time, 7-9, 39
philosophy and the self, 54
physics: Newtonian, 21-22; relativistic, 3
planning, 113-16, 226; and future, perspective, 39, 113; and tempo, 113; and time allocation studies, 6; and timing, 113; of the working class, 116-17
power, 99
present orientation, 35-37; of Chippewa Indians, 37, 77-78; of delinquents, 71; of neurotics, 70; of Spanish-speaking Americans, 69-70, 78
primary relationships, 92-93
Protestant work ethic, 126-27
psychoanalysis, 12, 53, 58
psychological time, 10-14
punctuality, 97, 130

religion, 120-21; and conflict over social time, 100-3; and temporal socialization, 61-

v

62, 94
ritual, 2, 9, 35
role, 45, 66, 86-87

self, 54-56
self-actualization, 53-54, 73-80
self-concept, 32, 63-66, 69-70
sequence, 14, 35, 144
Shintoism, 136-37
social class: and conflict, 106-7; differences in orientation and perspective, 44; harried leisure class, 92; and planning, 116-17; status relationships, 95-99
social control, 43-44, 139-43
social time, 17, 21-24, 25-29, passim; and act and action meanings, 27; and astronomical time, 13; and clock time, 21-26; and conflict, 45, 103-7; and power relationships, 99-103; and social control, 43-44, 139-43; and status relationships, 95-99; symbols of, 43-45, 139-41, 143
socialization, temporal, 57-64
space, 3, 95
spatial orientation, 67-68
status, 95-99
stress, 73
structure: hunger for, 74-75; temporal, 28-41, 60-61, 76, 103-4
symbolic interactionism, 86-87
symbols, 43-45, 138-41, 143

tempo, 31-32, 40, 43, 64, 113, 120, 144; of change in China, 130, 132-33; of change in Japan, 135-36; of change and stress, 72-73, 144
temporal orientation, 26, 35-37, 43; and definition of the situation, 68-70; and economic development, 128-45; of juvenile delinquents, 71
temporal pattern, 28-35, 42, 105, 117; disruption of, 102-3; and social planning, 113-15
temporal perspective, 38-43; and definition of the situation, 68-70; of Japanese youth, 65-66
temporality: and anxiety, 15-17; Balinese, 88-89; and Brazilian reform, 119; Chinese, 129-35; class differences in, 45, 107; human awareness of, 2; Japanese, 135-38; and self-concepts, 63-64; sex differences in, 63; social versus individual, 76; source of, 57-63, 117 (see also social time)
time: American concept of, 29, 34; astronomical, 13; clock, 14, 21-26, 61, 67, 68, 76, 77, 87-88, 91, 92-93, 94, 130, 135; compact of Micmac, 106; conditioning of, 10; as defense mechanism, 70-71; as dependent variable, 14-15; as a destroyer, 16-17; discretionary, 6, 97-99; diffuse of Micmac, 106; as a god, 23; as independent variable, 14-15; intentional, 73-74; and legitimation, 43; linear concept of, 39; as a measure of consumption, 4-5; as a measure of employee commitment, 15; as a measure of human activity, 87; measurement of, 22, 140; metaphors of, 16; as money, 35, 64, 89, 91-92, 102, 103, 128; mystery of, 1-2; Newtonian, 3, 16, 21, 22; perception of, 10, 27, 34, 67-68; reality of, 9; as a religious value, 61-62; as a resource, 4-5, 14, 99, 103; social (see social time); and television news, 23-24; waiting, 95-97, 104, 129-30; watch, 13-14

time allocation studies, 4-6
Time League, 93-94
time pressure, 75
timing, 32-34; and adjustment to change, 120-21; and family life, 94; in planned change, 113, 142
tradition, 139
traditional orientation, 119-21
Triviality, Law of, 34

utopian mentality, 112-13

women: less future oriented than men, 63; time allocation of, 5-6; time and status of, 97-98
work: effects of shift work, 72-73; preferred periodicity of, 30-31, 118; tempo of, 32; temporal socialization to, 60-63; and theory of surplus value, 100-1; time obsession of executives, 91; and women, 5-6